KT-406-652

Essential
Study Skills

AWN FROM
LIBRARY
UNIVERSITY OF
WINCHESTER

KA 0385636 4

SAGE has been part of the global academic community since 1965, supporting high quality research and learning that transforms society and our understanding of individuals, groups and cultures. SAGE is the independent, innovative, natural home for authors, editors and societies who share our commitment and passion for the social sciences.

Find out more at: **www.sagepublications.com**

SAGE Study Skills

Essential
Study Skills

The Complete Guide to
Success at University

Tom Burns & Sandra Sinfield

3rd Edition

UNIVERSITY OF WINCHESTER
LIBRARY

Los Angeles | London | New Delhi
Singapore | Washington DC

© Tom Burns and Sandra Sinfield, 2012
Chapter 7 © Debbie Holley and Chapter 26 © Christine Keenan

First edition published 2002
Second edition published 2008
Third edition published 2012

Apart from any fair dealing for the purposes of research or private study, or criticism or review, as permitted under the Copyright, Designs and Patents Act, 1988, this publication may be reproduced, stored or transmitted in any form, or by any means, only with the prior permission in writing of the publishers, or in the case of reprographic reproduction, in accordance with the terms of licences issued by the Copyright Licensing Agency. Enquiries concerning reproduction outside those terms should be sent to the publishers.

All material on the accompanying website can be printed off and photocopied by the purchaser/user of the book. The web material itself may not be reproduced in its entirety for use by others without prior written permission from SAGE. The web material may not be distributed or sold separately from the book without the prior written permission of SAGE. Should anyone wish to use the materials from the website for conference purposes, they would require separate permission from us. All material is © Tom Burns and Sandra Sinfield, 2012.

SAGE Publications Ltd
1 Oliver's Yard
55 City Road
London EC1Y 1SP

SAGE Publications Inc.
2455 Teller Road
Thousand Oaks, California 91320

SAGE Publications India Pvt Ltd
B 1/I 1 Mohan Cooperative Industrial Area
Mathura Road
New Delhi 110 044

SAGE Publications Asia-Pacific Pte Ltd
3 Church Street
#10-04 Samsung Hub
Singapore 049483

Library of Congress Control Number: 2011938241

British Library Cataloguing in Publication data

A catalogue record for this book is available from the British Library

ISBN 978-1-4462-0324-8
ISBN 978-1-4462-0325-5 (pbk)

Typeset by C&M Digitals (P) Ltd, Chennai, India
Printed in Great Britain by MPG Books Group, Bodmin, Cornwall
Printed on paper from sustainable resources

UNIVERSITY OF WINCHESTER

03856364   378, 17
            BUR

Contents

List of Checklists, Figures and Tables

About the Authors

In a previous life **Tom Burns** led the Hainault Action Group, setting up adventure playgrounds for young people and devising Community Events and Festivals for the local community. Tom has always been interested in theatre and the role of theatre in teaching and learning; whilst still a student at Essex University he set up and ran the first ever International Dario Fo Festival – with academic symposium, theatre workshops for students and local people – and full dramatic performances by the Fo-Rame theatre troupe of *The Tiger's Tale* and *The Boss's Funeral*.

Sandra Sinfield has worked as a laboratory technician, a freelance copy writer, an Executive Editor (*Medicine Digest*, circulation 80,000 doctors) and in the voluntary sector, including with the Tower Hamlets Information Research and Resource Centre and with the Islington Green School Community Play written by Alan *Whose Life is it Anyway?* Clarke and produced at Sadler's Wells.

Together Tom and Sandra have taken a production of John Godber's *Bouncers* on a tour of Crete music venues, written and made a feature film (*Eight Days from Yesterday*), and produced teaching and learning materials in a variety of settings. Their 'Take Control' video won the IVCA gold award for education – and has recently been embedded in an online study resource (six steps to success). They are both Senior Lecturers in Learning Development actively involved with the Association for Learning Development in HE (http://www.aldinhe.ac.uk/) and the LearnHigher Centre for Excellence in Teaching and Learning (www.learnhigher.ac.uk).

Working in the Centre for the Enhancement of Learning and Teaching at London Metropolitan University, they continue to develop teaching and learning resources, and are particularly happy with the launch of the Get Ahead student conferences – a programme of events designed to promote student success that are run by and for students – and their 'Tell us the secret of your success' project, which produced a whole range of creative products including a website built by students passing on their study secrets and a student video, 'The Z–A of university' … All of these materials will be shown on the website accompanying this book.

This third edition of *Essential Study Skills* has two guest chapters – 'Computers: Any Place, Anywhere, Any Time' and 'PDP: Becoming Who You Want to Be', by **Debbie Holley** of Anglia Ruskin University and **Chris Keenan** of Bournemouth University and five new chapters, including the Bibliography.

Acknowledgements

The authors would like to thank all the students and staff with whom they have worked, the Association for Learning Development in Higher Education and LearnHigher.

A huge thank you goes to Andy Mitchell who has acted as a critical friend to this edition, who has produced some lovely diagrams and pattern notes – and who has helped give it additional life and energy.

A very special thank you goes to our families whose love and support has made everything possible.

Companion Website

Take advantage of a wealth of additional learning tools to support both students and lecturers by visiting the Burns and Sinfield companion website at: http://www.sagepub.co.uk/burnsandsinfield3e

Online you will find:

Printable handouts featuring key activities, checklists, diagrams, and much more from the book. These are ideal for promoting in class discussion and individual student study.

Additional web links to a variety of useful learning resources provide advice on a range of study skills techniques.

Videos on how to make the most of your Study Skills book and how to take effective notes.

Journal articles guide you through selected topics in more depth, while introducing you to using journal articles in your study.

Excerpts from Selected Student Essays introduce you to real papers, written by real students, to help you get to grips with the dos and don'ts of academic writing.

Study Skills packs on presentation skills, effective reporting, and essay planning give you step-by-step advice on how to prepare for these type of assignments.

PowerPoints on selected topics give you a more in depth look at specific study skills.

Podcasts from the authors give you more detailed look at selected topics.

For instructors, we are also including access to selected chapters from Burns and Sinfield's teaching book, **Teaching, Learning and Study Skills** which includes practical advice on how to encourage students to engage with study skills.

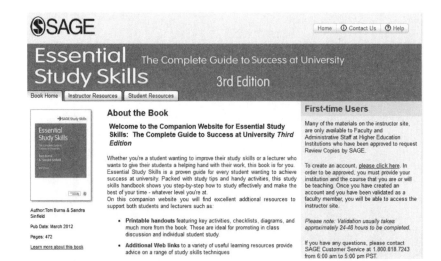

Section I

Overview

Chapter 1   Introduction

Chapter 2   Succeeding at University: Quick Steps to Success

Chapter 3   Places to Go and Things to Do

Chapter 4   Make Sense of Your Course

1

Introduction

Aims

To welcome you to ESS3 and to explain its aims and intentions.
To help you get thinking about your strengths, needs, hopes and fears as a student.
To prompt you to get the most from this book.

Learning outcomes

After reading this chapter and engaging with the activities you will:

- have gained a sense of how this book 'works'
- understand how to get the most from this book
- appreciate your own strengths, needs, hopes and fears and have begun to see a positive way forward for your own study success.

“ This really sets students up to succeed! **”**

Welcome

Welcome to *Essential Study Skills: The Complete Guide to Success at University* (ESS3). This book is designed to help you become a more effective and happier student by uncovering some of the mysteries of university life and revealing the 'what, why and how' of learning, studying and succeeding at university as quickly as possible.

Both of us (the authors) were the first in our immediate families to go to university and whilst we really enjoyed ourselves, we also found many aspects of university life strange, difficult or alienating. Life at university is even more fraught now than when we were students: there are loans to take out, enormous fees to take on board – and the job market is unpredictable. In these troubled times, this book is designed to help you understand and succeed at university. We look at all the different things you will be expected to do as a student – from independent learning to group work, from essays and reports to presentations and seminars, from dealing with your hopes and fears to being successful in creative, analytical and critical thinking.

It may take some time to work through the book – but you will be a much more productive and successful student if you invest a little time in yourself now.

Style warning

We have tried to be user-friendly without over-simplifying or, worse, being patronising. But this is difficult. There is no one writing style or way of explaining university life that will work for everybody.

Book warning

Becoming a successful student is a little like learning to drive. You would not expect to just read a book on driving and leap into a car ready to whizz up the M1. You would expect to have many, many driving lessons as well. Hopefully you would see your driving instructor as a critical friend, there to give you advice, tell you where you were getting it wrong – and guide you towards being a better driver... We hope that that is the role of this book for you.

We do pass on successful techniques to you and steer you as quickly as possible to academic success; but this is not a quick fix. We cover techniques that need practising and refining to work for you.

Out of your comfort zone

It is hard to change and it is hard to take criticism: but being a student requires both. Embrace change as a positive. Take feedback from tutors as good advice designed to help – not to put you down. Make mistakes and learn from them.

As human beings we learn by trial and error, by having a go, getting it wrong – then having more and more goes until we get it right. As we get older, this feels uncomfortable: we feel foolish or embarrassed. Yet, if we can get over those feelings, if we can force ourselves out of our comfort zones, and consciously decide to take risks, make mistakes and improve, everything else gets better. There are only two big mistakes:

- To be so frightened of making mistakes that we do nothing.
- Not to learn from our mistakes.

Web support

This book has been written with a companion website where we have put vidcasts, PowerPoint presentations, Study Packs, resource links and much, much more. Check out the website http://www.sagepub.co.uk/burnsandsinfield3e to see what we have for each chapter of the book.

LearnHigher

We are also part of LearnHigher, a centre for excellence in teaching and learning that has researched and produced resources for teaching, learning and study skills. You can explore the LearnHigher space as well as our companion website when you want to explore a topic further.

When searching online – or when we ask you to look – we will use this website icon for the following:

- COMPANION WEBSITE – our own online space with resources, links and work packs for you to use.
- LEARNHIGHER SPACE
- OTHER SITES – we will suggest sites and searches that you can use to find more things online.

tip

Use our Essay, Report and Presentation Packs to help you write your real assignments.

Resources: Pens, paper and the internet

The book is designed to give information, activities and links to online resources. Work through the book with notepad and pens at the ready. Make notes of the good stuff. Get involved with the activities.

When you start reading – think first: what do I know – what do I need? This gets you tuned in for success.

As learning is now multimodal – we learn by reading, talking, writing and also by exploring the web for additional reading and online tutorials – we will direct you to additional resources online when we can.

Using this book

This is a book that you can work through step by step but it has also been designed so that you can dip into different sections when you feel they will be useful to you. The trick is to know what you want from each section of the book at any particular time.

Each chapter looks like this

Each chapter in this book has an overall theme and whilst there might be some slight changes in the presentation of material, certain things will recur throughout the book. Typically there will be:

- Aims and learning outcomes that clearly state what we think the chapter will achieve
- An introduction to and presentation of information – coupled with, variously:
  - o activities for you to do
  - o questions to answer
  - o student and staff quotes
  - o queries, discussion and commentary
  - o further reading and guides to resources, including online resources and work packs
- A conclusion that draws the chapter together and to a close
- Reflection points.

Examiners

" This changes students' lives, not just their study skills. "

Course Leaders

" The effect on our students was like stardust. "

Strengths, needs, hopes and fears

This section of the chapter has a range of activities for you to do; they are designed to set you up to make the most of the book. Work through them – be spontaneous... See how the information will help you be more successful, more swiftly. Good luck.

Students

❝This was the best piece of learning I have ever done!❞

1. Activity: Personal skills review – a focusing questionnaire

To get you started complete the following questionnaire – but do it quickly. Don't think too much about your answers. This is not about getting it 'right' – it's about having a quick brainstorm.

1	How do you feel about yourself as a learner at the moment? Are you good at it?
2	How positive do you feel about being a student? How committed are you to developing your skills? What are you prepared to do to improve? How much time and energy are you prepared to put in?
3	How organised are you? (If you have brought up a family or juggled work with a hobby or family, then you are used to organising your life. This is a useful, transferable skill.)
4	If you have studied before, did you have set times to work? Do you have a place to study – a room, a desk, a table? Have you got an overall *approach* to studying? Do you feel you have successful strategies overall? What do you need to enable effective study?
5	What reading do you do at the moment? Are you happy with your reading skills? What do you think you need to make you a more successful academic reader?
6	How confident do you feel about using the library? Can you do successful online searches? Have you used journals or e-journals yet? What do you need here?
7	Do you make notes when you study? Are you happy with your notes? What do you do with your notes? What do you need to learn about notemaking?
8	What sorts of writing do you do at the moment (e.g. letters, blogs, emails, tweets, texts)? Have you written essays before? What sort of marks did you get? Are you happy with that? What do you want to get from the sections of the book that cover academic writing?
9	Have you ever had to make a presentation to a group of people? (A talk of a set length to a specific audience, usually on a specific topic.) How did it go? What do you feel about the idea of having to do presentations on your course? What do you want to know about presentations?
10	Have you revised for and sat exams? How did it go? How do you feel about your memory? How do you feel about exams? What do you need to know about revision and exam techniques?

FIGURE 1A   Personal skills review

 Photocopiable:

Essential Study Skills, Third Edition © Tom Burns and Sandra Sinfield, 2012 (SAGE)

Query: How do you feel now? Hopefully you have gained a better picture of what is required of you as a university student.

Discussion: The questionnaire outlines the sorts of things you will need to do to study effectively – you cannot write an essay, for example, if you cannot organise your time, make useful notes or read academic texts. The rest of this book will take you through these so that you understand them and get the opportunity to practise and reflect upon them.

tip

Your answers to the questions in Figure 1A will tell you what you want to get from each section of this book. Use them!

2. Activity: How to use this book

Reading an academic text is not like the reading we do for pleasure where typically you will read a book from cover to cover. Here's a quick introduction to active reading – focusing on this book. Work through the questions – and reflect on the exercise at the end.

1 Read the Contents pages of the book and ask yourself:

- What will I read first?
- What will I read later?
- When? Make a note in your diary…

2 Scan the Index pages (at the back – they highlight key words that appear throughout the book – with page numbers):

- What looks interesting?
- Look at some of those pages.
- What have you discovered?

3 Look over the notes you made in answer to the directions above.

Make sure that you have a list of things you want to study – and some dates in your diary indicating when you will work through this book.

➡

Query: Is this the way that you normally approach a book?

Discussion: Reading for study is not about the pleasure of 'what happens next'. Typically we do not ever read an academic book from cover to cover. We dip into books – looking for specific bits of information.

This can feel very uncomfortable: we can feel that we are cheating if we do not read the whole book, or we're afraid that we will not understand the subject properly – or that we will be missing something important. But we have to do it anyway: there's so much to do and so little time.

So, did you find it uncomfortable or was it okay? Don't forget, change is uncomfortable – but we can push through that. Hopefully you now feel more in control of this book – and if you use other texts in this way, you will be more in control of them as well.

"It opened up different strategies, learning strategies, and now I don't feel inferior.**"**

3. Activity: Hopes and fears

1 Read these statements and jot down your own responses to them: note whether you agree or disagree with the statement.

2 What advice would you give to the student concerned?

Statements

I'm not sure that I'll find enough time to study. I'm so busy – how will I fit everything in?	*I'm apprehensive that my studies will affect the rest of my life.*
Advice	**Advice**

I find it hard to concentrate for long periods.	I'm really looking forward to the challenge of studying again.
Advice	**Advice**
My memory isn't as good as it used to be.	I haven't written an essay for ages and I'm anxious about putting pen to paper.
Advice	**Advice**
I'm worried that the work will be difficult and I won't be able to understand it.	I was never good at school in the first place – how will I cope with this?
Advice	**Advice**
I enjoy working with other people – and discussing things.	I'm worried because English isn't my first language.
Advice	**Advice**
I'll find it hard to get down to work.	I'm not sure how my friends and family will react to my studies.
Advice	**Advice**
I'm good at organising my time.	I'm worried that I'll find it hard to cope with the difficult reading. I wish I could read faster.
Advice	**Advice**
I bet everyone on the course will be more used to studying than I am.	I'm not sure how to cope with the distractions at home.
Advice	**Advice**
I'm afraid that I'll fall behind with my work.	I'm glad that I have somewhere quiet to study.
Advice	**Advice**

➡

➡️

I'm not sure how much to discuss my work with other people. Isn't that cheating?	*Deadlines give me the energy to do things.*
Advice	**Advice**
I get a real sense of achievement out of finishing things.	*I'm not very good at spelling.*
Advice	**Advice**
I'm never sure when to use a comma or a full stop.	*I've forgotten all the rules of grammar.*
Advice	**Advice**
I can write letters but I don't know the sort of language you have to know to write essays.	*I know what to say but I can't find the right words.*
Advice	**Advice**
I don't have a wide enough vocabulary.	*I have plenty of ideas but I don't seem able to put them together.*
Advice	**Advice**
I'm all right once I get started, but I have a block about starting.	*I just don't know how to set about writing an essay.*
Advice	**Advice**

FIGURE 1B   Hopes and fears activity

Photocopiable:

Essential Study Skills, Third Edition © Tom Burns and Sandra Sinfield, 2012 (SAGE)

Query: How do you feel now? Here are a couple of things that might have happened:

- Just writing your fears down or saying them out loud made you see that they are not so bad after all.
- Seeing a list like this was reassuring – you are not alone.

Did this happen for you? Why don't you try to find someone to discuss your list with?

Make a friend, write a blog

We will ask you to discuss things quite a lot throughout this book – talking is really good active learning. Don't worry if you haven't got a university friend just yet – but do look out for one.

Even if you do have a friend – why don't you use your Facebook, Twitter or other online accounts as a space to talk through and reflect on your learning? You could set up a new blog or Wiki and use that to make useful notes on your student journey.

"Use or read student blogs or student video diaries: see what other people are writing about out there.**"**

4: Activity: Review the hopes and fears statements from Figure 1B and what other students have said about them

- *I'm not sure that I'll find enough time to study.*
  I'm not organised yet and I'll have to be if I want to work, study and maintain my family and friends.

- *I'm apprehensive that my studies will affect the rest of my life.*
  Well, being a student is going to have a dramatic impact on my life, I can see that. But I wanted to do this course – so I'll have to grin and bear it.

- *I find it hard to concentrate for long periods.*
  I shall start by concentrating for short periods and try to build up to longer study periods.

- *I'm really looking forward to the challenge of studying again.*
  So am I! It makes me feel good about me.

- *My memory isn't as good as it used to be.*
  I've heard that the main problem is that we were never taught how to learn in the first place.

- *I haven't written an essay for ages and I'm anxious about putting pen to paper.*
  But that's why I'm using this book.

- *I'm worried that the work will be difficult and I won't be able to understand it.*
  I am going to try to be brave and learn from my mistakes. I'm also going to ask questions if I don't understand.

➡

➡

- *I was never good at school in the first place – how will I cope with this?*
  I know what you mean – but I didn't like school, maybe that's why I didn't do well there. It's different now.

- *I enjoy working with other people – and discussing things.*
  I'm going to have to make a friend because I really do like talking things over.

- *I'm worried because English isn't my first language.*
  My daughter is better at English than I am and she has said that she will help me. She also thinks that I'm being very brave studying in English – which makes me feel strong instead of foolish.

- *I'll find it hard to get down to work.*
  It is hard to study – for everybody. I have a place where I 'feel' like a student. I trick myself into sitting there. I think, just sit there for five minutes and see what happens. Before I know it I'm working away.

- *I'm not sure how my friends and family will react to my studies.*
  I do know people who have a hard time: their friends think they'll become snobs or their children play up every time they try to work … I guess we have to explain what we are doing and make time for them as well.

- *I'm good at organising my time.*
  I find I have two approaches: one is to be very organised – I make lists and work through them. The other is I sit down amongst a pile of work and plunge in. Both systems seem to work sometimes.

- *I'm worried that I'll find it hard to cope with the difficult reading. I wish I could read faster.*
  I've heard that academic reading does get easier with practice – I certainly hope so.

- *I bet everyone on the course will be more used to studying than I am.*
  I also bet that I'm the only one who's frightened and I'm the only one whose family doesn't understand them … It's not true really, is it?

- *I'm not sure how to cope with the distractions at home.*
  You have to turn off the phone – not answer the door – and just work. My problem might be that I want to be distracted because that is easier than doing the work!

- *I'm afraid that I'll fall behind with my work.*
  I'm hoping the section on organising my time will help me with that.

- *I'm glad that I have somewhere quiet to study.*
  Lucky you. I've heard that some people work best in the quiet, others like noise … I'll experiment and see what works for me.

- *I'm not sure how much to discuss my work with other people. Isn't that cheating?*
  I know the answer to this one. Talking isn't cheating, it's active learning. I like the sound of that.

- *Deadlines give me the energy to do things.*
  Without deadlines I can't do the work. At the same time I know that I mustn't leave it all 'til the last minute – I must pace myself through an assignment. Hah!

- *I get a real sense of achievement out of finishing things.*
  I love it when I hand a piece of work in on time. But I do know other people who hate finishing things off. They just keep on reading and reading.

- *I'm not very good at spelling.*
  I'm going to use the spell checker on my computer. I've also heard that you need to build up your own dictionary of difficult words. I've already bought a small exercise book to do this.

- *I'm never sure when to use a comma or a full stop. I've forgotten all the rules of grammar.*
  My trick is to write in relatively short sentences. I use new words when it is easier to use the word than not. Like everything else, I hope it gets easier with practice.

- *I can write letters but I don't know the sort of language you have to know to write essays. I know what to say but I can't find the right words.*
  I'm going to get that exercise book to jot down the new words and use them when I understand them.

- *I don't have a wide enough vocabulary.*
  A friend of mine wrote all the new words on Post-its and stuck them up all over his flat. He said he got to learn them really quickly that way.

- *I have plenty of ideas but I don't seem able to put them together.*
  Another tip apparently is to write all those ideas on to separate index cards and shuffle them about till they make sense.

- *I'm all right once I get started, but I have a block about starting.*
  I've heard that just 'free writing' an answer to a question, without censoring or really thinking about it, is a good way to get started.

- *I just don't know how to set about writing an essay.*
  Again, I don't think that I have to know about this just yet. If I worry about too many things at once, then I get nothing done at all.

➡

➡

> **Query**: How do you feel now?

There are many ways to be a successful student and we hope that this has got you thinking about some of them.

The whole of this book goes on to look at successful study, learning and assignment strategies; everything from free writing to crafting beautiful analytical and critical essays; from preparing and rehearsing your first formal academic presentation to succeeding in your dissertation. **But to get you off to a quick start, there is a study tips checklist at the end of this chapter.**

❝And you go, yes, and it really spurs you on!❞

Conclusion

Universities can be mysterious and change can be uncomfortable; but we can sort these things out. In this first chapter we explained that ESS3 is designed to help you understand and succeed in university. We helped you to explore you own strengths, needs, hopes and fears – and you should now be in a position to get the very most out of this book. Good luck – we really hope that you enjoy using ESS3 – and that it helps you as much as these techniques have helped us.

Review points

You should now have:

- A sense of the book and its goals
- An idea of what you want from the book
- A successful way of reading
- A sense of purpose and a willingness to work through the book and become a happier and more successful student.

Study tips checklist

☐ Enjoy being a student.

☐ Help your family and friends realise how important being a student is to you.

☐ Have a regular place to study: when you sit there your body will learn to work.

☐ Move out of your comfort zone – make mistakes and learn from them.

☐ Work for half an hour every day

☐ Make some time to study every day. Turn off your phone, don't answer the door. Focus.

☐ Concentrate for 15 minute blocks at first and build up.

☐ Write something every day – your reflective blog?

☐ Develop your memory (Chapter 24).

☐ Discover if you like working alone – or with other people.

☐ Discover if you like working with noise or quiet.

☐ Discover if you like working in the morning, afternoon, evening or night.

☐ If English isn't your first language join an Academic English class.

☐ Buy an English dictionary, a subject dictionary and a dictionary of sociological terms.

☐ Buy an exercise book and make your own subject dictionary.

☐ Write new theories, words and phrases on Post-its and stick them up all round your home. Take them down when you know them.

☐ Prioritise; make lists; use a diary; use a 24/7 timetable. Be very organised … Sometimes sit amongst a pile of work and plunge in.

☐ Enjoy studying, do not see it as 'work'.

☐ Use deadlines to keep you on track.

☐ If unhappy with your spelling, punctuation or grammar, buy a simple grammar book and use it.

☐ Keep a small notebook with you. When you have a bright idea or insight, write it down.

☐ Find a friend, get a study partner, use online discussion boards, set up your own Wiki or blog and write about your studies and your learning.

 Photocopiable:

Essential Study Skills, Third Edition © Tom Burns and Sandra Sinfield, 2012 (SAGE)

Section I

Overview

2

Succeeding at University: Quick Steps to Success

Aims

To build on the goal setting in Chapter 1.
To jumpstart your study success with our 'six steps to success' strategy.

Learning outcomes

After reading this chapter and engaging with the activities you will have:

- reflected on common feelings about going to university
- been introduced to our six steps to success strategy and begin to succeed as quickly as possible.

Introduction

Are you the first in your family to go to university; an international or a mature student and worried that you won't fit in; leaving home for the first time; fed up that you are *not* leaving home; worried that you're too young and inexperienced; really bad at managing your time? Well you are not alone. In this chapter we outline our 'six steps to success' strategy – a thumbnail sketch of successful study practices that you can put into practice immediately.

Coming to university feels like...

Starting university or college or returning to study after a break can make you feel anxious: how will you cope with it all? How will you manage the reading, notemaking, organising your time, the assessments – essays, reports, presentations, exams? Everyone else looks as though they know what's going on and you are the only one who looks, sounds and feels like a fool. Everybody else is a *good* student – and no one has the same fears and worries as you. What can you do?

Here's what other students say:

" I think I'm going to be the oldest one there – I'm going to feel so out of place. **"**

" Well, I don't suppose I'll be the 'only gay in the village' – but how will I meet up with other people like me? **"**

" Is there any help for people who never really succeeded at school the first time round? **"**

" What happens if I find out I really hate my course? **"**

" Do you think I'll be able to share a flat with other people – I really, really want to leave home? **"**

" I've heard that it's really important to get to the Freshers' Week, but I'm still working – am I going to miss out all year? **"**

" Will I have problems because of my beliefs? **"**

And of course there are many more worries and fears than those. One thing you should be reassured of right away, whatever your fear, you will not be alone. Whatever you are worried about, frightened of or sure that you are hopeless at, there will be many others like you out there. The trick is to accept your fears as normal and take steps to do something about them.

Talk to other people about what's worrying you, don't bottle your fears up on your own. Make a friend or get a study partner or set up a study group so that a bunch of you can support each other. And always, always check out the Students' Union to see what help and advice they might have for you... For if there isn't already a Society or Club or meeting place for people like you, you can create one. And if there is any help or advice going at your university they can point you in the right direction...

Worst case scenario: if you really feel that you are on the wrong course, your Union, Students' Services and/or your Personal Tutor are all there to help.

❝ If you are in halls, make friends with the people there. If you are in a student flat, make an effort to integrate and make friends there. If you live at home, make sure you have freed up time to go to the Freshers events offered, especially those for your course. If you have a part-time job, now is the time to book holiday. ❞

Six steps to success

Our work has revealed that there are certain approaches to life and to study that promote active learning and study success. We call these the six steps to success and have shaped our book around them. For a quick overview, read the sections below and think about how you can put them into practice in your studies – and what chapters you might read first.

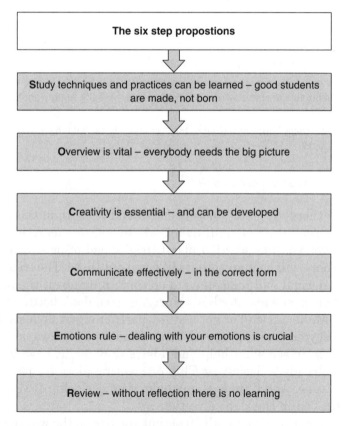

FIGURE 2A   Six steps to success – **SOCCER**

By the way, just because these ideas are in a list (Figure 2A) does not mean that the first thing mentioned is more important than the last – they are all equally important. In fact we have organised the book itself with the 'Overview' section first ... But the mnemonic (something designed to aid memory) **SOCCER** is more memorable.

We discuss the six steps briefly here and refer to other sections of this book that develop the ideas even further.

Study techniques and practices can be learned – good students are made, not born

It is all too easy to think that we are not 'cut out' for studying. Bad school experiences can make people believe that studying is not for them – they are not good students. But why should you know how to study effectively? If you wanted to be a firefighter or a farmer or a chef or a carpenter you would know that you would have to learn how to be one. If we think of studying like this it can become easier. All the way through this book we will look at the constituent study and academic skills that can help you to succeed. In terms of developing your study techniques consider:

- Chapter 5: How to learn effectively
- Chapter 6: Get organised for independent study
- Chapter 7: Computers: Any place, anywhere, any time
- Chapter 8: How to succeed in group work
- Chapter 10: How to survive academic reading: targeted research and active reading
- Chapter 11: How to make the best notes
- Chapter 25: How to understand and pass exams

" Why didn't they tell us this before? I left school feeling like a complete failure – but it was just that I didn't know how to learn. These techniques have given me such a boost. I feel really confident now. **"**

Overview is vital – everybody needs the big picture

Whilst it is true that we tend to learn things in pieces, one step at a time, this is helped if we have the big picture first; if we know how the subject will be covered. It's like a jigsaw puzzle, it is much easier to put the pieces together if we have the picture on the box. If we understand how universities work and how our courses have been put together, we will be able to achieve more, more swiftly. Have a look at more 'overview' chapters and then find:

- Chapter 3: Places to go and things to do
- Chapter 4: Make sense of your course
- Chapter 27: Moving on: what to do when you finish university

❝ I really hated school; not knowing what was going on and why. Using the 'overview' has made all the difference. I'm now on top. **❞**

Creativity is essential – and can be developed

There is a lot of 'common sense' about being a successful student – it is common sense to be well organised, to make time each day for study. There's nothing wrong with common sense, we know students who have gained good 2:1 degrees with common sense and sheer hard work. However, if you want to do that little bit more, if you want studying to be a little bit easier and more interesting, then a touch of creativity is needed.

If you give back to lecturers what they have told you, if you just use their examples and read the books that they recommend, then you will be a strong, average student.

To get a little further you have to be creative, you have to go somewhere or think something different. How can you do that? We discuss creativity generally, and explore creative ways to approach assignments and notemaking. We take you through techniques that encourage a different or more original approach to your studies. Look at:

- Chapter 11: How to make the best notes (especially the section on pattern notes)
- Chapter 12: How to be creative in your learning
- Chapter 13: How to think effectively: analytical and critical thinking

❝ At school I was told to go away and get a job in a shop [sorry shop workers!], that I would never be able to learn anything. Putting colour and life into my university work has made all the difference; now I get As for my assignments. **❞**

Communicate effectively – in the correct form

Just as we cannot 'know' how to study, we may not 'know' what an essay, report or presentation is. These things have specific shapes to them (what), they have specific purposes (why) and there are tried and tested ways of approaching them (how). In order to help you develop successful assessment techniques, we devote a whole section of the book to effective communication. We look at essays, reports, dissertations, presentations and seminars and also how to overcome writing blocks and avoid plagiarism. See:

- Chapter 13 on analytical and critical thinking
- Chapters 14–21 on how to prepare successful assignments

❝ I used to get comments like 'too descriptive' and I never knew what they meant. It's about critical thinking – I get that now! ❞

❝ They used to write things like 'there's no introduction' or 'there's no conclusion' on my essays. But no one ever told me what these were – or why they wanted them. Now I only have to worry about my ideas, I know how to present them. ❞

Emotions rule – dealing with your emotions is crucial

Studying and learning may be cognitive or intellectual activities, but for most of us they are fraught with emotion also. Certain tasks exhilarate us whilst others will bore us. When we first start a course we are apprehensive, nervous or even terrified. If we do not acknowledge and address our own emotional responses to the different things that we encounter as students, we will never be able to benefit from our positive responses or overcome our negative ones.

We explore the emotional dimension of study and the roles of fear and self-confidence in the academic environment. We will ask you to think about your own emotional highs and lows as a student – and what you intend to do about them.

Positive thinking is useful for all our studying and learning activities – but you may draw on positive thinking tips and tricks even more when approaching your first presentation and your exams. If this is a big issue for you, first read:

- Chapter 9: How to interact and build relationships at university
- Chapter 22: How to deal with your emotions

❝ You ask what the first day was like? I was het up, frightened, terrified ... I thought 'Why the hell have I done this to myself?' I just wanted to run away ... Oh I love it now, I don't want to leave! ❞

Review – without reflection there is no learning

Learning involves an active selection of what to learn and how to learn it. Throughout the book we will be examining different memory and revision strategies, including reflective learning logs and Personal Development Planning (PDP). You might also notice that each chapter ends with 'Review points' that encourage you to explore not only what you have learned but *how* you learned it. Learning and remembering are not necessarily automatic or simple, but we can learn how to do these effectively and we have structured the book to reinforce this. To explore this in more depth go to:

- Chapter 23: Reflective learning and the learning log
- Chapter 24: Memory and effective revision
- Chapter 25: How to understand and pass exams
- Chapter 26: PDP: Becoming who you want to be

" I love doing my learning logs, it makes me make sense of what I'm doing. If I didn't do my logs, I don't think I'd understand anything at all. **"**

Conclusion

In this brief chapter we looked at some typical hopes and fears about becoming a university student and explored the six steps to success – making links to other sections of the book. We have argued that good students, like you, are made, not born. If you build SOCCER into your study habits every day, you will make real progress.

Review points

By reading this chapter you should now have:

- An understanding of how your own hopes and fears about becoming a student are shared with others
- An awareness of the six steps to success – the propositions that shape and inform the rest of the book
- An idea of which chapters you want to read first – and why.

Section I

Overview

3

Places to Go and Things to Do

Aims

This chapter is designed to explain the unwritten 'rules' of university and how to study successfully.

Learning outcomes

After reading through this chapter you will:

- understand university and the unwritten 'rules'
- know about the key teaching and learning strategies – lecture, seminar, tutorial, VLE… – and how to make the most of them
- have been introduced to the places to go and things to do at your university – from the librarian to your personal tutor, from Careers to the Students' Union
- hit the ground running.

Using this book will make university easier for everybody – but it might be especially useful if you are the first in your family to go to university, if you are unsure of exactly what it means to be a student and if you are unclear about what to do at university, why to do it, and when.

University – what and why

A university is a research institution where lecturers don't just teach their subjects, they also *research* them, they create new knowledge. Going to university used to mean that you had access to the knowledge 'owned' and created by the university. The university validated your degree and acted as a gatekeeper to the careers and jobs that you could get with it.

Times have changed and more of us are going to university than ever before. One thing this means is that there are more people entering Higher Education (HE) who may not have been prepared for it by either their families or their schools.

One of the key purposes of this book is to reveal how to succeed in the strange and mysterious world of HE – even if you are the first in your family to go or if you never enjoyed school. The strategies work for all students – even if you are not the first in your family to go.

Why are you at your university?

Going to go university is a big decision: you must change your life – you may change yourself. Your time is no longer your own – and being at university is hard work.

If you do go to university you should know why, you should know how to succeed – and you should know what you want to do with your degree once you have got it. So what about you:

- Are you at a high status institution that will plug you into a high-powered network of contacts?
- Are you studying a subject because you're fascinated by it and couldn't imagine life without studying it?
- Are you studying in the hope of getting a better job?
- Do you want to plug into up-to-the-minute research?
- Are you more interested in a supportive teaching and learning environment?

Maybe none of these things seems important to you – but you have found a very interesting course at the place down the road and you are happy with that? Well, that's fine, too. The point is to know why you are where you are.

 **tip**

Not sure what your university is good at? Use its website. Find out what staff and students say about being there. Discover what support services exist. See what resources are available online. Research Institutes and postgraduate courses tell you your university's fields of expertise.

Universities have lives of their own

When you go to university many things are expected of you, including that you study differently from the way you did at school or college. Going to university means joining an institution with rules, regulations, requirements, conditions and habits. Often no one will actually tell you what the rules are, but there are rules none the less. This section is going to tell you what some of those rules are!

" The biggest secret of university life is that it should involve your whole life while you are there – it should be a 40 hour per week commitment! University is a full-time job. I wish I'd been told this at the beginning! **"**

The rules

As with all groups, academic communities have ground rules, traditions and a sense of self. These inform and influence the way that you are expected to behave as a student generally – and as a student of a particular subject. History, business, pharmacology, computing – all the subjects that you can study have specific ways of being researched and of being studied, understood and written about. As well as knowing how to learn and how to study generally, you will need to know how to study your subject: you will have to become familiar with the history, the epistemology and the academic practices of your subject.

1. Activity: The 'Unending Conversation'

(With thanks to Jackie Pieterick, Senior Lecturer, Creative & Professional Writing, University of Wolverhampton, for sharing this with us.)

1   Read through the following description of being an academic or a student; for it is a metaphor for joining an academic community.
2   What is it telling you about being a student?
3   How can you use that metaphor to help you understand what to do at university?
4   Make notes of your thoughts and make sure you understand the metaphor by the end of this chapter.

Imagine that you enter a parlor. You come late. When you arrive, others have long preceded you, and they are engaged in a heated discussion, a discussion too heated for them to pause and tell you exactly what it is about. In fact, the discussion had already begun long before any of them got there, so that no one present is qualified to retrace for you all the steps that had gone before.

You listen for a while, until you decide that you have caught the tenor of the argument; then you put in your oar. Someone answers; you answer him; another comes to your defence; another aligns himself against you, to either the embarrassment or gratification of your opponent, depending upon the quality of your ally's assistance.

However, the discussion is interminable. The hour grows late, you must depart. And you do depart, with the discussion still vigorously in progress.

(Kenneth Burke, *The Philosophy of Literary Form*, 1941: pp. 110–111)

> **Query**: Have you made your notes? Do you think you've understood it? Don't forget to discuss ideas with someone else if they are proving difficult – or interesting. Now read on.

So, it's about talking… or is it epistemology?

Joining an academic community is like joining a conversation that started before you got there – and will carry on after you have left. To feel like you can join in the conversation, it helps if you have a sense of the history of your subject – who are the key players – and what are their 'big ideas'? What are the main arguments?

By argument we do not mean the everyday use of the term – to disagree or fight – we are talking about how propositions or knowledge-claims are put together, the epistemology of your subject: and how you get to 'put your oar in' or say something in your subject.

This will also mean that you will have to make an effort to learn how to communicate: how to discuss and write about your subject.

The epistemology and academic practices will be slightly different depending on whether you are a biologist or an historian, a student of film or English literature. But one basic rule will be the same for all subjects: it helps to develop an understanding of what has gone before (the existing literature) before you move on to explore up-to-date knowledge and theories.

2. Activity: Joining my academic 'group'

So take a moment to think about the subject that you have chosen to study and why you have chosen to study it.

Bring to the front of your mind why you are interested in it.
Recall what you know – and what you might need to find out.
Make notes of your first thoughts here:

tip

To get a grip of a new subject, use a subject dictionary or see if there is a reader's and writers beginner's guide. You will come across publications with names like *Philosophy* or *Freud* or *Biology… for Beginners*. If you are not on top of your subject yet, get yourself some of these, read them, understand them, make notes and use them.

The first year doesn't matter does it?

A big mistake many students make is to think the first year doesn't count. But this is the year to get a basic understanding of your subject – and it is the year tutors meet you for the first time. Make a good impression. Be interested, engaged, enthusiastic … This is the year you start to make your mark – use it!

" When I first got here, I kept thinking that I would be 'found out', that someone would realise that I didn't belong and would throw me out. I don't think that any more, I know I can do it now – and my tutors know it too. **"**

So what are these rules then?

University is supposed to be a full-time occupation – using up 35–40 hours of your time per week – every week. Even if the taught part of your course only occupies 10–12 hours, you are expected to fill the other 28–30 hours with reading, talking and writing. You are supposed to be studying and learning full time, through lectures and seminars, but especially through your independent study. So the rules involve working full time – and making the most of the following teaching and learning opportunities.

The lecture

One lecturer plus a large group of students – 150 or more. The lecturer is an expert, a researcher at the cutting edge of the subject. The lecturer gives the students a short-cut to key information – and successful students make notes – and use those notes to seed further reading, thought and writing.

tip

Always prepare before you attend a lecture. Think – what is it about? What do I know already? Why *this* topic? How will it help me with my assignment?

Seminar

A seminar usually consists of a lecturer plus 10–30 students. A seminar is supposed to seed your thinking and develop your ideas through discussion.

 **tip**

Be an active learner – join in the discussions. Prepare before you attend. Know what you are supposed to be doing – and do it. Learn seminar survival strategies: know how to present your opinions assertively, not aggressively; learn how to interrupt the person who never stops talking; and learn how to draw out quiet people who may actually have much to offer.

The tutorial

Some universities still offer tutorials – they act like the seminar but with one tutor to four or five students.

tip

There is definitely no hiding place in a tutorial. You will have to be prepared and you will have to join in.

Virtual learning spaces

Universities include virtual, blended or e-learning experiences as part of their teaching and learning practices. Some may not have lectures at all, having the 'lecture' available only as a podcast or an online PowerPoint. Some may have whole courses delivered only via their Virtual Learning Environment (VLE) – and you will be expected to join in discussions, to write and post answers to questions and even to conduct group tasks through the VLE. Find out how your course is going to be delivered – and how to make the most of it.

tip

Your notes will be your lifeline when studying. Even if your course offers you the option of printing off the PowerPoint slides of your lectures, try not to. This only costs you money and gives you more work reading all the slides again. Or, worse, you'll feel like a failure because of all the things you are not doing. Just learn to make good notes and to use them.

Independent learning

No one source is ever designed to give you 'all you need to know' on a topic. Lectures and seminars, and all the reading that you can bear, are all designed to spur you on to discussion, to thinking, to writing – to yet more reading... Thus there is much emphasis on independent learning. That is, you will be expected to follow up ideas in various ways, including reading around a subject, *on your own and on your own initiative*.

Some people are now using the term inter-dependent learning – this indicates that we cannot learn in a vacuum. We could not have access to useful texts (books, journals, internet material) without the librarian, we could not have meaningful discussions without other people: we are inter-dependent, social beings and we can benefit from this inter-dependency if we use it actively; more on this below.

Some more places to go and things to do

The library – find your university library. Find where the books for your subject are kept. Make a habit of spending some time there every week. Notice the books that are available on your subject. Have a look at the books that are available on other subjects. Ideas can be inter-dependent as well. Thus if you are studying sociology, you might find useful material in the psychology section of your library. If studying literature, you might try some quantum mechanics.

tip

Check out your reading list. Courses come with reading lists that the tutor has put together. This list is often divided into essential and recommended reading. Essential is that which you *should* read for any assignment question. The recommended list shows books or journal articles that you might like to dip into. When the reading list is huge – share it. Read one or two things each and report back.

The **Counter Loans section** – there are never enough books to satisfy all our students. Therefore, universities have a special mini-library within the library proper. This is where all the essential reading is usually kept – and you can actually get your hands on it because these books are only allowed out for an hour or two. Use this area.

tip

If there are books that you need that are always out on loan, request that at least one copy be placed here.

Books and e-books – become aware of the most up-to-date and useful texts on your subject. Get used to picking these off the shelves and having a quick look in the index – what is in the book? Can you make a few quick notes now – or will you have to read it later? When? Put a date in your diary.

Journals and e-journals – the most up-to-date books are always several months old by the time they are actually written and published – to keep up to date with your subject read the latest journals.

tip

Find your subject librarian and ask them to recommend the best journals and e-journals for you. Make a habit of reading them. When reading don't just look at the information and ideas, look also at how arguments are constructed, how articles are written – this will be a model for your writing.

Quality press – many subjects are covered in the quality papers in sections headed Education or Financial Issues or the Media, and so on. Whilst such articles may not be academic enough for direct use, they do keep you abreast of current thought on your subject. There will be names dropped that you can then research in the books and journals.

tip

Start a press cuttings file for your subject. Get into the habit of looking in the papers every week and of putting relevant cuttings into your file. Always source your cuttings: put the date and the name of the paper.

" My development plan is to read broadsheet newspapers like the *Guardian, The Times* and *Independent*, and I'm currently working on it. If I compare me now to when I got here, I have improved my communication skills already. **"**

Electronic information systems: the web and all that. Ask your subject librarian for the best search engines and the best sites for your subject. Make a habit of checking the best sites and seeing what's new.

Networked information and **VLEs** – the networked computers and/or intranet systems are where key course materials and resources can be accessed. Many journals and newspapers can also be found more easily online than in paper-based format. Again it is helpful to discuss this with your subject librarian or your course tutor and ask them about these things. Once you have discovered which of your journals are online, or which key resources you can access through your VLE make a habit of dipping into them and seeing what's new.

tip

Do a quick journal search putting in key words from your assignment question – see what happens. Every time you start a new course or module, check what resources and materials are in the related VLE.

Other **media** – television, radio, films, video and audiotapes, online tutorials – all have a role to play in your learning. Your university library may well offer access to a whole catalogue of useful material that comes in special forms.

Don't limit yourself to electronic or paper-based approaches – explore *all* the sources of information that your institution offers.

tip

Do a quick search of the television pages: what programmes are there that might support your studies? BBC2's business programmes might help business students, various culture or film programmes might help film or literature students, Teachers' TV might help education students… Make a habit of viewing these programmes or channels – and enjoy doing it. You chose to be a student – make the most of every bit of it.

"When I first got here, I thought everyone was looking at me thinking, what's she doing here? I don't think that anymore. It's my university now!**"**

Networking at university

Remember, whatever your university is like, you and your fellow students are going to be the people that will earn more, live longer and be healthier. Being a student opens doors – and it allows you to meet people and make contacts that you could not make in any other way. Grab the opportunity.

As well as attending lectures and seminars, workshops and classes, you will be able to make contacts that could support and enrich you throughout your working life. Even if this idea does not appeal to you – perhaps it is not how your community normally operates – you should still investigate becoming a Student Representative or doing Volunteering or Work Placements. Join a Club or Society – or set one up.

Degrees are awarded according to your marks, typically as follows:

- First class degree – 70% or more
- Upper second (2:1) – 60–69%
- Second class (2:2) – 50–59%
- Third class – 40–49%

Typically the marks for your first year are not included in your mark average, whilst the second and third year marks are aggregated.

➡

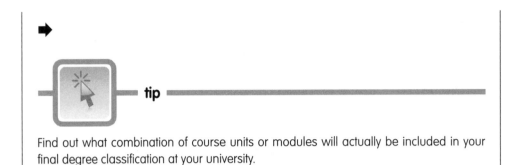

Find out what combination of course units or modules will actually be included in your final degree classification at your university.

People to see and more things to do

We've looked mainly at sources of information – from the lecture to the library – and how to use them. Here we are looking at all the people that might prove useful when a student.

Personal and/or academic tutor: Your personal and/or academic tutor gets to know you as a person and as an academic. This is the person who can advise you if things are going wrong – or who can write that glowing job reference if things went very well. However, they can't do this if they have not met you.

Go and see your personal tutor before a problem arises.

Subject librarian (Academic Liaison Library): The subject librarian is a specialist in his or her own right. They have knowledge of *your* subject, they may have put course materials and study resources online for you and they will be able to direct you towards useful books, journals and websites.

Find out when your librarian is holding a help session – and go there. Ask them about the books, journals and websites that will be most useful to you.

Learning and writing development and support: Most universities have some form of learning and writing development help – go there and use their courses, resources and help sessions to get you on course for that good degree.

❝ I just wanted to tell you that your Preparation course had me hit the ground running. I'm on track for a first class degree and it's due to the help I got before I even started! **❞**

If you missed your university's pre-sessional courses, don't despair because courses and workshops typically run semester time, too. Check out the university website to see what is running, when and where. And don't just think about study skills and writing support – many offer maths and IT sessions also – be there or be square.

Student support services: Universities typically offer Chaplaincy, Careers, Counselling, Dyslexia Support, Disability Support, Financial Advice, Peer Support, Volunteering and Work Placement opportunities... Find out exactly what yours has and how you can use student services to help you make the most of your time there.

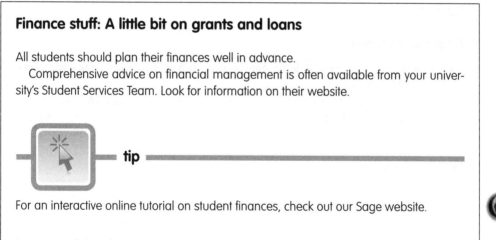

Finance stuff: A little bit on grants and loans

All students should plan their finances well in advance.

Comprehensive advice on financial management is often available from your university's Student Services Team. Look for information on their website.

— **tip** —————————————————————————————————

For an interactive online tutorial on student finances, check out our Sage website.

Loans explained

Students from the United Kingdom can take out student loans to help them with their university fees and living costs.

You will not have to start repaying your fees until after you graduate and are earning more than £15,000 per year, although you can start repaying them sooner if you wish.

➡

➡️

For fees:

- A loan covers the full amount of university fees
- Apply using a PN1 Form (continuing students should use the PR1 form)
- Fees are paid to the university direct by Student Loans Company
- Not linked to household income
- No upper age limit.

For living costs:

- Apply using a PN1 form (continuing students should use the PR1 form)
- All students receive 72% of loan. How much of the remaining 28% you receive depends on your household income
- If you receive a maintenance grant and no other benefits, your loan entitlement will be the maximum loan minus half of your maintenance grant
- You must be under 60 at the start of the course.

Students starting in 2012/13

A new loans system will operate for 2012/13 entrants onwards: visit the Student Loans Company website.

Help and enquiries

Your university Student Services Team may be able to help if you have any enquiries or problems with your loans.

Muslim students might like to research Muslim students and undergraduate funding before deciding on taking a student loan. Again, visit the Student Loans Company website.

What is a grant?

A grant is an amount of money given to students from low income families to help them pay for their living costs while at university.

For students starting in 2012 visit http://studentfinance-yourfuture.direct.gov.uk/ for detailed information on grants.

What is a bursary?

Most universities award some form of bursary to UK students from low income households. The bursary is given to help pay for living costs. All students may be eligible, dependent on their financial circumstances.

Do I need to apply for a bursary?

No: the Student Loan Company tells the university about your financial circumstances and this information is used to calculate if you are eligible.

When you complete your application for student funding, you have to sign a declaration that you are willing for your financial details to be shared for bursary purposes. It must also be signed by anyone else whose finances are taken into account in assessing your application, e.g. parents or partners.

I don't know if I gave consent to share the information – is it too late to do so?

No: if you ring the Student Loan Company on 0845 607 7577 they can accept this by phone. If someone such as a parent or a partner needs to provide financial details they will also have to phone this number.

How do I know if I have had my final assessment?

Check your assessment letter carefully – it will say either 'final' or 'provisional'. If your assessment is 'provisional', this means Student Finance England is still waiting to receive information from you.

More information

If you have any queries about bursaries phone the Student Fees Office on 0845 603 4016.

For more on grants and bursaries, please see http://studentfinance-yourfuture.direct. gov.uk/ for detailed information.

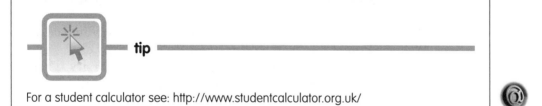

tip

For a student calculator see: http://www.studentcalculator.org.uk/

Student services – quick tips

Careers: Have up-to-date information on career opportunities, job requirements and how to plan and prepare curriculum vitae (CV). One of the most useful things that you could do would be to make an immediate appointment with the Careers people – we are talking in your first year here, not three weeks before the end of your degree programme. Find out what employment opportunities are open to you, now. Get advice about how best to tailor your degree programme to the sort of career you are likely to take up. If you are on a modular degree programme, this will help you choose the best modules for the career that you want.

tip

Start collecting information for your final CV the moment you read this. Have a folder (paper-based and/or online) where you keep key bits of information about yourself – jobs you have done, your responsibilities and how you developed; courses that you have taken and how you have utilised the information learned; modules that you took – and how they fit you for a specific job... Go through this file every so often so that you always keep it up to date.

Work Placement or Volunteering: The Work Placement or Volunteering Officers are the ones who find placements for you whilst you are still on your degree programmes. Once you know what career avenue seems best for you go to Work Placement (where you are paid) or Volunteering (which is unpaid). Find out how to get a placement in the best place. This is the key way of finding out whether or not you actually like the work. This gives you great experience to use both in your degree and in your CV – and if you make a good impression you may even find you have a job lined up whilst you are still taking your degree.

Counselling services: Offer confidential help with study, personal or social problems. We have hinted that being a student is not necessarily easy – so find out what counselling support might be available at your university. There is no stigma or shame involved in getting support when you need it.

tip

If you find that you are having problems adjusting to being a student, if you are homesick or if you feel overwhelmed by things – go and see the counsellor.

Students' Union: The Students' Union (SU) runs the Clubs and Societies that serve your extra-curricular needs. If you really want university to work for you, join a Club or Society and get involved in your SU. Why don't you think about standing for office? As far as we know, Ricky Gervais became a success not just because of his degree, but because he was involved in the Entertainments side of his SU.

Query: How much of the above was new information to you? How much were you aware of already? Has any of the information changed your mind about anything? What are you going to do now?

Discussion: Remember, the point with learning is that you *use* information in some way. You might use that information to form an opinion or to take action. Here we are hoping that this information will form or inform your behaviour. We hope that you will do something with and about the above information.

3. Activity: Do something with the information

It is not enough just to notice bits and pieces of information – you must do something with it. Here are some suggestions about what to do with the information above:

1 Make a list of the points above that will be useful to you.
2 Make a list of the key people – the ones that you want to see.
3 Set aside time in your schedule to go and do something – find the Counter Loans Area of the library or the Learning Development Unit; make appointments with some of the key people noted above.
4 Set goals for each activity that you plan – why are you going to the Counter Loans Area or the Learning Development Unit? What will you ask the person that you have booked an appointment with? How will you know that you have got what you wanted?
5 Complete the checklist at the end of this chapter (Figure 3B in Activity 5), noting what you have done, who you have seen and what you got from the experience.

Conclusion

In this chapter we have unpicked the unwritten rules of university life – focusing on the places to go, people to meet and things to do to hit the ground running. Don't forget to quickly review what you have read and done, why you did it – and what you feel that you have learned. Make a few notes so that you do not forget. Make those appointments so you get started on making the most of your university experience. Don't forget to use the checklists at the end of this chapter to make sure you make the most of this information.

Review points

When reflecting on this chapter you might notice that:

- Universities are academic communities with their own rules. Understanding them is part of the art of being a student.
- You know something about lectures, seminars, tutorials, the VLE; about librarians and personal tutors; about Support Services and the Students' Union. There are places to go and people to meet who are there to help you as a student – and to help you get a job when you leave.
- You now understand some of the rules – and you are prepared to hit the ground running.

4. Activity: Worried about money?

Use the projected income and expenditure checklist to work out your income and outgoings. Take control of your finances.

Projected income and expenditure for academic year

Income

	£
Loan/grant/bursary	
Family support	
Job	
Other	
Total yearly income	£
Monthly income	£

Expenditure

	£		£
Rent or mortgage		Toiletries	
Water		Newspapers/magazines/coffees	
Insurance (e.g. contents, phone)		Books/stationery	
Electricity		Miscellaneous course costs	
Gas		Laundry	
Phone/mobile/internet		Public transport/Oyster card	
TV licence		Clothing	
Car tax		Sports/hobbies	
MOT		Christmas/birthdays	
Car servicing and general maintenance		Holidays/trips	
Parking		University Ball/Socialising	
Food		Other	

Total yearly expenditure	£
Monthly expenditure	£

Deduct total yearly expenditure from total yearly income to work out your surplus or shortfall

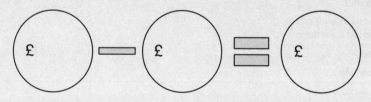

FIGURE 3A   Projected income and expenditure for academic year

Photocopiable:

Essential Study Skills, Third Edition © Tom Burns and Sandra Sinfield, 2012 (SAGE)

5. Activity: Studying at university checklist

Use this checklist to reflect on the different places to go and things to do, or that you have done.

Teaching and Learning

I have been to my first:

Lecture

It was about:

It linked to this bit of the assignment question:

I learned:

I will now read:

Seminar

It was about:

It linked to this bit of the assignment question:

I learned:

I will now read:

Tutorial

It was about:

It linked to this bit of the assignment question:

I learned:

I will now read:

Independent learning and inter-dependent learning

I have explored the following:

library

Counter Loans (Key Text Area)

books

journals

quality press

electronic information systems

I was looking for:

It linked to this bit of the
assignment question:

I learned:

I will now read:

People and places to go

I have now met with:

Personal tutor	Name:	Room:

It was about:

I learned:

I will now:

Academic tutor	Name:	Room:

It was about:

I learned:

I will now:

Subject librarian(s)	Room and/or Building:

It was about:

I learned:

I will now:

Learning development and support	Name:	Room:

It was about:

I learned:

I will now:

➡

➡

Student support services

Careers	Room and/or Building:
It was about:	
I learned:	
I will now:	

Work placement/volunteering service	Room and/or Building:
It was about:	
I learned:	
I will now:	

Counselling	Room and/or Building:
It was about:	
I learned:	
I will now:	

Students' Union	Room and/or Building:
It was about:	
I learned:	
I will now:	

FIGURE 3B   Studying at university checklist

Photocopiable:

Essential Study Skills, Third Edition © Tom Burns and Sandra Sinfield, 2012 (SAGE)

Section I

Overview

4

Make Sense of
Your Course

Aims

To help you make sense of your course, take control of your learning and succeed.

Learning outcomes

After reading this chapter and engaging with the activities, you will:

- know how your course has been put together
- know how to use an overview of a course to take control of it
- see how the overview promotes active learning and assignment success.

" I never enjoyed school, not at all. I never understood what we were doing or why. It was all so frustrating and I felt so powerless. Now I'm at university because I want to be, studying what I want to study, and everything is so different. It's great! **"**

Even the most engaged and excited student still benefits from understanding how to get the most from the different courses and modules they study. That is the goal of this chapter. We take you through a detailed examination of course information and show you how to use that to develop a successful study strategy.

1. Activity: What do you know about your course?

- What do you already know about the course you're on?
- What jobs can you do when you get your degree?
- How many modules will you have to take?
- How much choice will there be for you?
- How many weeks and how many hours per week are you in a classroom?
- How many assessments are there? What form will they take?
- Is there a reading list? Have you got any of the books on it? Have you read anything for this course already?

Query: Do you have enough information to be successful?

Discussion: If not, what are you going to do about it? Read on…

Take control

❝ Not knowing what to expect from university was my problem. I had no idea what to expect which made me anxious. ❞

Once you are at university you are thought to be an active learner in control of your own learning. You need to understand how your degree has been put together and to which jobs or careers it is leading. You need to understand exactly what you have to do and learn to pass each module you take – you need to engage. To get the most out of life and out of your studies you must be active and interactive; you must become an active student in control of your own learning. Here we explore how to make this happen.

❝ I didn't care who had designed or validated the course! To me, learning outcomes came to my notice through module booklets. ❞

❝ What was important to me was knowing what my course assessments were going to be, plus what the course would lead to in terms of future career and education. ❞

Use the module handbooks!

Once you join your course there are several really useful things to do immediately to gain your overview and take control of the course:

- **Read the module handbook**. Make sure you have a copy of the handbook for your course – usually this means downloading it from your VLE. Once you have a copy – read it! If you can access information before you even get to university – do so!

   " The uni didn't give me any way to prepare before I went, which didn't help ... even if it's false courage, I would have liked to have felt ready to go. **"**

- **Aims and outcomes**. Most handbooks spell out overall aims and the learning outcomes – the things you have to do and learn to pass that course. We also do this at the beginning of each chapter of this book. Don't put the handbook in your bag or file it away neatly. Read it – make sure that you do know what you have to do and learn.

 **tips**

Highlight key words – make notes.

Make a list of everything that you will have to do or learn to pass the course. Pin this list up in your study space to help keep you focused on the goals of the course.

Look at the learning outcome words when preparing for a class or lecture, for your reading and for an assignment.

- **Assessment**. Once you have analysed the aims and outcomes, look at how the course is going to be assessed. The course may be 100% coursework, 100% exam-based or a mixture of the two. Coursework tends to involve the production of one or more of the following: essay, report, write-up of a practical, presentation, etc.

   Exams can be just as varied, comprising seen or unseen papers (with the former you receive the exam paper in advance of the exam itself, with the latter you receive the paper at the beginning of the exam proper).

   Exams can be one, two or three hours in length. They might involve you writing essay answers, short answers or responding to multiple choice questions. They may be 'open book', where you can take certain books into the examination room, or 'closed book', where you can't.

 **tip**

In assessments, even exams, you must answer the questions but you must also meet the learning outcomes.

- **Read the question(s)**. Often coursework questions or assignments are given at the beginning of the course, in the handbook. Read them. You are not expected to know the answer yet – but if you read the question you will know what the course is designed to get you to be able to answer.

 **tip**

Write out the question.

Underline the key words.

Pin the question on your wall.

Free write a response to the question in your first week on the course.

Read up around one word at a time using your active reading strategy; listen for information on the key words in lectures and classes.

Make notes.

- **Look at the reading list**. Note essential reading – you should read some or all of these. Note the recommended reading – you should read some of these.

 **tip**

When reading, keep a word from the question in your mind. These act like hooks and help you catch the information you need. Make notes that help you answer that part of the question.

- **Look at past papers**. If there is an exam on your course, find past exam papers and read them. These tell you what you should be able to answer by the end of the course. They help you to set your learning goals for the course.

tip

Draw up weekly and termly timetables – put all your assessment dates on them.

- **Examine the syllabus**. If you have a timetable, syllabus or scheme of work, read it. Notice how the course has been put together. When attending lectures or seminars, have a word or phrase from the question in your mind, this should help you make relevant notes as you attend.

tip

Colour-code your learning outcomes – and colour-code your syllabus. Again, this makes you a more focused and successful person.

- **Work on your PDP, CV and career options** from the beginning:
  - Make an appointment with Careers to see what jobs are open to you.
  - Decide to engage in Volunteering or Peer Mentoring.
  - Think what extra-curricular activities you will do – for interest and pleasure, but also to develop your CV.
  - Check out your university's PDP process and decide to treat it as an opportunity not a problem.
  - Start a PDP/CV file – even if you just start with an old A4 envelope and start collecting information about jobs you are beginning to take control of your learning.

2: Activity: Try it with this book

1 Get an overview of this book: look at the Contents pages – check out the Index.
2 Set your own goals – what do you want to get from reading it?
3 Make a list of what you want from the book. Pin it up.
4 Tick items off as you achieve them.
5 Blog about what you are doing and learning.

This information really helps

Handbooks are designed to make sense – they are designed to tell you what you need to do and learn to pass. We want students to succeed! But if your handbook is confusing:

- Work through the learning outcomes and assessment criteria with a friend or study partner.
- Ask the course tutor to help you make sense of the outcomes and criteria.
- Ask the learning or writing development people for help.

Conclusion

In this section we have explored how to take control of your course – with a focus on using module handbooks to shape your strategies… Good luck!

3. Activity: Use our Get Ready for Exams checklist

Photocopy a copy of the exams checklist from Chapter 25, or download a copy from our website, and use with every module or course that you do.

Review points

When reviewing this chapter you might realise that you now have:

- An understanding of how to make sense of your course
- An understanding of how to use that to take control of and pass a particular course
- A sense of being in control of your own learning.

Section II

Study Techniques and Learning Effectively

5

How to Learn Effectively

Aims

To enhance your study success by exploring learning and learning styles.

Learning outcomes

After reading through this chapter and engaging with the activities, you will have:

- deepened your understanding of learning
- explored your own approach to academic study
- gained an understanding of learning styles – and how to make them work for you.

Introduction

We have discussed the six steps to success and looked at the 'rules' of universities, with very specific advice on places to go, people to meet and things to do in your university. In this chapter we are going to look at effective learning strategies and how to harness your learning style to promote active learning and study success.

1. Activity: Good and bad learning

Before moving on, we'd like you to think back to your own past learning experiences. In particular, think about the conditions that helped you to learn – and the things that got in the way of your learning. Make brief notes to answer the questions below:

1 Think back to a previous successful learning experience. It does not have to have been at school – it could be learning to drive or sky dive. Now try to work out why it was successful – why did you learn?
2 Now think back to an unsuccessful learning experience. What was it? Why did little or no learning take place?
3 Looking over these good and bad experiences of yours – can you sum up 'things that help learning to happen' and 'things that prevent learning'? Make a list.
4 If you wish, use your list to write two paragraphs: one on 'Things that help me learn', and one on 'Things that stop me learning'.
5 Once you have completed your own thoughts, compare your paragraphs with those written by another student, below.

" Things that helped me to learn were an interesting course with a good teacher – you know, one that had enthusiasm for the subject and lots of energy. It also helped that I knew why I wanted to do that course, I had chosen it for myself and I actually wanted to learn. I was committed – I'd turn up and do the work – because I wanted do. Not only that but there was a really supportive atmosphere – I felt challenged and stretched – but it was also safe to make mistakes ... Nobody laughed at you or made you feel a fool. **"**

" The worst learning experience I had was at school. I had to be there – it was compulsory – but I never really saw the point of it. I just felt so powerless all the time. I never knew what we were doing or why or when or how. It was a nightmare and one of the reasons that I left school the minute I could! **"**

Query: Were these points like your own? What does this tell you?

Discussion: One thing we can see is that if we are going to be successful when learning, then we must want to learn: we must be interested and motivated and we should have our own clear goals. On the other hand, what seems to stop people from learning is feeling unmotivated, confused, unhappy, fearful and powerless.

Now look at your points again – how can you use the information to help yourself be a more effective student? Things to ask yourself:

- How do I learn best?
- What subjects do I enjoy?

- What job do I want later on?
- What sorts of courses will help me get where I want to go?

Things that other students have said are their reasons for studying:

- I want to know more about this subject
- I want a better career
- I want to earn more money
- I want to make new friends…

These reasons may or may not be like your own. The trick is to understand your own reasons for doing something and then to use those as motivation – especially when your energy is low.

 **tip**

Whenever you start to study anything – from a long course (like a three- or four-year degree programme) to a short unit of a course (a 15-week module) – sit down and write your own personal goals for that course. Put them on Post-its and display them over your desk. Cut out pictures that represent your success to you and stick these up also. Use these to keep you motivated and interested.

What is learning?

Learning is not about the empty student coming to university to be filled with knowledge and wisdom: it is a social, interactive and constructivist activity; something active that you do with other people and with ideas. Now that you have reminded yourself of your own learning experiences – and brought to the surface what you think learning is – we are going to explore learning some more and consider what it involves for a university student. As always, as you read on, think, 'How does knowing this help me to be a more effective student?'

Devine (1987) argues that learning is not one thing but a series of activities:

- gathering new ideas and information
- recording them
- organising them
- making sense of and understanding them

- remembering them
- using them.

You might notice that this list consists of many verbs – *doing* words: gathering, recording, organising, making sense of and understanding, remembering and using. Learning is doing – it is active. It is not just storing bits of information in the brain ready to spill out onto an exam paper and then forget. Everything in this book is designed to build your active learning skills: we will encourage you to engage with, question and understand your coursework and to express yourself successfully within the academic conventions of your subjects. But first, let us see how Devine's list might help us.

Gather

Learning is about gathering new ideas and information. This is research and it can involve actively acquiring information from classes, lectures, seminars, tutorials, discussions, practicals, reading (texts, journals, newspapers and more), and watching documentaries, films, videos and television programmes.

Record

You have to record, organise and make sense of information for yourself. Recording involves some form of notemaking activity where you note points that you have heard, read or seen, in order to use the information in your assignments.

Organise

When we research we encounter information in many forms, in many places and at different times. We are encountering the various accepted and contested knowledge-claims for our subject. We have to *reorganise* the information to make sense of it for ourselves.

Make sense of – analytical and critical thinking

Rearranging and recording information involves playing with the 'flow' of ideas and thinking about all the different things that we have heard, read or seen. We analyse information, break it down into its constituent parts and try to understand the arguments. Ultimately, we have to decide for ourselves – we create knowledge for ourselves.

tip

Good notemaking strategies can be part of gathering, organising, making sense of and recording information: make great notes!

Remember

All this information is not 'yours', however, unless you remember it. So, you have to develop the ability to learn and remember what is important in your subject or discipline.

tip

Use a revision cycle, build your memory.

Use it

Finally you have to be able to *use* the information yourself for it to be really your own: you have to be able to discuss it with other people and use it in your assignments: you have to be able to explain it and write about it.

tip

See your writing as part of your learning process – write to learn, rather than worrying about learning to write.

However, it's not quite that simple:

> 'Education' involves the integration of knowledge with the self, where knowledge is defined by and helps to define the self. (after Noble (2002) *Digital Diploma Mills*)

Of course, the different aspects of learning listed above do not happen in isolation from each other, but are happening all at the same time. We are *using* information when we gather, reorganise and understand it: when we *read*, *talk* and *think* about it. We also use, process and learn information when we write about it – especially when we write our assignments.

Reading, talking, listening, thinking and writing are all *using* information; as we struggle with new ideas and information we are also struggling to understand and learn them. When we prepare assignments, we do not pour out ready formed ideas and already polished words – what we actually do is struggle to understand and use information; we struggle to form our own opinions and we struggle to express our ideas, often using the ideas of other people. This struggle is the learning process and we are changed as we learn.

tip

Don't rush home after a lecture or class, but go to the canteen and talk about it. Get a study partner or form a study group. Discuss lectures and seminars. Discuss your reading. Write before you know or understand it all. Discuss your writing. This is all active learning.

Surface and deep learning

In education we talk about surface and deep learning. 'Surface' describes where you might record key bits of information – names and dates of battles, for example; 'deep' describes where you understand the significance of the events that occurred – 'this battle was actually the turning point in the war and brought about...' or 'that bit of evidence contradicts what I read in...'

➡

➡

Of course, to be really successful we need both surface and deep learning, for we will need to remember important names, dates, theories and concepts – and we will need to understand their significance.

An active learning approach means that you continually ask questions of and do things with the information that you acquire. An active learning style ensures that both surface and deep learning occur; it helps you both to remember those important names, dates and events and to understand their significance.

❝Tell them about notemaking! Great notemaking saves time!❞

 **tip**

If you know your notemaking strategies are not working for you at the moment, see Chapter 11.

Learning style

If you went to a Montessori primary school, you would have been encouraged to see, hear, say and do in order to learn effectively. All of us at any age can benefit from that sort of approach, for we learn *some* of what we see or hear or say or do – but we learn 90% of what we see, hear, say *and* do. This has been developed into a theory of learning style. It is argued that we all favour either visual (sight based), auditory (sound based) or kinaesthetic (touch, feel or movement based) learning styles. But to make our learning effective, we should use all the learning pathways – we need to employ see, hear, say and do techniques.

Using your learning style

To really succeed as a student you not only need to be organised, as we suggest in Chapters 4 and 6, or to communicate effectively, as we cover in Chapters 14–21, you also have to be aware of and develop your own learning styles – and to build them consciously into your learning strategies. We do re-visit learning styles in relation to developing your memory in Chapter 24, but we are also going to look here at learning styles in connection to becoming an effective learner.

2. Activity: What's my learning style?

For a quick check on what your learning style might be consider the following:

One way to check your primary learning pathway is to examine the language that you use. For example, are you the sort of person who says:

- I see what you mean? or
- I hear what you're saying? or
- It feels good to me?

  I see what you mean' indicates that you use sight-based language, and you might favour the visual learning pathway.

  'I hear what you're saying' indicates that you could favour an auditory pathway (hear and say).

  'It feels good to me' possibly indicates that you are a kinaesthetic type person (touch, feel, movement).

  Still not sure? Well, if remembering a spelling would you:

- See the word in your mind, possibly write it down, and see if it looks right? (Visual)
- Sound out the letters and hear if it sounds right? (Auditory)
- Look at or say the word – but check if it feels right? (Kinaesthetic).

 **tips**

- **Sight:** If you remember mainly by sight, you may enjoy learning by reading and watching television, film or video. You could use pictures in your learning and revision activities: draw pattern notes, put in colour, and put in memory-jogging cartoon images or visuals.
- **Sound:** If you remember sounds best, you may enjoy learning through listening and joining in discussions or explaining things to other people. You could benefit from using audiotapes to support your learning and you could use songs, rhymes and jingles that you write yourself as learning and revision aids. Tape yourself and sing along.
- **Feel:** If you remember the feel of things, you may enjoy practical learning activities, from making something, to performing a science experiment to role-playing. Making charts and patterns of the things you want to remember will help your learning and revision – as will acting out in some way.

> **Query:** So, are you auditory, visual or kinaesthetic in your approach to learning? How are you going to build see, hear, say and do into *your* learning?

Not sure about your learning style? See the useful learning styles websites below:

Learning styles – with reference to Kolb & Gardiner:
http://www.i-learnt.com/Thinking_Learning_Styles.html
Learning styles test:
http://www.ldpride.net/learning-style-test.html
Learning styles & multiple intelligences explained:
http://www.ldpride.net/learningstyles.MI.htm#Learning%20Styles%20Explained
Another learning styles site – with longer test:
http://www.learning-styles-online.com/

Learning styles for students

When studying you should build on all the learning styles – see, hear, say and do – to make sure that you perform at your best.

Visual learners may prefer:

- To see the lecturer – their body language and facial expressions
- To sit near the front with nothing blocking their view
- Learning through visual media, film, television and video and the visual aids that a lecturer will use in their teaching
- To make notes full of pictures and cartoons; to make notes funny, bizarre or unusual
- To learn how to make notes that are visually stimulating and memorable (Chapter 11).

Auditory learners may prefer:

- Verbal lectures, listening carefully
- Tuning in to the nuances of voice: tone, pitch, speed, passion
- Taping lectures (and making shorter versions to revise from)
- Rather than reading, finding audio versions of books (really useful in English Literature)
- Learning by discussion, explanation – talking and listening
- Making their own audiotapes of things that they want to remember – utilising silly voices, tunes, rhythm and rhyme.

Kinaesthetic (touch or feelings based) learners may prefer:

- Hands-on learning – engaging with the real world. These learners will typically prefer practical courses, experiments, activity and role playing in their learning

- To care about or 'feel' something for the subject
- To move about as they study – or move from room to room for different parts of assignments
- To make diagrams and charts of the key things that they need to remember.

tip

As you cannot roam around in a lecture or class, have an object to squeeze (rubber ball) to allow some movement

All learners should try to see, hear, say and do!

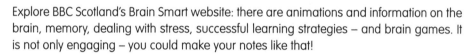

tip

Explore BBC Scotland's Brain Smart website: there are animations and information on the brain, memory, dealing with stress, successful learning strategies – and brain games. It is not only engaging – you could make your notes like that!

http://www.bbc.co.uk/scotland/brainsmart/

Some things to do about your learning right now

Hopefully, we have encouraged you to think of learning slightly differently from how you might have thought about it before. We encouraged you to see that learning is interactive, involving a series of activities designed to get you actively engaged with information and ideas, rather than passively remembering them (or not). This can be facilitated by your active use of visual, auditory and kinaesthetic techniques. We have further stressed that you have to be an active, analytical and critical student in order to learn. We now want you to use that information to draw up your own Learning Contract, where you set your own study goals.

The Learning Contract

A Learning Contract that you write for yourself for every course that you study is not the same as one that your institution might ask you to sign. Those contracts typically focus on your attendance or punctuality. Your contract with yourself is not like that – it is your own motivating tool designed to help you get the most out of your studying for your own reasons.

Your Learning Contract is where you make clear to yourself:

- Your reason for doing something: 'What I want from this course (or job or whatever) is…'
- What you are prepared to do to achieve your goals: 'What I'm prepared to do to make this happen is…'
- What might interfere with your progress or prevent you from achieving your goals: 'What might stop me is…'
- What you will actually get from the activity (course or job) in the long term: 'What's in it for me is…' (station WiiFM).

Now that we have looked at the elements of the Learning Contract, why don't you complete a Contract for reading this book.

3. Activity: How to learn and study – ESS3: The Learning Contract

Answer the following questions to write your Contract for ESS3.

1. Why am I reading this book?
2. What am I prepared to do to get the most from this book?
3. What might stop me?
4. What's in it for me?

 **tips**

- When you have drawn up your ESS3 Contract stick it on the wall.
- When you settle down to read another bit of this book, look at the Contract and remind yourself of your own goals.
- Always do your own Learning Contract for any course that you do – use it whenever you need to push yourself a bit to get the work done.

Discussion: Your Learning Contract for this book could help you when you don't feel like doing anything, let alone reading a Study Skills book. It could help you when you feel you *should* be reading, but don't actually *want* to read. When these things occur, look at your Contract and see if that gives you the motivation to proceed. Figure 5A is an example of a Learning Contract.

tip

Now look back at your personal skills review (Chapter 1). Can you add things to your Learning Contract in the light of your answers there?

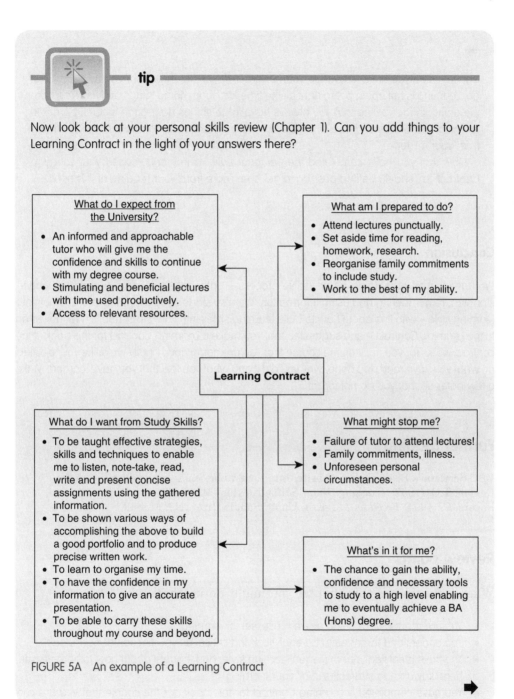

What do I expect from the University?
- An informed and approachable tutor who will give me the confidence and skills to continue with my degree course.
- Stimulating and beneficial lectures with time used productively.
- Access to relevant resources.

What am I prepared to do?
- Attend lectures punctually.
- Set aside time for reading, homework, research.
- Reorganise family commitments to include study.
- Work to the best of my ability.

Learning Contract

What do I want from Study Skills?
- To be taught effective strategies, skills and techniques to enable me to listen, note-take, read, write and present concise assignments using the gathered information.
- To be shown various ways of accomplishing the above to build a good portfolio and to produce precise written work.
- To learn to organise my time.
- To have the confidence in my information to give an accurate presentation.
- To be able to carry these skills throughout my course and beyond.

What might stop me?
- Failure of tutor to attend lectures!
- Family commitments, illness.
- Unforeseen personal circumstances.

What's in it for me?
- The chance to gain the ability, confidence and necessary tools to study to a high level enabling me to eventually achieve a BA (Hons) degree.

FIGURE 5A   An example of a Learning Contract

➡️

Don't worry if you have to change your Contract, if you didn't get your contract 'right' first go. Learning is not about being right all the time, it's about doing things and learning from the doing. In fact feeling that you always have to get things right is the biggest barrier to learning that we know; it prevents you from taking risks, making mistakes and learning from your mistakes.

Now that you have completed the personal skills review and revised your Learning Contract you should be in a position to get even more from your reading of this book.

Conclusion

We have looked at learning as an active process – gathering, recording, organising, under-standing, remembering and using information. We also started you on your exploration of your learning style – with tips about how to build learning styles into your study habits. We moved on to the Learning Contract – and suggested that you make a Learning Contract for this book. If the contract works for you, try it on the course that you are doing now. Finally we'd like you to reflect on what you have read and done, why you did it and what you feel that you have learned. Make a few notes so that you do not forget.

Further reading

BBC Scotland's Brain Smart website: http://www.bbc.co.uk/scotland/brainsmart/
Devine, T.G. (1987) *Teaching Study Skills*. Newton, MA: Allyn and Bacon
Rogers, C. (1994) *Freedom to Learn*. Upper Saddle River, NJ: Merrill

Review points

When reflecting on this chapter you might notice that:

- You are more aware of the active processes of learning
- You understand the need to be analytical and critical as you encounter new ideas
- You have identified your preferred learning style, and thought about how to harness see, hear, say and do strategies in all your learning
- You have completed a Learning Contract for this book, for the course that you are cur-rently on and will do so for other courses.

Section II

Study Techniques and Learning Effectively

6

Get Organised for Independent Study

Aims

This chapter covers really practical advice on when, where and how to study. Get rid of your time sponges – do not procrastinate – read it now.

Learning outcomes

After reading this chapter, and engaging with the activities, you will have:

- tackled deadlines, motivation, time sponges and procrastination
- engaged with very practical advice on when, where and how to study
- sorted out a study space – and got organised to succeed.

" I'm a mum, I work, I've got my parents to look after ... I guess I'm organised! **"**

How organised are you?

Studying is really hard work – there are notes to make, reading to do, and essays and other assignments to plan, prepare and produce. Far from feeling fun and exciting, sometimes this can feel really overwhelming – sometimes it even feels quite frightening. We are going to explore when, where and how to study and provide you with very practical advice and tips. We will begin by asking: Are you motivated by deadlines? How often do you feel like studying?

Are you taking it all in your stride – or do you feel overwhelmed? Let's see what other people are saying.

"I can only work under pressure of a deadline."

" I know we are supposed to start work weeks before the deadline, but I usually start two or three days before. **"**

Many students do not start work until a deadline really frightens them. These students do not give themselves any time to produce the work they are really capable of. Their assignments never reflect what they truly can do and they never receive the grades they might get. They never get to feel good about themselves as students.

 **tip**

Get used to doing a little bit of work every day: reading, writing a paragraph, talking new material over with others. This may seem impossible at first, but working consistently in this way ensures that you make the most of your time and produce really good work.

" The best tip I ever got was to do at least half an hour's work each day. This has put me on top of all my studies ... And usually once I start I get a little bit more done and I feel so much better. **"**

"It all seems too much, I just can't start!"

" I know what I should do, I really know ... but I just can't face it. **"**

Studying can feel like climbing a mountain. But there is more than one way to face a mountain! For some a mountain is so large and dangerous that they are afraid of it. For some a mountain is an exciting challenge. For some a mountain is just a thing to be tackled sensibly one step at a time.

How do you view the mountain? Whatever your normal attitude, try to approach the mountain – and your assignments – one step at a time.

 **tip**

If you feel that it is all so overwhelming that you cannot even begin your work, read Chapter 12 on creativity – this will give you ideas on how to start assignments.

"But I have no time and never seem to *feel* like studying."

"I have a job ... or I'm looking for a job. I have my family. I have no time."

Nobody leaps out of bed in the morning going, 'Wheee – this is the day that I tackle that huge assignment!' So do not rely on *feeling* like studying or *finding* time. You have to put a study system in place and you have to make the time. Every university student has to work out for themselves just how much time they are prepared to give to their studies (35 hours or more each week). They have to decide how much work they are prepared to put in, to get the results – in crude terms the grades – that they want.

Want to do well? Study to a timetable – even when you don't feel like it.

So when should I study?

When planning out your time think about:

- Whether you are a morning, afternoon or evening person. Try to fit your study times around your maximum performance times. Work with your strengths.
- How much time you spend travelling: reading on the bus or train is a really effective use of time.
- How much time you would like to give to friends and family. Your studies are important – but most of us would like to have friends and family still talking to us when our studies are over.
- How much time you have to give to chores. We need to keep our homes at least sanitary. Watch out though – housework and all chores can become excellent excuses for not working. They become displacement activities – sometimes it feels as though it is easier to completely re-build the house rather than write an essay!
- How much time you have to give to work. These days we need to earn money whilst we study and sometimes universities help by fitting lectures and other classes into one or two days a week. Beware – this does not mean that all your studying can fit into two days. Remember you have to give 35–40 hours a week to your studies, if you cannot do this, you will be in trouble.

- Whether you will be able to keep all your hobbies and interests going. Do you fight to keep up your hobbies now or do you plan to take them up again after your studies? Do you acknowledge time limits and decide that in the short term your studies become your hobbies? Or can you juggle time effectively and so fit more in?
- Time for rest and relaxation. As we have said studying is hard work – it can also be very stressful. It is important to get sufficient rest whilst you study and it is useful to build stress relief activities – dancing, exercise, gym, meditation, massage, yoga – into your time-tables right at the beginning of your studies.
- Timetables. Timetables give you a strong guide to your work – if you keep to them. But more than that, without timetables you may feel that every time you are not working or spending quality time with friends and family you *ought* to be studying. You may not do that studying, but you worry – and this is exhausting in itself. Eventually it may feel that your whole life is work, work, work. Something will have to go – and it could be your studies!
- Make lists and prioritise tasks.
- Keep a diary – note when you plan to read or write.

Timetables to think about:

- **Study timetable:** This is a 24/7 timetable (24 hours a day, seven days a week) that covers how many hours per day go to non-study and how many go to your studies. It is where you can plan which subjects to study and for how long. It takes some trial and error and experiment to get this right – so do give it that time.
- **Assignment timetable:** This is a record of all the assignment deadlines that are coming up either in a term, a semester or across a whole year. Fill in deadlines and pin up on your wall – and place in your folder and diary. Never let a deadline take you by surprise.
- **Exam timetable:** Similar to the assignment timetable, this is a record of all the exams you will be taking. Note dates, times and locations. It is all too easy to turn up at the wrong time, on the wrong day and in the wrong place!
- **Revision timetable:** At the appropriate time, each student should devise their own revision timetable where they work out when they are going to test their knowledge and practise for the exams that they are going to sit (more on this in Chapter 25. Tip: follow the Checklist there – now!).

 **tip**

Photocopy the timetables on pages 85–89. Experiment with using them to help you focus on your work and get the most from your time.

Overwhelmed? Try the five-step plan

(With thanks to our LearnHigher colleagues at Reading University.)

1 List everything that you need to do. This may feel like a really bad idea and that you'll be even more frightened; but the opposite is true. Once you write the list, and you can see the reality of the 'problem', it becomes more manageable and less overwhelming.
2 Divide each big task that you have to do into smaller steps. So do not just put down 'write essay', break it down: 'brainstorm question'; 'read up on…'; 'write a paragraph on…' etc.
3 Organise your big list into things that must be done now; soon; later.
4 Do one of the NOW tasks immediately and cross it off. You will instantly feel more calm and in control.
5 Prioritise your list and put into a 'to do' order.

 **tip**

If you are really worried about time visit the Time management pages on LearnHigher.

Procrastination

So, are you still not convinced? Are you a procrastinator? Try this activity suggested by Michelle Reid of Reading University.

1. Activity: The time sponge

Try this with a group of friends, especially if they are fellow students. You will need Post-it notes and pens.

1 Everybody takes one large Post-it and writes their biggest time sponge at the top (a time sponge is anything you find yourself doing instead of working e.g. updating your Facebook status).

2 Everybody passes their Post-it to the person on their left. You all read someone else's time sponge problem and write a possible solution.

3 Pass to the left again and write another solution to another problem…

4 Keep going until you have run out of space on the Post-its.

5 Everybody takes a turn to read out the problem on the Post-it they have been left with – and the various solutions offered.

6 Everybody says one thing they will now do differently after listening to all the sponges and solutions.

One more thing: If you tackle this activity with a group of friends, go around the group one more time. Each person has to give their best re-focusing tip – that is, the one thing that works for them when they find they are losing concentration (for our friends at Reading University, it would involve taking the wheels off their chairs so they spend more time working and less time whizzing around the office).

Query: How has this exercise made you feel?

Discussion: Advice can feel more relevant when it pops out of activities like this. Note the good ideas – and do something with them. Moreover, if you found that you like working like this, organise a 'successful study group' of your own. Each week focus on a study issue: understanding your course, organising yourself for study, reading, notemaking, giving presentations... As well as reading the information in here, see what good strategies and tactics you and your friends can come up with.

Where to study

Everyone deserves a nice place to study, but real life is not always as convenient as that and sometimes we just have to adapt to what we have and make it work. And, just as it is important that you decide when to study – and work at it until you get it right for you – it is important that you work out where you are going to study and you make that place work for you. With most of these things there is no right or wrong, there is only what works for you. So take the time to find out what does work for you. There are some things that you may need to think about.

Your study space

Negotiate a space with family or flatmates: your studies are part of your life now – and they must fit in. Creating a study space helps everyone in your life – including you – realise just how important your studies are.

A good place to study needs light and air – you need to see and breathe – but does not necessarily have to be a completely quiet place, as some people really do work best with a little bit of background noise going on.

You will need space to lay out your work, pin up your timetables, deadlines and notes. Have your textbooks out and visible. Have subject files neatly labelled and ready to hand. Post up all the new words that you are learning, so that you are immersed in your learning. All this is practical and also helps you to feel like a student.

Leave out work; do not tidy it all away. Having your work visible keeps it alive in your mind whereas putting it all away can give the false impression that you're finished.

You need pens and pencils, also highlighters, a stapler and staples, paper clips, correction fluid, Post-its, coloured pens – and all sorts of different sizes of paper. All these resources make it easier to write notes, annotate source material, mark important pages in books and so forth. The different sized paper gives you paper to make notes on, paper to make plans on, paper to print work on. Further, if you play around with materials and colour, you feel an injection of energy and enthusiasm, and this just makes the job easier.

You should also have access to a computer. A computer makes it easier to draft and redraft work until you get it right and allows you to word process work so that it looks neat and tidy; if your tutors can actually read your work, your chance of getting the grade you deserve improves. Also, as you know, a PC or laptop means that you can access research materials online and gives you access to your university's VLE and the additional study resources in there. This makes studying from home more productive than it has ever been before.

A positive space

Once you have a study space sorted out you should practise using it positively. Say to yourself as you sit down: 'Now I am working', 'I enjoy being a student'. Try to avoid those old negative thoughts: 'I don't want to be here.' 'This is too hard.' 'I'd rather be…' Negative thoughts have a negative effect – positive thoughts have a positive effect.

Make that study space work for you. Get into the habit of giving 100% whenever you sit down to study. Act as if you and your studies are important – they are – so are you.

 **tip**

Experiment with working at home, in the library and when you travel (being a commuter adds hours of study time to your week, if you take your books with you). But whether you want to work in a library or on a bus, you will also need a study space at home.

2. Activity: Sort out your study space

1   If you have not already done so, sort out a place to study. Make sure that you can use this space at the times that you have planned to study in your timetable.
2   Over time, collect the resources that we have mentioned above.
3   In the meantime, make a list of all the resources that you need. What materials do you have already? Which ones are you going to buy? Which books can you get easily from the library? Which ones are so important that you ought to buy them? Can you buy them second hand from the Students' Union? How many can you afford? Etc.

Having that study space – some comments from other students:

" It felt really good having my own study space. It made me feel like a real student. **"**

" I felt that at last I could settle down to some real work. **"**

" I felt a bit frightened at first – you know? Like now I couldn't put it off any longer! I'd have to take it seriously. **"**

" Sometimes I use my space to sort of trick myself into working. I think, I'll just sit there for a minute... Next thing I know I've been working away for an hour and I feel really good. **"**

" I felt guilty at having to cut myself off from the kids. It just felt so selfish. I have to work really hard at still giving them some time. **"**

" I used to get so frustrated; it was like every time I sat down to work they would start demanding things from me. Now we all sit down to work at the same time – even if they are just crayoning or reading a storybook. This has helped us all feel better. **"**

" I still like going to the library to work – but it's great having a proper place for my stuff at home. It really does help. **"**

> **Discussion**: As you can see from the student comments, there is no right or wrong response to having your own study space. For each of us there is only our reaction – and what we choose to do about it.
>
> If having your own space makes you feel like a 'proper' student then you will only have to sit at your table or desk to put yourself in the right mood to study. You can always do what one of the other students does and sometimes 'trick' yourself into getting some work done.
>
> If it makes you feel a bit lonely or frightened, console yourself. New experiences are often frightening, at first. It might help to say to yourself several times 'I am a proper student', each time that you sit down to study.
>
> If your family always chooses that moment to want something from you – again, do what the other student did, and try to get them to 'study' (or draw or read) at the same time as you.

How to study

This whole book is designed to get you studying in more successful ways, but here are some very practical things to do right now.

Want it: Everyone should know what they are studying and why. Make sure that you do know what you want from each course that you are studying – and how your life will be changed when you reach your goals.

tip

Remember to write your goals on Post-its and stick them up in your study space. Write your Learning Contract (Chapter 5) for each course, module or unit that you do.

Get the overview (Chapter 4): Know what is happening week by week. Know how the course is being assessed. Read the assignment question at the beginning of the course, not the end. If there are to be exams, check out past papers at the beginning of your studies, not the end. All this gives you a sense of how the course has been put together and where you are going each week.

Use the 'Getting Ready for Exams checklist', Chapter 25. The advice there will help you to plan and use your time throughout your course.

Epistemology: We mentioned this in Chapter 3. Remember every course has its own theory of knowledge – what counts as argument and evidence. Make sure you know the what, why and how of all your subjects.

Read the journals to get a model of how to argue and write in your subject. Use a dictionary and a subject dictionary.

Be positive: Just as an athlete will perform better if they feel like a success and think positive thoughts, so a student will learn more if they can adopt positive attitudes and develop self-confidence.

When your motivation runs low, role-play, or act like, a successful student. Remind yourself that you can be a successful student. Read Chapter 22 on dealing with your emotions.

Timing: Prioritise tasks and set your study timetables in motion. Long study sessions work for some people but are not always the most effective way to work. One study myth is that this is what we *must* do. We might sit there for hours but not much work is getting done. This belief can make you very frustrated, angry and tired but it rarely produces good work. Work out if you prefer to dip into your work – juggling several different things at once – or if you prefer to give one day a week to each of your different courses. Whichever you do, remember, work for an hour then take a break. A short break will recharge your batteries and make your work profitable.

tips

We concentrate best in 15-minute bursts. When we study we have to get into the habit of regularly recharging our mental batteries to wake up our brains. We can do this by:

- taking a short rest
- changing what we do
- making the task very important
- making the task interesting, stimulating or more difficult.

Prioritise time: When working we need to be strategic – note which assignments carry the most marks, note which deadlines are coming first. When you make lists of what needs to be done and when – do that first with the nearest deadline; give more time to the assignment which carries the most marks.

tip

Use a diary – note when you are going to do what. If you don't do it, re-schedule.

Use the time: We know students who sit down to study – out come the pens and paper – they get rearranged. Out come the books and the highlighters – they get rearranged. They go for a coffee. They go for a glass of water. They put one lot of books away and get out another set. They look at the clock – oh good! An hour has passed – they put their materials away. But they have done no work! This is a time sponge. Watch out for this.

tip

Goal setting will help you benefit from independent study time.

One worry at a time

One thing that can stop people achieving enough when they sit down to work is too much worry. They sit down to write an essay and worry about the two other essays that they also have to write. They worry about the weather or the bills. They worry about anything and everything.

If we worry about everything – we do nothing. One of the hardest tricks to being a successful student is to learn how to worry about one thing at a time.

It is as if we need to set up a set of shelves in our brain. We then need to put all our different worries on the shelves. Learn to take down one thing at a time and give it our total concentration. When we have finished with that, put it back on the shelf and take down something else.

Like everything else recommended in this book, this is a skill that develops through practice.

Goal set: Before you sit down to study, set yourself some goals. Know what you are doing and why. Do not just start reading a book because it is on the reading list. Know why you are reading a section of that book. If you are not sure have a look at the assignment question and find a bit of the book that will help you with that bit of the assignment. Then you will know what you are doing and why. This makes all the difference.

tip

Read Chapter 10 on reading. Each time you read, brainstorm first: What do I know? What do I need? Which bit of the assignment will this help me with?

Be active: When studying independently be just as active as when you are in a lecture or joining in a class discussion. Read actively, asking questions as you go. Think about the information that you are receiving: What does it mean? Do you understand it? If not, what are you going to do about that? How does it connect with what you already know, including things that you have heard in class or read in other places? How will you use it in your assignment? Connecting up information in this way is a really important part of active learning. Make active notes – typically, key word notes – in patterns (more on this in Chapter 11). Revise those notes actively.

Before reading, re-read the assignment question and then make notes that would help you answer that question.

Review actively: At the end of each study session – independent study or a lecture or class – take some time to reflect on what you have read or heard. Check what you have done. Recall what you have learned. Make brief notes to make the learning conscious (see Chapter 11).

Complete a learning log at the end of every day or week (Chapter 23).

Study partners and groups: Study is best when undertaken actively and interactively; this is where a friend, study partner or a study group can be invaluable. Talking over new information with other people is the easiest way to understand and learn it – to make it your own. Further, if you encounter a problem you can talk to your partner. Probably they will not know the solution either. Oh the relief! You are not alone and you are not stupid. Then the situation changes as you work on the problem and sort it out together.

If you don't have a study partner persuade a friend or family member that they are interested in your course and talk to them. If your course has an online chat space or discussion board, use that to air your views and ask your questions.

Don't end on a sour note: Try not to end a study session on a problem – it is de-motivating and it can make it that little bit harder to start studying again. As suggested, use a study partner, friend or online discussion space to talk it over.

tip

Make a note of the problem and sleep on it – sometimes the solution comes to you when you wake up. But don't lie awake fretting all night; this does not solve the problem and you have made everything worse by losing sleep and gaining stress.

Relaxation and dealing with stress: Remember to make time to rest, relax and let go of stress. This is important. You need rest to carry on. Stress relief allows you to let go of tension and this helps you to perform better. When we are stressed our body releases cortisol – a hormone that has a direct impact on the brain causing the cortex to shrink – and adrenalin – the flight or fight hormone. The combination of these hormones eliminates short-term memory and produces the narrow, tunnel vision necessary for fight or flight. This might save our lives when escaping from a burning building, but works against us when studying where we need breadth and depth of vision.

tip

Read Chapter 22 on dealing with your emotions. Practise positive thinking. Take up yoga.

Do it! Review it!

As always, the advice given above will only work if put into practice. But much of it is there to be played with and adapted to suit you. So note the useful points and try them out. After a while, review how they are working for you and adapt them so that they become more tailored to the sort of student that you are: become a more effective student.

Conclusion

In this chapter we have considered some basic organisation and time management techniques via a discussion of when, where and how to study. Remember, though, that none of this will mean anything unless and until you put the ideas into practice. If it seems too difficult to put them all into practice at once, sort out one thing at a time. As you do this, take the time to reflect on how the things that you are doing are working for you. If something is not working – or stops working – change it. These tips work best once you adapt them to suit yourself.

3. Activity: Filling in your timetables

On pages 85–89 there are several timetables including two blank 24-hour timetables. Complete all your timetables but first follow the guidelines for your 24-hour timetables.

Filling in the 24-hour timetable:

1. Fill in the first one, indicating when you expect to work, sleep, do chores and so forth. Think about the time that you have left. Put in times for study and relaxation. Think about it – are you being realistic? Make sure that you are not under- or over-working yourself. Run that programme for a few weeks.
2. After a couple of weeks, review your success in keeping to the study times that you set and in achieving the goals that you had in mind.
3. Change your timetable to fit in with reality. Use the second blank timetable for this.
4. Remember to do this every term, semester, year.

Keeping a timetable

Mark in the following details:

- time which must be spent in college
- time spent travelling
- personal/family commitments (children, shopping...)
- any important, regular social commitments
- hours of sleep required
- time for independent study.

 **tip**

Use a colour code.

Blank 24-hour timetable

TIME	MONDAY	TUESDAY	WEDNESDAY	THURSDAY	FRIDAY	SATURDAY	SUNDAY
1.00							
2.00							
3.00							
4.00							
5.00							
6.00							
7.00							
8.00							
9.00							
10.00							
11.00							
12.00							
13.00							
14.00							
15.00							
16.00							
17.00							
18.00							
19.00							
20.00							
21.00							
22.00							
23.00							
24.00							

 Photocopiable:

Essential Study Skills, Third Edition © Tom Burns and Sandra Sinfield, 2012 (SAGE)

Blank 24-hour timetable

TIME	MONDAY	TUESDAY	WEDNESDAY	THURSDAY	FRIDAY	SATURDAY	SUNDAY
1.00							
2.00							
3.00							
4.00							
5.00							
6.00							
7.00							
8.00							
9.00							
10.00							
11.00							
12.00							
13.00							
14.00							
15.00							
16.00							
17.00							
18.00							
19.00							
20.00							
21.00							
22.00							
23.00							
24.00							

Photocopiable:

Essential Study Skills, Third Edition © Tom Burns and Sandra Sinfield, 2012 (SAGE)

Course events and deadlines timetable

EVENTS AND DEADLINES				
Write down the dates of the following events each term:				
	Course 1	Course 2	Course 3	Course 4
Course title				
Exam(s)				
Essay deadline(s)				
Laboratory report deadline(s)				
Seminar presentations				
Field trips/visits				
Project report or exhibition deadlines				
Bank holidays or other 'days off'				
Other events (specify)				

Photocopiable:

Essential Study Skills, Third Edition © Tom Burns and Sandra Sinfield, 2012 (SAGE)

Term plan timetable

Term Plan – what is happening over your terms/semester?							
	Mon	Tue	Wed	Thurs	Fri	Sat	Sun
Week 1							
Week 2							
Week 3							
Week 4							
Week 5							
Week 6							
Week 7							
Week 8							
Week 9							
Week 10							
Week 11							
Week 12							
Longer term deadlines:							

Photocopiable:

Essential Study Skills, Third Edition © Tom Burns and Sandra Sinfield, 2012 (SAGE)

Weekly plan timetable

Keep a WEEKLY PLAN: Key events and activities each week							
Week Number:	Mon	Tue	Wed	Thurs	Fri	Sat	Sun
8am							
9am							
10am							
11am							
12 noon							
1pm							
2pm							
3pm							
4pm							
5pm							
6pm							
7pm							
8pm							
9pm							
10pm							
11pm							
12 midnight							
1am							

Photocopiable:

Essential Study Skills, Third Edition © Tom Burns and Sandra Sinfield, 2012 (SAGE)

Review points

When you reflect on this chapter you might notice that you have:

- Thought about your own approach to study – including motivation and procrastination
- Decided on when, where and how you study best
- Started the process of organising yourself for effective study.

Section II

Study Techniques and Learning Effectively

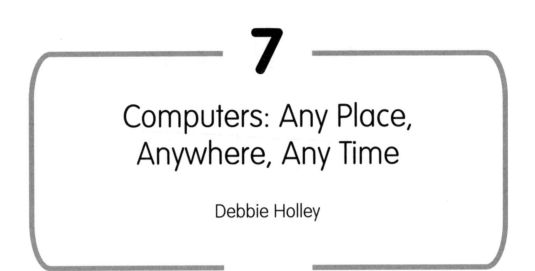

7

Computers: Any Place, Anywhere, Any Time

Debbie Holley

'Young researchers are increasingly using free web technology to help with their research – but they are not active in creating content,' says a major British Library/JISC generation Y, 'Researchers of Tomorrow' report. (http://www.jisc.ac.uk/news/stories/2011/06/researchersoftomorrow.aspx)

Aims

This chapter offers insights into using a range of technologies to help you study when you want, where you want – and as effectively as you can.

Learning outcomes

By the end of this chapter you will:

- understand that enhanced technology skills are important both for study and future employment
- know more about your university Virtual Learning Environment (VLE)
- have effective web research techniques at your fingertips
- understand how social media can enhance academic study
- have no fears about trying out new technologies.

Introduction

This chapter has four key sections:

1   The first is about using a computer for study
2   The second is about researching for your studies
3   The third is about presenting your research findings in different ways
4   The fourth is about using social media to assist with your studies.

There is a 'box of tricks' at the end of the chapter, with ideas about how to use blogs, IM, Twitter and Wikis in your studies.

The Sage companion website has all the web addresses used in this chapter and in the other chapters in this book.

---

1. Activity: Start this chapter by taking the 'test your web knowledge' quiz

1   What is the World Wide Web?
    a   A computer game
    b   A software program
    c   The part of the internet that enables information-sharing via interconnected pages
    d   Another name for the internet

2   Which of the following is a use of search engines?
    a   Searching an online library catalogue
    b   Searching the World Wide Web
    c   Searching the contents of a specific website
    d   All of the above

3   Web portals (or gateways) are:
    a   Lists of websites by topics
    b   Subscription databases
    c   Search engines
    d   All of the above

4   Which of the following is probably the most logical sequence to do research for an essay on cloning?
    a   Periodical articles > background information > opinions
    b   Background information > periodical articles > opinions
    c   Opinions > periodical articles > background information
    d   All three sequences are equally effective

➡

➡️

5 Which of the following would probably be the best search for finding the health effects of smoking?

   a   Smoking OR tobacco OR health
   b   Smoking AND 'health effects'
   c   'Smoking health'
   d   Information AND smoking OR tobacco

6 Google is an example of:

   a   A URL
   b   A subscription database
   c   A portal
   d   A search engine

7 The words 'AND' and 'OR' are examples of Boolean operators:

   a   True
   b   False

8 Which of the following is a true statement?

   a   You are free to copy information you find on the web and include it in your research report.
   b   You do not have to reference internet sources you use in your research report.
   c   You should never consult internet sources when you are doing a research report.
   d   Just like printed sources, web sources must be referenced in your research report. You are not free to plagiarise information you find online.

9 Which of the following is a factor to consider when using a search engine?

   a   How many pages it searches
   b   If it uses Boolean searches
   c   If it allows phrase searches
   d   All of the above

10 Using AND between keywords gets:

   a   More results
   b   Fewer results

11 Quality control of the World Wide Web is low:

   a   True
   b   False

12 Which of the following are the best keywords for the topic, 'A comparison of business management styles in Japan and the United Kingdom'?

    a   Comparison/business management/Japan/United Kingdom

    b   Management/Japan/United Kingdom

    c   Business/Japan/United Kingdom

    d   Styles/business/management/comparison

13 Which of the following information sources is usually the best for background information?

    a   Reference materials

    b   Periodicals

    c   Email materials

    d   None of the above

14 Which of the following is a true statement about the internet and the library?

    a   They both have an expert librarian or specialist to answer your questions

    b   They both provide up-to-date news and information

    c   They both close when it gets late

    d   They both provide access to newspapers, magazines and journals

Now check your answers.

Answers: 1(c), 2(b), 3(a), 4(d), 5(b), 6(d), 7(a), 8(d), 9(d), 10(a), 11(a), 12(a), 13(a), 14(d)

Photocopiable:

Essential Study Skills, Third Edition © Tom Burns and Sandra Sinfield, 2012 (SAGE)

Query: How did you do in the test?

Discussion: Most of us can learn something new and useful about Information and Communications Technology (ICT), so the score is not that important; but it can show you the areas that you might like to focus upon.

❝I took one look at the banks of PCs in the university laboratories – and all those very confident students sitting there working – and panicked.❞

This chapter is designed for everyone, from those who want to extend their skills as well as those who are just starting at university.

1: Using your computer for studying

The findings of a recent EU project, MATURE (http://mature-ip.eu) suggest that learners are moving towards developing their own Personalised Learning

Environments (PLEs) where they manage both the content and process of their learning, communicating with others as they move across multiple contexts of work/life/learning and appropriate digital tools and media to achieve their learning goals. (Interview with Professor John Cook, August 2011)

No matter what the level of your existing computer and information skills, one of your aims should be to leave university with excellent ICT skills. Not least because most employers expect graduates to be confident with seeking, handling and interpreting electronic information as well as having their specialist subject knowledge. This chapter is designed to introduce you to the what, why and how of the key ICT skills you will need both to be a successful student and to get and keep that great job.

❝ I found out that employers have the first stage of their selection process online. I'll need ICT skills just to apply for a job. **❞**

Customise your PC or laptop

To start your own learning journey, you must have access to a computer or laptop, and then customise and personalise it to help you study and reflect your own learning styles. It helps to have compatible software with your university systems and most universities' student machines have Microsoft Office as the default software, a package containing Word (a word processing package), PowerPoint (for presentations) and Excel (spreadsheets). Different subject specialisms will have their own particular computer software requirements: students taking more creative subjects may find they use Apple, for example.

If buying a new laptop or PC, your new purchase could have a higher specification than your university's; find out if they provide a statement of their minimum requirements to help you decide what to buy for your studies. Additional devices such as printers, scanners and webcams are useful, and modern laptops will come with cameras and webcams built in.

When using the university PCs, even though you will have secure storage space on one of their servers, make sure you back up work on a USB stick and email it to yourself; you may not be able to access the university servers outside the university buildings.

Many universities have free WiFi hotspots to enable you to access materials online; some will be networked throughout to enable you to access materials in class; some will already have bespoke iPad/iPhone/mobile phone applications to help students settle in.

tip

Check out what hardware and software your university supplies, how easy it is to access WiFi and any free downloads or recommended sites. Find out where the printers are and the cost of printing documents.

Organising your computer for your own learning

Different browsers offer different kinds of customisations and tools, and Google has a number of features that can help you customise your own PC/laptop for study. By creating a free account, you can access the iGoogle software, and make your PC/laptop more user-friendly using the huge range of free gadgets. Customise your iGoogle page with maps, images, currency convertors, jokes, quotes, a calculator, a thesaurus, free Sudoku puzzles and lots more (http://www.google.com/ig).

The advantage of this is wherever you have an internet connection, you can login and access your own customised screen, set out with the information that is useful for you. You can use this space to collate your links to your selected communication tools, such as Facebook, Twitter, Google+, email, Skype and links to the essential university pages you will need.

tip

Bookmark the ALLE page to get an overview of some of the technologies used for learning: http://www.jisc.ac.uk/whatwedo/programmes/elearning/ltig/alle.aspx

---

Anytime Learning Literacies Environment (ALLE)

This project has three different learner journeys to help students starting with their studies:

(a) The academic journey
(b) The library learning journey
(c) Digital tools for learning.

Explore it and use it.

E-learning and Virtual Learning Environments (VLEs)

E-learning, blended learning and virtual learning are all terms used to describe learning activities supported by or accessed through electronic channels – computers, CD-ROM, DVD, internet, intranet and so forth. If you are a full-time, 'face-to-face' student, you may well be a little surprised to find sessions on e-learning being discussed in your 'Welcome Week' or 'Induction' activities. These are for you! As well as attending lectures and classes, you are expected to use any online materials or resources that your tutors provide.

"When I did my Globalisation course, we were required to do a group blog. I also had to access all the handouts from my tutor's website. My presentations were put online and I was expected to discuss the merits of my peers' work online as well. Some students also have to make videos/ podcasts as part of their assessments. We were all directed to learning resources and external websites through the tutor's Blackboard site.**"**

E- or online resources for students are often gathered together in one place in a university Virtual Learning Environment (VLE). On your university VLE you may find some combination of lecture notes, seminar materials, course information, discussions, blogs, online assessment, a calendar, revision tasks, announcements, links to other resources, assessment information, and lots more.

Make the most of your VLE

Once you have access to your VLE, check you have access to your modules, and also if you have access to any more general resources. Some librarians put information up on the VLE, and many learning development or study skills units put material up for all students to use.

Then for each module check:

- Is my lecturer using the VLE for this module mainly to store lecture notes?
- Does this lecturer use a bulletin board to communicate changes?
- Is there a facility where I can add my questions?
- Is there a frequently asked questions (FAQ) section?
- Is there an area where I can get in touch with my fellow students?
- Is there any assessed work on the site?
- Do I use the site to submit my coursework?
- Are there any quizzes or other tools available to help me check my knowledge?
- Which areas will be useful when it comes to revision?

Use your VLE!

Virtual Learning Environments help lecturers track your progress, so if you forget to login for a few days you may well get an email asking if you are having any difficulties. Make sure you are working through the online material regularly, and report any problems you have quickly to maximise your learning from these supplementary resources.

tip

Attend the university IT training sessions to maximise the use of the VLE. At the start of each module explore the resources available through the VLE – not all modules are the same, and different lecturers may use different tools.

Types of VLE

VLEs can be divided into two types – open-source based ones such as Moodle and Bodington, and commercial packages like Blackboard.

The open source VLEs (http://moodle.org/ and http://www.bodington.org/) are available for use by anyone, which could be very useful if you are on a course where *you* are developing materials and need somewhere to place them, for example if you are a student teacher or if a module assessment involves you in designing teaching and learning materials instead of writing an essay, but typically will not be used by students themselves.

Blackboard is a commercial VLE that universities purchase because it can be linked into other university IT systems. Universities can then offer their students a **portal**, which is one point of entry to personalised online information about your learning, your courses, administration, exam results, graduation and so on.

The advantages of a VLE are that you can access these 24 hours a day, 365 days a year. They are easy to access via a high-speed internet connection and can be used even if you only have basic computer skills. To maximise this resource plan regular visits to make sure you are up to date with any changes. Most students login daily to check up on any changes.

Many universities have their own Open Educational Resources (OER) initiatives which allow them to share digitally and freely a wealth of knowledge. Oxford is one such university and much of the content available through their initiative is in the form of mp3 podcasts – which makes them part of mobile learning. Their initiative 'Open Spires' is supported by JISC (Joint Information Systems Committee) and HEFCE (Higher Education Funding Council for England), and it contains learning materials on a wide range of subjects.

tip

Bookmark Oxford Open Spires: http://openspires.oucs.ox.ac.uk/

2: Using your PC for research

" Then there is using the internet for researching. We were always told not to use Wikipedia, but we were rarely told good ways in which to research online, other than to use Google Scholar. This is where Delicious enters the conversation as being one tool we use, but that site, although good, is now just one of 100s of similar sites/gadgets/applications. One of the problems I have now online is determining authenticity of information. It gets harder and harder the more advanced the internet gets. There is also the subject of plagiarism ... **"**

Using library electronic resources

University libraries are so much more than a collection of books. Today they spend millions of pounds on buying in peer-reviewed journals and databases, and newspapers and current periodicals like the *Economist* are also available online for free from your library – or from your home. You can also check to see if any of your course main textbooks are available online as an e-book from the university library; or at a small cost from Amazon if you have a Kindle (a digital book reader).

Your lecturer will expect you to show you are reading broadly across your subject as well as deeply to gain expertise in particular areas; so usually a mix of traditional (paper-based) and peer-reviewed e-learning resources are needed to show you have effectively researched your subject.

Mini case: Government statistics. These can be found in your library, but by entering the website there is so much more information at your fingertips. For example, there is a summary of the most recent statistics released, a search facility and a facility to customise your search, a key statistics explanation, as well as links to other useful sites. It is far more effective in this case to access the information online.

tip

Bookmark http://www.statistics.gov.uk/

Meet your librarian

Your subject librarian is a really important person. He or she will usually do a presentation at welcome week or in one of your first lectures. Find out his/her email address, because, like your lecturing staff, there will be specific days and times when they are available for consultation. Subject librarians can give you advice and assistance with all kinds of research, helping you to find a book or explaining the best key words to enter for successful searching of a particular online database.

tips

- Most libraries have *subject indexes* as well as having search tools to enable you to search by journal, by author and by topic.
- Your librarian may also put useful subject information on the library web page.
- Check to see if your reading list is online – this is often in with the library resources.

Open an ATHENS account: ATHENS is a personal username and password that verifies you as a student at your university and allows you to access the full range of online resources remotely. All you need is internet access, so this makes working on the move far easier. From ATHENS you can browse online journals; databases for your subject; access e-books and lots more. Most universities now have ATHENS as part of your standard student ID and login; it is worth checking so you can study anywhere, anytime.

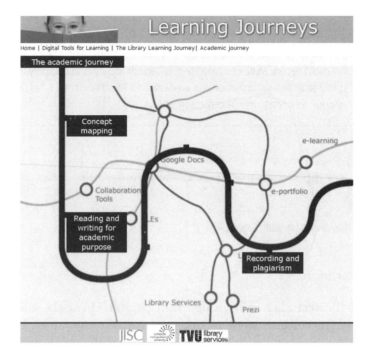

FIGURE 7A Learning journeys

Adding tools to help you with your own research

As a successful student, you need to demonstrate that you are skilled in researching not just paper-based books, journals and newspapers, but to be equally skilled at extracting relevant information from online resources. With so much information available on the World Wide Web, you can make the most of the web by using a few simple tools to manage and store your information. There are numerous gadgets and applications available free for students, or that can be downloaded for a small charge.

Google Scholar (http://scholar.google.com) provides a simple way to broadly search for scholarly literature. From one place, you can search across many subjects and sources: peer-reviewed papers, theses, books, abstracts and articles, from academic publishers, professional societies, preprint repositories, universities and other scholarly organisations. Google Scholar helps you identify the most relevant material across the world of scholarly research. It can be very useful for mapping out the key writers on your chosen area of research, and will assist you to identify the relevant 'key words' for using when you refine your research later. This site is great because it flags up where free copies of the documents can be accessed online.

tip

Using too few key words will bring up thousands (or even millions) of websites. You will need to refine your research to get a more manageable number.

Try **Google Books** (http://books.google.com), and see how the site finds a book whose content contains a match for your search terms, and automatically links to it in your search results. By clicking on a book result, you will be able to see a few short excerpts to the entire book. Each book includes an 'About this book' page with basic bibliographic data like title, author, publication date, length and subject. For some books you may also see additional information like key terms and phrases, references to the book from scholarly publications or other books, chapter titles and a list of related books. For every book, you will see links directing you to bookstores where you can buy the book and (non-academic) libraries where you can borrow it.

Bookmarking

Having refined the key words and identified key authors using the Google tools successfully, you can source **textbooks** from your university library; check the **electronic peer-reviewed journals** for your area; and search for your lecturer by name in case they have published on the topic! You will find that you can gather quite a number of resources. It is useful to **collate** these resources, to keep them together in one place, and, if you choose, share them with others.

Bookmarking is an essential academic skill to develop, and it will save you hours of time trying to remember where you read or saw a piece of information later, when you are editing your work for final submission, and creating a reference list or bibliography. Many universities have systems available via their catalogue to do this (Endnote and REFworks are the most common) but you may wish to use some of the free tools available.

Bookmarking tools work by marking or 'tagging' the websites, resources and even books you read and find useful. You can store all your electronic bookmarks in one place, and more importantly, categorise them into topics.

Whatever your area of study, you will find that over time the same authors and themes keep re-emerging, and each time you locate a new source you can bookmark it. Over time, you will create a whole database of your reading. By the time you are writing your final year projects or extended essays you will have a whole collection of bookmarks in one place, covering various aspects

FIGURE 7B Delicious – an example of social bookmarking

of your subject. Even better, you can view the bookmarks of others on the same topics, which makes this a very effective tool to learn about. **Delicious** is an example of a free bookmarking tool (see Figure 7B).

Go to http://www.delicious.com and create your own account.

Keep your references!

Always make sure you list your references as you draft your work – trying to find out where you got some information from weeks later is onerous and time consuming. You can use a free online referencing tool such as **Zotero** (http://www.zotero.org/). Zotero can collect all your research in a single, searchable interface. You can add PDFs, images, audio and video files, snapshots of web pages, and really anything else. It will automatically index the full-text content of your library, enabling you to find exactly what you're looking for with just a few keystrokes. The icons illustrate the different uses this tool can offer, so it can act as a personal research assistant as, once installed, one click will save and store your references, ready for exporting in the style you require.

Collate your webpages – get updates!

So now you have got to grips with searching for information, storing information and collating information for your own use, or to share with others. The next stage is to start to think about collating the web pages you regularly visit, and getting updates when the web page changes and new content is added. There are a number of online aggregator tools, and these work by automatically linking to your site when the material changes.

Learning how to set up and use **RSS feeds** is a really useful skill. Feeds are known as RSS or 'Really Simple Syndication'. In essence, the feeds themselves are just web pages, designed to be read by computers rather than people. The first thing you need is something called a news reader. This is a piece of software that checks the feeds and lets you read any new articles that have been added. There are many different versions, some of which are accessed using a browser, and some of which are downloadable applications.

RSS feeds

One of the best sites for getting started with news feeds is the BBC. Here is their explanation of RSS feeds:

> News feeds allow you to see when websites have added new content. You can get the latest headlines and video in one place, as soon as it is published, without having to visit the websites you have taken the feed from. (http://www.bbc.co.uk/news/10628494)

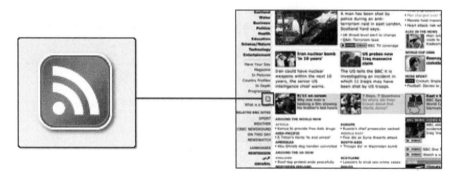

FIGURE 7C RSS feeds

Go to http://www.bbc.co.uk/news/10628494. Now scroll down the BBC site to the section called 'How do I get a news reader?' to check which news reader will work with your computer operating system. Then follow the instructions and you will have your first RSS feed. An RSS aggregator is useful when you start to develop your skills. This will automatically update you when a new posting appears on one of the sites you have visited. This will help you to keep up-to-date when information on a favourite website changes and alert you to new information on a subject. It will also save you lots of time by managing the information sensibly and you can check at a time and place that suits your own learning pattern.

YouTube if you want to

Another favourite study application is, of course, **YouTube** (www.youtube.co.uk). YouTube can be customised and personalised by you – simply **create your own YouTube Channel** and save all the videos clips you find useful for your studies. These can be 'tagged' and sorted – for example into themes, including sites you want to keep as part of your social life for your own hobbies and interests. There are tips and tutorials on all kinds of subjects and areas; however, be aware that these are not peer-reviewed, and you will need to make an academic judgement as to the quality of the resources you locate.

YouTube

Since its inception in 2005:

- YouTube has 490 million users worldwide (unique visitors per month).
- It generates an estimated 92 billion page views each month.
- The average user spends an average of 25 minutes on the site each time they visit.
- The number of advertisers using display ads on YouTube increased by 1,000% in the last year.

Mini case. For understanding social media see, for example, Lee Lefever and his 'Commoncraft' YouTube clips. These are great for simple, illustrated tutorials on all the different social media tools (http://www.youtube.com/watch?v=6a_KF7TYKVc).

Evaluate your sources

FIGURE 7D Evaluate your sources

Having located and collated a range of materials from different sources, materials that have been accessed via open access (i.e. not university provided), resources need to be carefully evaluated before inclusion in your work. There is an invaluable free resource to assist with the process, an online resource called 'The Internet Detective' (http://www.vtstutorials.ac.uk/detective/) – work through this early in your studies. The tutorial looks at the critical thinking required when using the internet for research and offers practical advice on evaluating the quality of websites. It is really important to develop your critical skills and learn how to judge how reliable a website is for your studies.

Specialist study resources

The Higher Education Funding Council for England recently funded 73 projects to develop materials for students around a range of subject areas and disciplines. The Centres of Excellence in Teaching and Learning are all listed here: www.hefce.ac.uk/learning/tinits/cetl/final/ and each has a supporting website with resources for students.

Mini cases

1   LearnHigher (www.learnhigher.ac.uk) is an excellent resource that has hints, tips and online materials for students on all aspects of studying, from time management to mobile learning to group work to being creative.
2   WriteNow (www.writenow.ac.uk) is all about student writing, and has a free book on writing designed by students, for students, available to download.
3   Reusable Learning Objects (www.rlo-cetl.ac.uk) has a website containing a whole range of small multimedia resources on a huge range of topics, from languages to maths to nursing to science and study skills. One especially useful section is the study skills section, where a series of multimedia resources takes you through the creation of Harvard system references.

3: Using your PC to present your research

Having discovered lots of different online tools to assist you to collect, manage and store your information, this next section talks through different ways of collating this information for different study uses. This could include working smart – and using mobile technology to keep in touch with your presentation group; using a tool such as 'Prezi' instead of PowerPoint to present; creating surveys using tools such as Google docs or survey monkey to share documents with others via a wiki or Google docs; or creating your own artefacts for revision.

Present it

Presentations are an essential part of most university courses, many being graded and utilised in group work. However, they have a habit of becoming dull and monotonous, largely due to the fact most presentations are made on Microsoft PowerPoint, where customisation and personalisation are limited. PowerPoint is a great tool for presentations and has stood the test of time, but many other presentational tools are overlooked. These include programs such as GLO Maker, Prezi and Xtranormal.

Presentations with a difference

GLO Maker

The RLO-CETL project developed free software to enable the free creation and/or repurposing of multimedia resources. The software can be downloaded for free from www.glomaker.org, and there is a blog with tutorials and examples at http://glomaker.wetpaint.com/. Students can now easily create their own resources to embed within a presentation; as a revision aid; or as part of coursework.

Xtranormal (http://www.xtranormal.com/) is another great tool, but instead of presenting your work in a traditional form, you use avatars to create a movie that gets your point across in a very effective way. There are examples on their website, and tutorials are available on YouTube with examples of current work.

Prezi, a free tool which can be accessed online at http://prezi.com, allows you to build your presentation into a website. It has been designed to help you build exciting and informative presentations and is particularly useful when you are presenting to an audience. There is a free tutorial in the ALLE digital tools learner journey (http://hermes.uwl.ac.uk/learnerjourney/journey2_prezi.html).

An example of students using the tool to present can be accessed here, where three Business School students were awarded a prize for their presentation (Student Prezi – LH bursary project – the secret of our success: http://prezi.com/ssuuvqkdx9uz/uni/).

4: Social media – starting to share your tools and communicate

Social media are about getting involved. It is about getting the web to work for you for fun, for work or to support your learning. The web is becoming far easier to use, navigate and take part in. It can work for you personally as well as you 'the student'. There are many different packages out there that will make your life much easier. You can organise your social life and keep in touch with friends by using one of the social networking sites such as Facebook (http://www.facebook.com/) or Twitter (http://www.twitter.com/). These packages allow you to keep track of friends back home, your group work team mates and anyone else you want to invite to join your network.

Future lab and find out

There are numerous social media tools. One way of starting to understand the different capabilities and uses to suit your own personal study needs is to explore one of the mapping diagrams; for example www.futureexploration.net maps tools out in terms of web applications; content sharing; social networking and recommendations/filtering. This website has a useful set of characteristics and definitions by which to sort the different technologies.

Futurelab (http://www.futurelab.org.uk) is an independent not-for-profit organisation committed to developing creative and innovative approaches to education, teaching and learning. They have excellent reports and resources on emergent technologies. The Government Funded JISC (http://www.jisc.ac.uk/) is the UK's expert on information and digital technologies for education and research, and has evaluations and reports into technological innovations.

Suggestions for getting started

- Watch: The machine is using us: http://www.youtube.com/watch?v=6gmP4nk0EOE
- Download: This four page overview of Web 2.0 technologies http://www.rossdawsonblog.com/Web2_Framework.pdf
- Cristina Costa (based at the University of Salford as the Research Technologies Development Officer) has a series of great presentations about all things web based on her slideshare account, so this is a good starting point (http://www.slideshare.net/cristinacost/social-media-for-newbies-8800689). Cristina also has examples of her different projects at her website here: http://knowmansland.com/

109

" Then we have the future with mobile phones/tablets entering the scene. At the moment they are still quite new but they have real possibilities as the operating software starts to merge with the operating software on your desktop. It is an area I know little about but it offers exciting opportunities. **"**

Mini case

A recent study by Bradley and Holley (2011) looked at how students liked to use their mobile phones for formal and informal learning. The project found students had lots of different uses for their mobile phones, including transporting files, recording lectures, taking notes, making short video clips, as well as using their mobile to keep in touch with friends and classmates. The results, with lots of hints for using your own phone for study can be accessed at www.londonmet.ac.uk/learningonthemove.

 **tip**

Most lecturers are experts in their own area. Check whether they, or other colleagues, have written anything that you could read, both in formal settings, such as books or peer-reviewed journals; but also informally – check if they have a subject blog, a Facebook page, blog or Tweet on Twitter for work.

Alternative spaces in Virtual Worlds

Some universities are starting to use 3D worlds for some aspects of teaching and learning. One of the best known is Second Life, a 3D online digital world that is imagined and created by its residents. The University of Ohio has combined representations of their 'real buildings' that are familiar to students and a virtual welcome site that is completely different. Their graduate students, part of the University's Russ College of Engineering and Technology, are designing a series of Second Life science activities for middle school children as part of a $1.7 million science project (http://vital.cs.ohiou.edu/vitalwiki/index.php/Ohio_University_Second_Life_Campus_Places_To_See).

Second Life – meet other students and find information in 3D

You can join Second Life and create a profile for yourself. You do not need to wait for a tutor to develop a Second Life course. If you are interested, go to the Second Life website (http://secondlife.com/), create an account and go and explore. The 'On the beach' project was sponsored by the authors of this book – the project blog can be found by searching 'slonthebeach' (www. slonthebeach.co.uk). Here you will find information on the project and the links to the spaces where you will be able to meet other students will always be up to date. The lecturing team continue to use the surrounding areas for engaging students in reflective learning; for language teaching; for fashion shows; to develop art galleries and other activities – so there is always something happening.

The video tutorials give you an idea about the kinds of things that are possible. See http://wiki.secondlife.com/wiki/Video_Tutorials to get started. Watch out for Sandra Sinfield (Sandra terasaur) and Debbie Holley (deb khaos)... Tom's a little more cagey about his ID.

Conclusion

The aim of this chapter is to give you a 'taster' of how your PC can be customised for your use – so you can study at a place and time of your own choosing. It has offered some ideas to assist with some of the key technologies and tools that may be useful for you in organising your own learning. With the growth of smart mobile phones, these technologies are at your fingertips. Mobile learning enables you as the student to personalise your education experience, with the use of mobile phones or with mp3 players. Podcasts of lectures made available by universities are a brilliant way to reinforce what you learnt in those lectures, and can be accessed whilst travelling or away from your home, making your learning a mobile and multisensory experience.

Putting together some of the tools from this chapter will help you to develop your own personalised learning environment. These tools can now be used for future career enhancement. The UK government are currently encouraging all universities to offer their students the opportunity to undertake Personal Development Planning (PDP) activities as part of their Higher Education Studies. Some universities offer paper-based PDPs, but others are starting to introduce electronic PDPs. These schemes are usually voluntary and are not assessed, but they offer you a fantastic chance to gather evidence to show prospective employers at a later date.

tip

Use your PDP to develop and demonstrate your ICT skills (see also Chapter 26).

Box of tricks

Some key web tools – and how to use them in your studies.

Blogs

There are numerous useful blogs for any academic subject. For example, the *Guardian* newspaper reporters also contribute to the blog: http://blogs.guardian.co.uk/news/. If you are interested in current affairs, and keeping up to date with current affairs should be part of your life as a student, create your own blog and add this link – or the link from your preferred broadsheet newspaper to your Delicious account. Then search for useful blogs to do with your subject area, and add these to the list.

 **tip**

Create your own blog – perhaps for your PDP entries – or to reflect on your learning on a particular module? There are a number of ways of setting up a blog – see Wikipedia for a list; www.blogger.com is quick and easy to use. Wordpress (http://wordpress.org/) has great free styles you can choose from, and an easy-to-use dashboard that will allow you to link up your social media.

Interesting blogs that we follow:

- University librarian blog: http://www.daveyp.com/blog/archives/1370
- Student Learning and Teaching Network: http://studentlandtnetwork.ning.com/
- The Student cycle blog – useful tips: http://www.thestudentcycle.co.uk/
- Postings from an e-learner: http://www.e-learningconfessions.blogspot.com/
- PhD student blog on producing a Literature Review: http://onlinelitreview.blogspot.com/2008/07/blog-entry-for-tuesday-22nd-july.html
- Psychology blog: understand your mind: http://www.spring.org.uk/
- Uses of technology for learning: http://cyber-kap.blogspot.com

IM – Instant Messaging

With IM, you can interact with friends or colleagues who are online when you are. As long as the person is connected to the internet, you can type messages to each other. These appear in a small window on both of your computer screens.

Most IM programs provide these features:

Instant messages – Send notes back and forth with a friend who is online

Chat – Create a chat room with friends or co-workers

Web links – Share links to your favourite websites

Video – Send and view videos, and chat face to face with friends

Images – Look at an image stored on your friend's computer

Sounds – Play sounds for your friends

Files – Share files by sending them directly to your friends

Talk – Use the internet instead of a phone to actually talk with friends

http://communication.howstuffworks.com/instant-messaging.htm

Twitter

Twitter (http://www.twitter.com/) is a social networking site where people tweet briefly about their research, up-to-the-minute articles and stories – or what they had for break-fast. The site is set up in a similar fashion to a blog page; however users are limited to 140 characters keeping posts crisp and easy to digest.

Twitter is a great way to keep up to date on current affairs through following pages such as BBC News and all the quality newspapers. Many researchers – and your lecturers – will have a Twitter account where they share links to useful websites, blogs and readings on their subject. If you 'follow' them, a few moments' viewing every day leads you straight to the most relevant research in the subjects you are studying. You can 'mix' your academic following by also following comedians, celebrities, authors, sports teams and also your university Twitter account to keep up to date.

Wikis

A Wiki is a collaborative (http://en.wikipedia.org/wiki/Collaborative) website (http://en.wikipedia.org/wiki/Website) which can be directly edited by anyone with access to it. There is a good example of Wiki use at http://evolvingessay.pbwiki.com/. Here a student is producing an online essay – and the accompanying blog captures her thoughts as she writes it. Visit the site to see how a real student essay evolved over real time.

Set up your own Wiki by visiting one of the 'Wiki farms' (http://en.wikipedia.org/wiki/Wiki_farm). Some of these are public, which means anyone can read them, while some can make private, password-protected Wikis. PeanutButterWiki (http://en.wikipedia.org/wiki/PeanutButterWiki), Socialtext (http://en.wikipedia.org/wiki/Socialtext), Wetpaint (http://en.wikipedia.org/wiki/Wetpaint) and Wikia (http://en.wikipedia.org/wiki/Wikia) are popular examples of such services. For more information, see the list of Wiki farms (http://en.wikipedia.org/wiki/List_of_wiki_farms) on Wikipedia. Note that free Wiki farms generally contain advertising on every page.

➡

➡

Wikipedia

Wikipedia (http://en.wikipedia.org/wiki/Wikipedia) for research is a useful tool. However, like all sources, not everything in Wikipedia is accurate, comprehensive or unbiased. Many of the general rules of thumb for conducting research apply to Wikipedia, including:

- Always be wary of any one single source, or of multiple works that derive from a single source.
- Where articles have references to external sources (whether online or not) read the references and check whether they really do support what the article says.
- In all academic institutions, Wikipedia, along with most encyclopaedias are unacceptable as a major source for a research paper.

(http://en.wikipedia.org/wiki/Wikipedia:Researching_with_Wikipedia)

 **tip**

Start your research of a topic with Wikipedia, but use other sources to support your arguments. Be careful – some lecturers will penalise you for citing Wikipedia as a source of information as it is not an academically peer-reviewed resource.

Review points

When reflecting on this chapter, you may realise that you:

- See just how much potential there is in using your PC, laptop and the web for studying
- Understand how enhanced technology skills are important both for study and future employment
- Know more about what a university VLE might offer – and what you will have to find out to make the most of your university's VLE
- Have some effective web research techniques at your fingertips – including information on how to bookmark and reference your sources
- Understand how social media can enhance your academic study – and have decided to follow some blogs to see how other people use them. You will be developing a blog of your own very soon
- Are opening a Twitter account straight away – and finding some people to follow as part of your learning/research journey
- Have no fears about trying out new technologies.

And finally: You can use the technology to make wonderful notes as shown in Figure 7E.

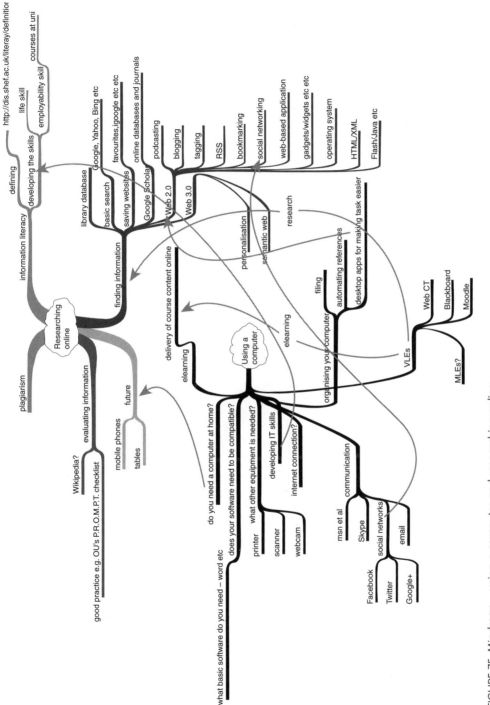

FIGURE 7E Mindmap – using a computer and researching online

Photocopiable:

Essential Study Skills, Third Edition © Tom Burns and Sandra Sinfield, 2012 (SAGE)

Section II

Study Techniques and Learning Effectively

8

How to Succeed in Group Work

Aims

Group work is one of the most emotionally charged areas of university life – and it is oh so important. Group work develops skills for study, work and life. This chapter will explore the role of group work in the academic environment and how to build your group work skills.

Learning outcomes

It is intended that after reading this chapter and engaging in the activities you will have:

- become aware of the what, why and how of group work – with a focus on academic groups
- strategies to help you make the most of all your study groups – and even to enjoy them
- made links between group work and the skills you can record in your PDP and for your CV.

Introduction

Group work can be brilliant or it can have you tearing out your hair! It is one of the most emotionally charged areas of university life. Many see group work only as a problem; perhaps they're the ones who do all the work or get the silent partners... whatever the issue, group work makes them unhappy. But group work is important, as it develops skills for study, work and life – and this chapter is designed to help you get the most from any group that you are in. If you have doubts about group work or if you don't know how to succeed in groups then this chapter is for you.

Groups – a fact of life

Universities are increasingly building group activities into their programmes:

- because they believe in collaborative learning; we are inter-dependent beings and should recognise and build on that
- because group work offers support; tasks are easier when they are shared
- because they are pragmatically preparing students for the world of work; if you cannot work with other people, you are unlikely to keep a job.

Whatever your university's reasons for asking you to engage in group work, see this as an opportunity and get the most from it. To help you, we are going to explore the what, why and how of group work.

What is group work?

A group has to have a membership of two or more people. There should be a sense of shared identity: you should all *feel* like a group with shared goals. You should feel a connection to and be able to interact with each other – with a sense that you can achieve your goals together.

Perhaps it is in these initial definitions that we have hit upon some of the problems with academic groups. How many people in an academic group do feel that sense of identity and inter-dependence? How many embrace the task and the sense of shared goals? How many resent and resist the whole group work process?

If the latter sounds like groups that you have been in – or that you are in now – what are you going to do to make your group feel and operate like a group?

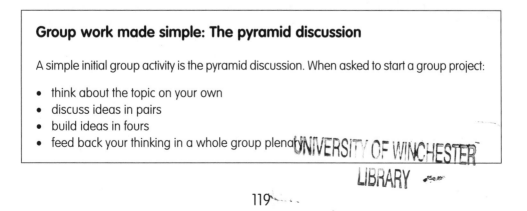

Group work made simple: The pyramid discussion

A simple initial group activity is the pyramid discussion. When asked to start a group project:

- think about the topic on your own
- discuss ideas in pairs
- build ideas in fours
- feed back your thinking in a whole group plenary

UNIVERSITY OF WINCHESTER
LIBRARY

Students in groups

In university there can be many forms of group work, from your own study partner or group, to the group activities organised by the tutor: class discussions, presentations and seminars, the formal, assessed group project. To get the most out of these things, the best thing you can do is participate in these as positively as possible.

Academic groups

There are many different forms of group that you might engage in at university. Here are some of them:

- Class discussion or activity: This is a simple collective activity that you are asked to do in class, with other people.
- Tutorials: Typically this involves two or more students meeting with a tutor and discussing, or working together on, a topic or task.
- Seminars: This is a group of students – around 15–30 working together usually with a tutor. This may involve whole-class discussion, activities or reading being undertaken or working on an issue together; often related to a lecture programme.
- Group assignments: This is where students are asked to produce something collectively. This may be to prepare and deliver a presentation or a seminar, or write and produce a report, magazine or a video. Perhaps you will be awarded a collective grade.

 **tips**

- Group work gives you real examples of collaboration for your CV – make notes.
- Group work is designed to reduce the workload whilst increasing the amount of active and interactive learning that takes place – take advantage of this.
- Sometimes the process, as well as the product, is assessed. Here, students will be asked to reflect on the whole group work experience. That is, how you worked as a group, roles that were adopted, problems that occurred and how they were solved. Make notes as you go along.

“ They keep making us work in groups, but university is a competition – why should I help other people? **”**

“ I love group work. I enjoy working with other people – I like the camaraderie and I like the fact that I'm not on my own as usual. **”**

Why groups?

Group work offers many advantages to students of all ages – yes, really. Group work can foster supportive, active learning giving you the opportunity to develop your personal and inter-personal skills. Working with others offers an opportunity to share the workload. It really is easier to do all the reading if you share it out and discuss it. When engaged in a group project, you can develop assertiveness rather than aggression; tact and diplomacy rather than bullying and hectoring; flexibility and compromise rather than intractability and stubbornness. You can learn to listen as well as to speak, to encourage others as well as to establish yourself; and to work co-operatively and collegially with others. Another advantage of group work is that a good group offers social support that can break down the isolation often associated with being a student.

Disadvantages

Of course, there can be disadvantages to group work. For one thing, many group activities are now assessed. Students have become increasingly aware of the importance of good grades and do not want *their* grade based on the effort – or lack of effort – of other people. Thus they are incredibly resentful of those in the group who do not pull their weight, who do not turn up, who do not stay on track, who dominate or bully or distract, who stay silent, or who talk too much, who are not interested or committed. None of this feels satisfactory and it causes much resentment.

Resolving conflict – and your CV

But, every disadvantage can become an advantage if you work out how to resolve the problems that you encounter. So notice what is happening in your groups. Notice how difficult situations are resolved. For example, if there are people who do not speak or don't turn up for meetings or do not contribute to the group task; instead of being angry and frustrated, try to discover the real problem – and see if you can find a solution. Be creative – can you use virtual meetings or blogs to take your projects forward?

Your attempts at finding solutions may not work, but that doesn't matter. That you recognised and attempted to address a problem is what will make you employable.

Put notes on your group activities – your problem solving and your project successes – in your curriculum vitae file. When applying for jobs, you will be able to *prove* that you are good at group work by giving examples from your time at university. It is the examples that you give – and the way that you tackled your problems – that will make all the difference in that vital job interview. And this refers to another 'why' of group work – it can and does prepare you for your future employment.

tip

If you have to write a reflective account of your group work: make notes of your group sessions, your conflicts and resolutions, your strengths and weaknesses, the plusses and minuses of the experience.

1. Activity: SWOT your group work

SWOT stands for Strengths, Weaknesses, Opportunities and Threats.

- What are your group work strengths? What do you already like about group work and the way that you perform in a group?
- What are your weaknesses? What do you really dislike about group work and/or your own performance in groups?
- What opportunities are there for you in group work?
- What threats?

Once you have answered these questions, think about your answers – discuss them with your study partner.

Query: What do they tell you about yourself? What do they tell you about how you should approach group work? What are you going to do differently next time? What are you going to do now?

How to 'do' group work

The best way to get the most from group work is to approach it positively, determined to get the most from it. If you really dislike group work, but have to engage in it, fake it to make it! Role-play being an active, positive student.

Another simple and very effective strategy is to choose your groups with care. Do not just team up with those people sitting next to you – or those nice chatty people from the canteen. Group tasks normally involve hard work: choose people who are as motivated, positive and industrious as you.

2. Activity: Belbin's group roles

There are eight key roles that management experts like Belbin (1981) have described in group activities. We have listed these below indicating the possible strengths and weaknesses involved.

- Company person: dutiful and organised – possibly inflexible
- Chair: calm and open minded – not creative
- Shaper: dynamic – but impatient
- Creative thinker: brilliant ideas – but unrealistic
- Resource investigator: extrovert, responds well to the challenge – may lose interest
- Monitor: sober, hard-headed, keeps everything on track – may lack inspiration
- Team worker: mild, social person, plenty of team spirit – may be indecisive
- Completer/finisher: conscientious, perfectionist – a worrier.

Query: When looking at that list:

- Do you recognise these roles? Are they helpful or unhelpful? Why?
- Is there a description that most fits you? Are you happy with that description? What are you going to do about it?
- How are you going to get the most from the roles that you play in group work?

 tips

- In a small group, make sure that you have a chairperson and that everyone knows what their task is, what they are doing and by when it all has to be completed.
- Experiment with group work. Adopt different roles in different academic groups. Each time you vary your role in a group you will develop different aspects of your personality; this is a good thing.

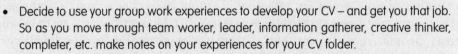

- Decide to use your group work experiences to develop your CV – and get you that job. So as you move through team worker, leader, information gatherer, creative thinker, completer, etc. make notes on your experiences for your CV folder.
- Whilst eight roles are indicated here, research indicates that academic groups work best if they only contain about five people – any more and you start to get passengers.

A business-like approach to group work

Management theorists like Belbin and Adair have worked to de-mystify group work so that businesses can run more effectively. Critics say that they offer rigid and inflexible descriptions of group work forms and processes which do little to help us either to understand groups or to perform better in them. Have a look at the information in Activity 3 and ask yourself, 'How will knowing this make me a more successful student?' For, in the end you must work out if and how knowing those things will help you to succeed in your group activities.

tip

If you are expected to reflect on your group work experiences, using the boxed information will definitely improve your grade.

3. Activity: Adair's processes

Belbin describes the *roles* adopted in group situations, Adair describes the *processes* that groups go through. Adair argues that groups pass through distinct transformations, as they encounter a problem and finally solve it. These have been described as forming, storming, norming and performing – some people also speak of a fifth stage, mourning.

Read through these descriptions and see how they might help you work better in academic groups.

Forming is where the group comes together and takes shape. It is a time of high anxiety as people work out:

- who is in the group – and what they are like
- what the assignment is – what it involves
- what the 'rules' are – about their behaviour and about the task
- what they will have to do to get the job done – and who will be doing 'all the work'.

 **tip**

In groups, keep in contact, share phone numbers. Make dates to meet. Work out who is doing what by when.

Storming is where conflict arises as people sort out all the confusions highlighted above. This is where people seek to assert their authority, and get challenged. Typically this is a 'black and white' phase – everything seems all good or all bad: compromise is not seen. At this stage people are reacting emotionally against everything as they challenge:

- each other
- the value of the task
- the feasibility of the task (you cannot be serious!).

 **tip**

If you do not like group work, ask yourself, is it because you do not like conflict? Perhaps you just find this phase uncomfortable? If this is so, remind yourself that this phase passes.

Norming, as the name suggests, is where the group begins to settle down. Here that sense of inter-dependence develops as:

- plans are made
- standards are set
- co-operation begins
- people are able to communicate their feelings more positively.

➡

Be a team player. Be punctual for meetings. Apologise if you cannot attend. Pay attention. Keep in contact with the whole group. Do what you say you will do.

Performing is where the group gets on and does what it was asked to do. Jobs get done – by everybody in the group. Success can be achieved as the presentation is delivered, the report written… Here it is useful if:

- roles are accepted and understood
- deadlines are set and kept to
- communication is facilitated by good inter-personal skills.

Use those phone numbers and email addresses. If group leader, learn how to chivvy people politely; if chivvied – do what you said you would do.

Mourning: The fifth stage, mourning, is supposed to follow a successful and intense group experience. As you work hard with people, you develop links and bonds. Typically you enjoy the sense of mutual support and commitment. The feeling of inter-dependence is very satisfying. When all this ends as the task ends, there can be a real sense of loss.

Be prepared for the sense of loss. Keep in contact with good team players, you may be able to work with them again.

Queries:

- Do you recognise any of these stages?
- Now that you know about them, think how you might use this knowledge to your advantage.
- How will you draw on this information in your next group activity?
- Make notes so that you do not forget.

Discussion: There is debate about these group work stages and whether or not they exist – or if the descriptions are helpful. If you want to approach group work from another perspective do go to the LearnHigher site.

LearnHigher's award winning 'Making Group Work Work' is a video resource that follows students going through group work struggles. It runs like a mini-soap opera – and has links to useful things to think about and do.

How to succeed in group work

When undertaking a group task it still helps to use the 10-stage approach to assignments:

1. Prepare to research. As a GROUP:
   - understand the task – know what you have been asked to produce
   - analyse the question – all of it – know what you have to cover
   - have the overview – fit the task to the module learning outcomes
   - use creative brainstorming and notemaking strategies
   - action plan – work out who is doing what, why, where and when.

2. Follow the action plan: do what you said you would do – when you said you would do it. Keep in contact with other members of the group. If a problem arises do not just disappear – talk to someone.

3. Review your findings: everybody should share their research – and share their ideas about how to finish the task.

4. Plan the final product – together. Know who will be doing which bits of the presentation or the report. Who will be writing which sections of the newsletter – or who is responsible for which bits of the video.

5. Prepare first draft or first version or first 'cut' of whatever it is you have to produce as a group. If working independently, meet up and show each other what you have achieved so far.

6　Leave a time lag. Have a break from this task (and work on something else). Let the brain know that the task is not over – but put it on the back burner.

7　Review, revise and edit – agree on a final draft. The group has to come together to agree the final version of the presentation or report. This is another difficult time for a group – typically everybody thinks their version or opinion is the best – and it takes real skills to agree a version that everyone is happy with. Ride the storm.

8　If producing a written product, proof read. If preparing a group presentation, put all your ideas together into one PowerPoint presentation – or one group website. And rehearse together as a group. Make sure everybody knows the whole presentation in case someone does not or cannot turn up on the day.

9　Hand in written work on or before a deadline – have your presentation ready by the deadline.

10　Review your progress (see reflective account of group work).

Developing your inter-personal skills: Useful things to say and do in your group

To move things along:

- Initiating: What about trying… What if we did…
- Questioning: Could you explain that? Could you elaborate a bit?
- Giving: This has worked for me before… What would happen if we…?
- Clarifying: Do you mean…? Is this like…?
- Summarising: Do you think this is what we have agreed so far…?

For a good atmosphere:

- Supporting: I see what you mean… I understand…
- Observing: We are making good progress OR We seem to be stuck…
- Mediating/reconciling: You two seem to be seeing this differently, but what about…? Is there anything that you can find to agree on?
- Compromise: What about if I gave ground on this… Would that work?
- Humour: Well obviously the UN lost a diplomat in me…

Reflective account of group work

If you are required to write a reflective account of your group work as part of the formal assessment of your course or module:

- Ask your tutor exactly what it is that they are assessing before you even start the group activity. In this way you can note the relevant things as they arise and have information there ready for when you perform your formal review of your group project.

- Do not just write things like, 'We all argued and did not agree on anything'. OR 'I really like group work'. You need to comment on how you made your group function effectively. It helps if you note problems and how you overcame them.
- Do mention Belbin and Adair and how their theories helped you do better in your group task.
- Do use theory and practical examples from your weeks working as a group to justify your arguments and make your reflective account sufficiently academically rigorous.
- Do read Chapter 18 on the report to see one way to report back on a practical experience.

4. Activity: Group building exercises

There are management team-building games to experiment with to develop your group work skills. We have included one below – with suggested variations. Have a go – and have some fun.

The Paper Tower

In this activity you will need to gather together some students who want to develop their group work skills and some simple resources. The goal will be for groups to construct a paper tower with a given supply of resources.

Variations on this exercise include: designing, producing and testing a non-breakable egg container or balancing a spoon on a paper tower. The egg container is the more dramatic.

The exercise is designed to develop group work skills through practical activity, observation and feedback.

By the end, participants may understand the social support and positive benefits of doing things with other people. They should be more aware of how they approach group work – they should also have had some fun.

Resources: Large quantities of newspaper, sticky tape, paper clips and rubber bands – sufficient for all participants.

The Paper Tower exercise

1 Divide participants into groups of 5–6 people. Each group has to choose an observer who will not participate but will note how the other people work together. The participants have to build a tower with the resources to hand. Each group will 'present' their tower to the other groups. Each observer will feed back how his or her group performed. (Allow 20–30 minutes' tower building time and two minutes' reporting back time.)
2 Whilst the students build their towers the observer makes notes as to the roles adopted by individual members or the processes engaged in by the group. The observer notes how people engage in the group task.

➡

➡

3 Groups report back on the criteria they had chosen for their tower, the tower itself – and how they felt the group performed. The observer feeds back (in constructive terms) on the roles and/or processes of the group.
4 Plenary: hold a plenary to discuss what the participants have learned from the activity – and how they will draw on this in the future.

When reviewing this activity, participants might note that they:

- enjoyed it – it was fun
- benefited from being part of a team
- have some idea of how they performed in a group activity
- have learned something useful about group work that they will build on in the future.

Conclusion

We have used this section of the book to explore group work in the academic setting. We have stressed that group work can be a positive, supportive and interactive learning experience – especially if you tackle group activities with enthusiasm and commitment and with the co-operation of similarly committed group members.

We stressed how an awareness of group roles and processes can help you understand and succeed in your group activities. At the same time we stressed that you can benefit even from problem groups by noting how your problems were overcome – and that you can use such reflections in a formal group review and in your job applications.

Finally, we suggested that where group activities require a formal reflective account, you will complete a better one if you make notes of all your ideas, problems and solutions as you go.

Good luck with your group activities. Enjoy your group work – groups really can be supportive, exciting and productive.

Further reading

If you are interested in this topic you may wish to have a look at the following:

 Check out the LearnHigher resources – especially 'Making Group Work Work'

Adair, J. (1983) *Effective Leadership*, (1987) *Effective Team Building*, (1987) *Not Bosses But Leaders* (3rd edn, 2003). See: http://www.johnadair.co.uk/published.html
Belbin, R. Meredith (1981) *Management Teams: Why They Succeed or Fail*. London: Heinemann

Review points

When thinking about what you have read and the activities that you have engaged in, you might feel that you have:

- Developed an awareness of how to use your group work experiences at university to improve your job applications and are ready to start putting group work notes into your CV folder
- An awareness of the forms and processes of group work – and are in a position to make the most of group activities in the future
- Developed an awareness of the potential of group work in the academic environment.

Section II

Study Techniques and Learning Effectively

9

How to Interact and Build Relationships at University

Aims

To explore the human and social side of being a student.

Learning outcomes

After reading this chapter you will have:

- thought about your own situation as a student – and what you might need from a chapter like this
- selected some useful things to do – and made dates in your diary to do them
- listed what you will do first, second and third – to get to know people and to experience the rounded, human parts of being a student.

Introduction

Being at university is not just about studying your subject and gaining a qualification that will help you to get a good – or a better – job. Interacting with a diverse group of people of different ages, classes and nationalities develops your personal and inter-personal skills – your abilities to work and communicate with other people.

Throughout this book we stress how helpful it is for you to make friends, to form study partnerships and study groups as part of your active and interactive learning strategies. In this brief chapter we are going to explore how to interact and build relationships at university as part of the human and social aspects of being a student.

 **tip**

For information on listening and interpersonal skills, as part of your academic repertoire, explore LearnHigher which has quizzes, questionnaires and video tutorials on body language, listening and paying attention, improving concentration in lectures, keeping conversations flowing, non-verbal communication and body language.

Shyness and making friends

❝ When it comes to reading about meeting people and making friends, less is more. There is a lot of hype about university being the best time of your life – giving the impression that everyone else is having more fun than you. Most of us just want reassurance that other people are also finding it tough to meet people, make friends and adjust. **❞**

❝ Going to university is a stressful and strange experience for most people. Typically it brings two responses: how will I cope with all the changes? Or – Pfffftttttt – it doesn't bother me, I'm not going to change my life at all. **❞**

Let us quickly tackle that last response. Why would anyone go to university – or do anything – if it isn't going to make a difference, if they are not going to change or grow or respond in some way? You may not conform to what you think the university expects of you. You may want to keep many aspects of the old you, because you are already proud of your culture and your identity... but a more knowledgeable you should be able to merge the old with the new in a creative and stimulating way. People who are totally resistant to change may be hiding quite significant insecurity – or they just don't understand what life is about. Life is change, growth, risk. Life in the west is dynamic or it is nothing at all.

That leaves us with all those people who are worrying about how they will cope. We are going to explore that by looking at some of the key personal and human rather than academic reasons for not coping.

First in family

One big reason for feeling swamped at university can be because you are the first in your family to go to university. You do not know what the 'rules' are and you are absolutely convinced that everybody is staring at you and wondering what on earth you are doing at 'their' university.

This is often called 'impostor syndrome' and we cannot tell you how common it is – and not just in students. Whether you are a 'non-traditional' student, or whether you come from a very university-orientated family, you can experience this sense of feeling like a fish out of water – of waiting for that hand on the shoulder and someone to say, 'get out, you don't belong in here'. Lecturers, too, often feel this and admit it either informally amongst friends they trust – or sometimes they confess it (like a disease). It is not just students who say they can't write because they are 'not academic enough'.

Given the commonality of this feeling, we can only reassure you that you are not alone and that the feeling passes – especially if you help by saying to yourself: I am a good student, this is my university, I can do this. You might feel a bit foolish doing this, but it really works. (See also Chapter 22.)

International student: New country, new language, new rules

As an international student you travel to a foreign country to study in a language that is not your own. You might be lonely and homesick – you might feel out of your depth with grammar and spelling: so many international students apologise for 'not being good enough'. Yet instead of focusing on what you cannot do as an international student, it might help to acknowledge how brave you are being and what you are good at before you move on to correct your weaknesses.

One thing you really need to do is get out of your room and meet other people. Check out your university's international office and go on the trips and other social activities that they set up for you. If there is not an international office go to the Students' Union and see how to set up an International Students' Club or Society. Bid for Union funds to hold social activities and run trips and events. If you are the one organising this, you will soon find that you have made friends.

However, you also have to make the effort to meet people who are not from your home country. Visit the Students' Union and join a Club or Society that has nothing to do with being an international student.

" And one thing I always remember two of my flatmates saying, one South Korean, the other Indonesian, is how important it was for them to make English/British friends, not just other International Students, as it helped them not only to learn and understand English better and more quickly, but to understand a bit more the country they were in. **"**

... and if you are really having trouble in studying in English, check out your university's support provision. Are there classes on English for Academic Purposes – actual or virtual? Is there an English language section in the library where you can take video tutorials on the language, access resources to teach yourself, or meet new people who could become conversation partners?

" Oh, while I am thinking about it, and not sure how to say this, one problem I came across was some International Students taking advantage of the newer International Students. Bullying, in other words. I took one Chinese girl up to the police station after she 'lent' £600 to another Chinese lad, because she was naive and he took advantage. This was a particular problem with International Students as they did not know how to resolve the problem and often felt isolated and afraid of reporting it to police or the university, for fear of losing their visas ... and because of the shame they thought it would bring. **"**

" Of course, being taken advantage of is not entirely limited to International Students! **"**

Left home ... living in Halls

You may not be an international student, but may still have left home for the first time – and boy are you feeling homesick. How come? You were so excited about the thought of leaving home; it never occurred to you that there could be a down side. If this is you, you really must put in an effort to get out of your room – whether in Halls or other accommodation – and meet people.

If possible, go to the Freshers' Week and see what clubs and societies are being advertised. Force yourself to join a couple of them. Go and see what the Students' Union stall is offering. Make a date in your diary to go to the Union offices soon and have a chat with someone there.

If once you have done all these things – you have forced yourself out of your room, you have met a couple of people – you still feel really homesick and it is stopping you from studying, make an appointment to see the counsellor. Talking it over with another person gives you human contact and helps you put everything into perspective. The bad feelings really do pass and one day you won't remember that you ever felt that way.

tip

Whilst it is good to get to know the people in Halls – or in your shared accommodation – it is also really good to make friends on your course. Go on, be that brave person who says, 'let's go for a coffee' – or 'let's go and get some food…'

Living at home and a student

Given that going to university can be so expensive, many students are not leaving home for the first time, but have the different problem of staying at home. It can be really difficult living at home and being a student. For you, everything is changing – your world has turned upside down and sideways – but for your parents, siblings and friends everything seems exactly as it was.

You will have to juggle the difficult challenge of growing up whilst other people are thinking that you are staying the same. You might have to deal with friends who resent that you have no time for them or who believe that you are now turning into a numpty or a snob. You might have to persuade parents that you are a responsible adult whilst still being dependent on them for help.

Again, the best advice is to try to get to know other people on your course. Talk with them about your course but about everything else that you normally talk about. Do social things with them – you be the one to invite someone else to go for a coffee or to join the gym.

❝I know many parents who are studying. It's important for them to make the time getting to know people and getting familiar with the university during the first few weeks. If they have child responsibilities, universities often offer crèche services. But, if not, it is often valuable to make arrangements so that they can be free to 'be a student' and get to know people and feel comfortable.**❞**

Making the most of your Students' Union

We have already mentioned that it is useful to check out the Students' Union at the Freshers' Week. Even if you miss this, find where your Union offices are; pop in and check out the lie of the land. See what sorts of things they do and work out if you want to get involved now – or at a later date.

Typically Unions have a political purpose, where they represent students on university committees and fight for your rights if they have to. They also have social wings: they are the ones responsible for the clubs and societies – and for entertainment, a student magazine, website, radio or TV station. All of these things are vital parts to student life. Offer to help with something – get involved in a small way at first and you will find that your isolation disappears and you really enjoy being an active student.

Become a peer (or writing) mentor

Many universities have some form of peer mentoring programme operating. This is where students help other students, their peers, in some way or other. This can include everything from being a 'meet and greeter' in Welcome week – wandering around helping new students to not feel so lost or out of their depth – to becoming a writing or study mentor where you help students with their assignments in some way.

Obviously these are not things that you tend to do in your first year but they are a great way of adding depth to your second- and third-year experiences. Not only do we learn best when we teach someone else, but this develops your interpersonal and communication skills and looks good in your CV.

“ When I ask other students if they have anyone to study with, they tend to say they don't know anyone in their subject as they have massive lectures and prefer to make friendship groups in halls instead. I can't emphasise enough how important it is to get to know people on your course... **”**

Conclusion

Trying to give too much guidance on friendship and meeting people is difficult for us – it is something better coming from students themselves, like on the Student Stories website (http://www.studentstories.co.uk/). When it comes from us, it runs the risk of sounding patronising. So this is short and sweet. But do put into operation some of the strategies we have suggested above – they do work and they help break the ice and get the ball of positive friendships rolling.

If you are interested in developing your interpersonal skills as part of your academic development, check out the LearnHigher pages... and all students should look at the Student Stories website, to see what real students have to say on this topic.

Review points

When reflecting on the information and advice in this chapter you might:

- Have noted some useful things to do – and have made dates in your diary to do them
- Have thought that making friends seems do-able – and you really will make the effort and put in the time to do the social and human activities that are so important in student life
- Have decided that you are off to click on Student Stories (http://www.studentstories.co.uk/) right now.

Section II

Study Techniques and Learning Effectively

10

How to Survive Academic Reading: Targeted Research and Active Reading

Aims

This chapter is designed to deconstruct academic reading for the sceptical student – and to give very practical guidelines about how to manage your research and reading throughout your time at university.

Learning outcomes

After reading through this chapter, and engaging with the activities, you will have:

- understood the purpose of academic reading – and developed some active reading strategies
- practised a range of engaging and fun reading activities
- thought about how to capture your notes from reading – in patterns, in small animations, in a reading dossier
- overcome your fear of academic reading – you can now read with a purpose.

Okay – so you are worried about the reading. We're not born knowing how to tackle a university textbook or journal… Brainstorm the questions below to set your goals for this chapter:

Why do we read?
How much should I read?
How can I read effectively?
What do I already know on this topic?
What do I need to find out?
How will knowing this make me a more successful student?

❝With the growth of the internet, we are reading websites, viewing YouTube clips, engaging in Facebook, Twitter, LinkedIn… And I still don't know how to read for university!❞

Reading for your degree

In the UK you are not *taught* your degree, you are supposed to research and read for it yourself. This means that, whilst you are given information in lectures, classes, seminars and tutorials, this will never be 'all you need to know' on a subject. You are supposed to develop your knowledge of the subject beyond that which the tutor has told you. This means reading. This reading gets easier with practice.

If you are just beginning to study a topic you may know very little about it and that's why the first reading that you do can be so difficult: everything feels new and uncertain to you. You're not sure who to read – or why. You don't know whether to read something really difficult – or to 'cheat' and try something easy… Here are some typical student reading worries:

❝I don't know what I'm reading or why. I hate this.❞

❝So what on earth does 'Read around the subject' mean then?❞

❝What are the basic things that I ought to know and understand?❞

❝Who are the people that I ought to read?❞

❝How much of my reading list must I cover?❞

❝Can I use Wikipedia? The tutor says no – but it's so helpful!❞

Quick tips would be: Read with the assignment question in mind. Read the ESSENTIAL books on your reading list. Read four to five textbooks and four or more journal articles per assignment in your first year. Read Wikipedia – but don't *only* read that...

" Have you considered why we students read Wikipedia? It's not just because it is a source of information, but also because it can narrow down the topic and focus the research. The danger being that if the subject they are looking at is missing elements from it or that the contributor has misunderstood the subject or context, it can throw a student in completely the wrong direction. It can also send the reader to some very suspect sources. This is what you ought to be telling us! **"**

Extending your knowledge

The first reading you do is designed to introduce you to the key ideas, people and principles of your subject. After that you will move on to the more recent and the more difficult ideas. You have to read more than one person's works on a topic – and you take the initiative by following up the people that your lecturer names in class and that are on your reading list.

For example, if this is the first Study Skills book that you have ever read, this subject might be new to you. But if you now pick up another Study Skills book and go to their section on reading, you will be able to see what they write. If it is different from this, you might ask yourself why. This might prompt you to look at yet another Study Skills book to see what they say – and so on.

This is the basic principle of academic reading. You start reading to gain an understanding – you then develop that by reading more. You engage analytically and critically with all your reading and you develop your knowledge and understanding as you bring the differing arguments together in your own mind. This is where your writing comes in (see Chapters 14–21).

 **tip**

Remember that you are supposed to be studying for 35–40 hours per week – this allows a lot of time for reading!

That week when you did that reading session I hated that: Thoughts on reading from another student

" That week when you did that reading session I hated that and I was really uncomfortable the whole lesson… because I was so unsure and not confident and, as I looked round, everyone seemed to be getting on with it and I thought I don't know what the hell she wants me to do.

And you know as soon as you're in that position, you can't learn anything, you can't take anything in. Things were being said, and I couldn't understand. And I was sitting with a couple of people who seemed to know what it was all about and I thought 'Oh crikey'. You know? And it was awful. It was horrible. I didn't like that at all. **"**

Yet when the same student was asked later about a positive learning experience she said:

" I was thinking about all those books on that booklist. I was thinking I had to read every single one of those books and I didn't know how I was going to manage that so I thought I'd just bluff it a bit you know.

But later on I found from you that I didn't need to do that. When you did that bit about reading – about books. I mean I wasn't aware that I didn't know anything about that first page bit, about this is the author and this is when it was published and this is where it was published. I didn't know any of that. I didn't have a clue because books have always been really alien to me you know?

And when you showed us about looking in the index and looking in the contents and then finding the bit that interests you and then going to your first paragraph and reading the first few lines and seeing if it's what you want. I found that really valuable. **"**

> **Query**: What are your reactions to this student's feelings about learning about academic reading? Are her reactions similar to or different from your own? Did reading this help in any way?
>
> **Discussion**: As tutors, we learned a lot from this student's reactions to learning how to read an academic text:
>
> 1 It was difficult.
> 2 The difficulty brought with it many negative feelings.
> 3 The negative feelings swamped everything else so that nothing could happen at that time.
> 4 Later the student did start to try the technique out.
> 5 Eventually it became one of the most useful techniques that she felt she got from the study skills programme.

Query: What does that tell you?

Discussion: Reading can be difficult – it can even be frightening. Worse, at first even learning how to read an academic text can be frightening. As always, we promise that these things do get easier with practice. Try to take comfort from this student's experiences. She managed to move from fear and loathing to confidence and assurance comparatively quickly. You can too.

Big reading tips – practical strategies to use right now

Here are some effective reading tips and strategies – as always – as you read through this section ask yourself how knowing that will help you as a student – make notes to remind yourself.

Academic reading tends to be tough – it is hard work and requires concentration, time and effort. So when you are going to read, get prepared mentally and physically:

- Have everything you need to hand: dictionary, key texts (photocopied); pens, pencils, highlighters; notebook for new names, words and concepts; index cards and notepaper for your references and key word notes.
- Have the lighting and sound tuned to your study preference.
- Have water and sweets available to keep you energised.
- Make sure you will be undisturbed. Unplug your landline, switch off your mobile. Do not look for a disturbance to get you out of reading!
- Work at your 'best' time of day. In-depth reading is hard work and should be done when you are at your most alert.

Set clear goals for each reading session: brainstorm – what do I know? What do I need? Which part of the question will this help me with? Use an active and critical reading system as shown in Figure 10A.

When we read we need to be active and interactive; we need to ask questions as we read and we need to mark up, annotate or scribble on texts as we go (obviously NOT the library books!).

"One of the most powerful things I ever learned to do was to photocopy chapters – and write all over them as I was reading. I really felt in charge – I took control of my reading. Everything changed when I did that.**"**

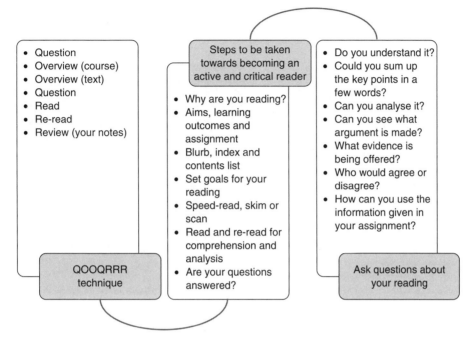

FIGURE 10A Using the QOOQRRR reading strategy

Read analytically and critically, engage with the text. Ask yourself questions about what you are reading. Do you *understand* it? Could you sum up the key points in a few words? Can you *analyse* it? Can you see what argument is made? What evidence is being offered? Who would agree or disagree? How can you use the information in your assignment? *Annotate*! (See Figure 10A.)

Read beyond the reading list – remember if you just give back to the tutor what they gave to you, you will only get an average grade.

tip

Use a variety of reading resources: books (printed and electronic: e-books), journal articles (printed and electronic: e-journals), academic websites, reports and conference papers, abstracts.

Read beyond texts that 'agree with' you. Make sure you cover a range of opinions and that you use a range of sources. Academic writing requires a balanced view, so your academic reading requires that also.

Keep a record of what you are reading. As soon as you sit down with a text, record the author, date, title, location (where it was published) and publisher

© Tom Burns and Sandra Sinfield, 2012
Chapter 7 © Debbie Holley and Chapter 26 © Christine Keenan

First edition published 2002
Second edition published 2008
Third edition published 2012

Apart from any fair dealing for the purposes of research or private study, or criticism or review, as permitted under the Copyright, Designs and Patents Act, 1988, this publication may be reproduced, stored or transmitted in any form, or by any means, only with the prior permission in writing of the publishers, or in the case of reprographic reproduction, in accordance with the terms of licences issued by the Copyright Licensing Agency. Enquiries concerning reproduction outside those terms should be sent to the publishers.

All material on the accompanying website can be printed off and photocopied by the purchaser/user of the book. The web material itself may not be reproduced in its entirety for use by others without prior written permission from SAGE. The web material may not be distributed or sold separately from the book without the prior written permission of SAGE. Should anyone wish to use the materials from the website for conference purposes, they would require separate permission from us. All material is © Tom Burns and Sandra Sinfield, 2012.

SAGE Publications Ltd
1 Oliver's Yard
55 City Road
London EC1Y 1SP

SAGE Publications Inc.
2455 Teller Road
Thousand Oaks, California 91320

SAGE Publications India Pvt Ltd
B 1/I 1 Mohan Cooperative Industrial Area
Mathura Road
New Delhi 110 044

SAGE Publications Asia-Pacific Pte Ltd
3 Church Street
#10-04 Samsung Hub
Singapore 049483

Library of Congress Control Number: 2011938241

British Library Cataloguing in Publication data

A catalogue record for this book is available from the British Library

ISBN 978-1-4462-0324-8
ISBN 978-1-4462-0325-5 (pbk)

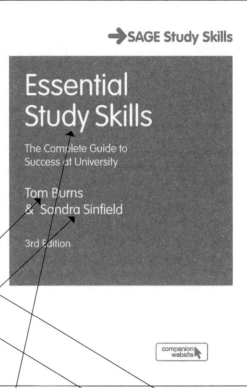

→SAGE Study Skills

Essential Study Skills

The Complete Guide to Success at University

Tom Burns
& Sandra Sinfield

3rd Edition

companion website

Author's name and initial(s)	Date of publication	Title	Place of publication	Publisher
When you write the author's name, always begin with the surname, followed by a comma and then any initials. Complete the author's name with a full-stop.	The date can normally be found adjacent to the copyright symbol. Make sure you are using the date referring to when your book was first published.	Make sure you always use the full title. If there is a subtitle, use a colon to separate this from the main title. The full title should be completed with a full-stop.	You need to find the publisher's name and the publisher's location. The location comes first and you separate this from the publisher's name with a colon. Complete the publisher's details with a full-stop.	

For example:

Burns, T. and Sinfield, S. (2012) *Essential Study Skills: The Complete Guide to Success at University*, Third edition. London: Sage.

FIGURE 10B   Referencing a book

 **tip**

 Visit http://www.rlo-cetl.ac.uk/whatwedo/rlos/completedrlos.php#studyskills for learning objects that will help with your referencing.

Author	Date of publication	Title of website	Website address	Date accessed on
The person or organisation responsible for the site.	This can be found at the bottom of the page close to the copyright or from a date headline.	This should be put into *italics*.	The **full** URL of the website.	The date you last accessed the website (in brackets).

For example:

LearnHigher (2011) *LearnHigher – resources for students*. Available at: http://learnhigher.ac.uk/Students.html (accessed on 21 August 2011).

FIGURE 10C   Referencing a website

tip

Visit http://www.rlo-cetl.ac.uk/whatwedo/rlos/completedrlos.php#studyskills for resources that will help with your referencing.

(A [D] T L:P). Make this an instinctive act that you do not even need to think about. If you use material from your reading without giving sources you will be accused of plagiarism – even if this is an accident.

tip

Record everything you read onto index cards and file them. Put the source (A [D] T L:P) at the top; summarise what the text was about; capture a couple of good quotes – with page numbers. Doing this means that you can use source material in more than one module and on more than one assignment.

A quick note on plagiarism

Plagiarism means kidnapping – and if you do not give your sources when you write you are in effect kidnapping someone else's work and passing it off as your own. Plagiarism is a major academic offence for which you can fail a module, be suspended from university – or even have your whole degree annulled.

'Well, I read it, I agreed with it and now I've put it in my own words – it's mine now. I don't have to give sources then, do I?' Yes you do – the ideas still came from someone else. And anyway, you are supposed to be giving sources – you are not supposed to be making it all up – you are supposed to be using and acknowledging the knowledge-claims of your subject.

If you are worried about plagiarism, use our online Preventing Plagiarism resource. In this there are student views on plagiarism, a tutorial and exit tests so that you can check out that you have understood it. Web search LearnHigher Preventing Plagiarism Course.

Make reading fun – and productive

When approaching reading, build in purpose and make sure you have some fun. Try some of these:

- After reading, sum up what you read in three sentences or construct a bare bones summary in no more than 25 words. Prepare a one minute presentation upon the text. Select one sentence from the text that you have found meaningful (a main point or an idea with which to argue) – say why you chose it. Highlight key points whilst your friend blacks out everything that is NOT necessary – discuss. Make an Xtranormal movie of the main ideas in the texts: Text to Movie resource: http://www.xtranormal.com/
- Instead of writing about your reading – make a visual summary. Draw a diagram or picture of the text using as few words as possible. As you struggle to capture the ideas in pictures you will find that you are really struggling to understand and learn what you are reading. See these online examples:

- o http://fixiefoo.typepad.com/.a/6a00d8345eaeee69e20120a590b9e8970c-pi
- o http://www.johnclapp.com/artw_pages/sketch_pages/sketch_eyeworks.html
- Build a READING DOSSIER or a READING NOTEBOOK over the whole of your degree programme. Make or buy a series of sketchbooks and each week write about what you have read, why you read it, what it made you think about, what you now know about your subject, how you now feel about your progress/knowledge/ assignments… Vary your reading entries by sometimes drawing what you think – or adding pictures from newspapers or magazines. Make this space as creative as possible. Make it a place or thing that you want to use. When you have to write assignments, your reading dossier should provide plenty of source material – and it should be easy to use because you have invested feelings in it as well as thoughts.

 **tip**

This can be a really creative, reflective process; see: http://www.arts.ac.uk/cetl/ visual-directions/

- Don't forget to construct your own subject dictionaries. As you study new material you discover new words, concepts and phrases, so note these. Make your subject diction- ary a key study and revision aid for yourself. Take control of your learning.
- Try textmapping (http://textmapping.org/). A fun way to start reading difficult texts is to take one chapter or journal article that is relevant to your assignment, enlarge it and turn it into a scroll that you explore with another person.

Now do some reading

We have put together several activities to get you thinking about and using our information on active and interactive reading: *using* the reading strate- gies; exploring online reading resources – including Internet Detective; a tutorial on evaluating materials you find online; a quick library checklist; and a prompt to get you using index cards to record your reading.

 **tip**

Put dates in your diary for when you will work through the activities… otherwise you won't do them!

1. Activity: Use the QOOQRRR reading strategy!

1 Photocopy the strategy below. Use it with all your reading.
2 Practise using it first as you work through the rest of this book.

Q: Question – think first: what do I already know on this subject? What do I need from this reading?

O: Overview – your course: read module aims and learning outcomes – read the assignment question: these all tell you **why** you are reading!

O: Overview – the book, chapter or journal: this will tell you **what** you are reading!

Look at – author, title, date; chapter headings; index. Chapter/article: introduction/conclusion – first sentence of every paragraph… NOTE your source here A (D) T L:P

Q: Question – So, in the light of all that, ask yourself, Why am I reading **this**, *now*?

R: Read the text actively and interactively – marking it up as you go.

Underline, highlight, circle key words or points – make notes in the margin: who would agree or disagree? What does it remind you of? Where will you use the information?

R: Re-read your own annotations and marginalia – now you are ready to make your key word/key point notes.

R: Review your notes – are they any good (are they sourced: author (date) title location: publisher)? Can you use them? What will you now read or write?

2. Activity: Try textmapping

Put the textmapping suggestion into practice with one or more friends from your course.

Resources: useful books and journals from which to choose one article to explore in depth. Module handbook – with assignment question annotated to highlight key words or phrases that you are exploring in depth. Sticky tape, highlighters, marker pens, blu-tack, paper and index cards for final notes.

1 Choose a chapter or article that is challenging but obviously relevant to the assignment you are preparing for.
2 Enlarge the article as you photocopy. You want A3 pages rather than A4.
3 When you have all your A3 pages printed tape them together into one big scroll (side by side rather than end on end is recommended).
4 Roll the article out over the floor or stick it up on your wall.
5 Together with a friend read through the enlarged version and mark up: what the whole article is about; headings and sub-headings; repeated words or phrases; main points; main arguments; evidence that is offered; names used by the writer… Things that it makes you think about and other things that you have read that might connect to this 'story'.
6 Once you have finished step back and review your annotations and marginalia. Discuss with your friend.
7 Remind yourself of your assignment question. Review your annotations again: how can that article or chapter help you answer your assignment question?
8 Make notes of your annotations – properly referenced – and plan your next steps.
9 Review this activity: see if it helped enjoy reading and if it made the reading more productive.
10 Plan to do it again!

3. Activity: Online resources to support academic reading

1 Explore these online resources and see how they help you to understand the reading process and develop your reading strategies.
2 Why not blog, FB or Twitter your positive thoughts about them to other students?

There is a correlation with stock usage and e-resource usage. Those who achieved a first borrowed on average twice as many items as those who got a third, and logged into Metalib/AthensDA to access e-resources 3.5 times as much. The correlation is fairly linear across the grades, although there is a noticeable jump up in e-resource usage (when compared to stock borrowing) in those who gained a first. (University of Huddersfield: http://www.daveyp.com/blog/archives/1370)

➡

Reading and evaluating information

- Leeds University tutorial on academic reading (60 mins): overwhelmed by the amount of reading you have to do and not sure how to manage it? Try this online tutorial: http://skills.library.leeds.ac.uk/tutorials/reading_tutorial/player.html
- Our interactive desk shows how to organise yourself for study – and reading: http://learning.londonmet.ac.uk/TLTC/learnhigher/desk/desk.html
- Our writing space: has links to our NoteMaker resource; a free write tool – so that you can practise quick writing about what you read; referencing resources; and much more. Explore it and see how useful it can be to you. See http://learning.londonmet.ac.uk/TLTC/connorj/WritingGroups/
- Critical reading towards critical writing: http://www.writing.utoronto.ca/advice/reading-and-researching/critical-reading
- How to read an academic article: http://www.lenmholmes.org.uk/students/how-2read/how2read_a.htm
- How to read a research article: http://cla.calpoly.edu/~jrubba/495/howtoread.html
- Internet Detective: tutorial on finding and evaluating information: http://www.vts.intute.ac.uk/detective/
- For summarising information: http://learning.londonmet.ac.uk/busdev/hq1001nc/ecdl/summarizing.htm

And MAKE CREATIVE NOTES WHILST READING.

- This allows for a messy, private online notemaking space: http://www.evernote.com/
- Or try CORNELL notes: http://coe.jmu.edu/learningtoolbox/cornellnotes.html
- Or visual notes: http://www.visual-literacy.org/periodic_table/periodic_table.html#
- Have you thought about making notes on a Prezi website? http://prezi.com
- Here's one constructed by some recent graduates: http://prezi.com/ssuuvqkdx9uz/uni/
- A student's thoughts on active reading – from Evolving essay: http://anessayevolves.blogspot.com/2007/02/active-reading.html

And (with thanks to Alice Gray):
If you want to develop speed-reading skills try the following resources:

- Short Burst Learning (accessed August 2011) – to find your current reading speed: http://www.speedreadingcd.com/reading-test.htm
- Doyle, D. (2010) Glendale Community College: Self Pacing Methods – for five useful methods (accessed August 2011): http://english.glendale.cc.ca.us/methods.html

If developing a summarising technique:

- http://learning.londonmet.ac.uk/busdev/hq1001nc/ecdl/summarizing.htm

Outlines

An outline is a list of the main features of a given topic, often used as a rough draft or summary of the content of a document. A hierarchical outline is a list arranged to show hierarchical relationships, and is a type of tree structure. (Wikipedia)

Outlines are used all the time in education and everyday use to organise content and show relationships among items. While creating an outline is nothing new, there are websites dedicated to increasing this skill and taking it to the next level.

Top 10 sites for creating outlines

1 Webspiration Classroom – From the creators of Inspiration, a wonderful graphic organiser that now allows for online collaboration and one of the best visual outline creators on the web: http://www.mywebspiration.com/
2 Quicklyst – A free user-friendly site for creating outlines. Quicklyst also integrates with a search engine and dictionary for enhanced note taking. Study queues can be made as well: http://www.quicklyst.com/
3 Knowcase – Create collaborative outlines with this easy to use site that features a drag-n-drop interface: http://knowcase.com/
4 Thinklinkr – A real-time collaborative outline creator that has a nice built-in chat feature to engage in project development: http://thinklinkr.com/
5 Checkvist – A great collaborative online outliner that has an abundance of features such as: gmail/browser integration, mobility, and nice import/export features: http://checkvist.com/
6 CRLS Outline Maker – A very easy to use outline creator that takes you through a step by step process: http://www.crlsresearchguide.org/NewOutlineMaker/NewOutlineMakerInput.aspx
7 Read Write & Think Outline Maker – A very easy to use outline creator that teaches how to create outlines: http://interactives.mped.org/view_interactive.aspx?id=722&title
8 Loose Stitch – A nice fun site for creating collaborative outlines that can be exported to a blog or website: http://loosestitch.com/
9 Wisemapping – More of a mindmapper than pure outline creator but still a great visual site that teaches the basic concepts of creating an outline: http://www.wisemapping.com/c/home.htm
10 Mindmeister – A fun site for real-time collaboration that is ideal for creating brainstorms, mindmaps, and outlines: http://www.mindmeister.com/

Referencing

- Harvard system: http://slb-ltsu.hull.ac.uk/awe/index.php?title=Harvard_system_of_referencing
- Avoiding plagiarism: Tutorial (also available via writing site): http://learning.london-met.ac.uk/TLTC/learnhigher/Plagiarism/

155

➡

4. Activity: Using your university library

Find your university library. If you find it an intimidating place hopefully this activity will take you through the library in a useful way so that you start using as much of it as possible, as soon as possible – and it will not be intimidating any more.

For each activity, tick the box when you have completed it, and write in details where indicated.

Books ☐

Find the part of the library that houses the books for your subject.

- My books are ....
- Write in the Dewey decimal number (the numbers on the spine of the book) for your subject...

Journals ☐

When studying it is important to read the relevant journals for your subject.

- Where are your journals kept? ....

Write in the title of two journals that you could be reading:

- Journal One...
- Journal Two...

Newspapers ☐

With most subjects it is also important to read the 'quality' press.

- Where are the newspapers kept?...

Counter Loans Area (CLA) ☐

The CLA holds the most important texts for each subject – find it.

- My CLA is ....

Study Areas ☐

What facilities are there for independent study in your library?

- My library offers quiet Study Areas?..
- My library offers group Study Areas?...

Workshops ☐

Some libraries contain student help workshops – does yours?

- My library does/does not have workshops.
- They are located ....
- Opening times are ....

Now that you have had a quick introduction to the library, list three things that you like about it:

1 ....
2 ....
3 ....

What would you tell someone else about the library?

1 ....
2 ....

Photocopiable:

Essential Study Skills, Third Edition © Tom Burns and Sandra Sinfield, 2012 (SAGE)

5. Activity: Completing your index cards

Author(s):

Date:

Title:

Place published:

Publisher:

Key quotes (and page numbers):

➡

➡️

Always note these essential details so you can cite them correctly in assignments – and in your bibliographies.

When completing your index card review of a book or journal always note the information above on one side of the card.

Experiment with the reverse: you could note what essay you used the book for; you could note the chapter or paragraph headings so that you have an outline of the book… The trick is to make this process as useful to you as possible.

 **tip**

Always make some form of active notes: for a pattern note on reading see Figure 10D on page 159.

Conclusion

In the UK we are not taught our subjects, we read for our degree – and thus special reading strategies are useful and necessary. We covered academic reading with a special focus on being analytical and critical readers of academic texts – and that we need to get physical, interactive, with our reading. We covered a whole host of advice and activities designed to get you reading happily and successfully – so it is up to you now to put this into practice.

Review points

When you reflect on this chapter you might notice that you have:

- Understood the purpose of academic reading – and you have already developed some active reading strategies
- Practised a range of engaging and fun reading activities
- Thought about how to capture your notes from reading – in patterns, in small animations – in a reading dossier
- Overcome your fear of academic reading – you can now read with a purpose.

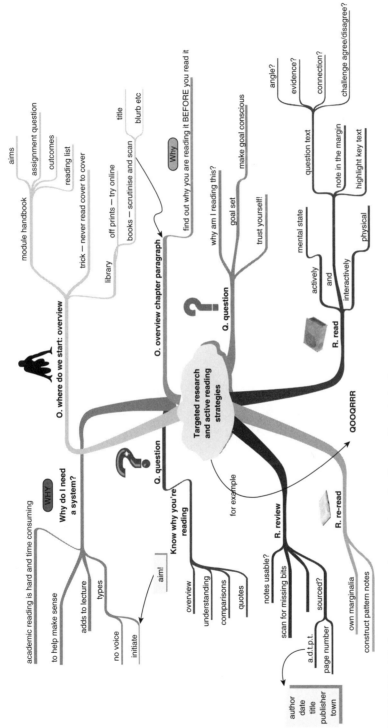

FIGURE 10D Mindmap – targeted research and active reading strategies

Section II

Study Techniques and Learning Effectively

11

How to Make the Best Notes

Aims

Nothing can be quite as empowering as active notemaking. Notemaking involves finding and reorganising information; it fundamentally changes the relationship between you and the information you meet. This chapter aims to introduce you to successful notemaking strategies, making connections with reading (Chapter 10) and creative learning (Chapter 12).

Learning outcomes

It is hoped that by the end of working through this chapter you will have:

- been introduced to notemaking theory – and ideas about the empowering potential of notemaking
- been introduced to notemaking practice – with the emphasis on creative, pattern notes
- realised the importance of active and creative learning strategies.

From notes to creative notes

Notemaking is fundamental and one of the most empowering things you can learn as a student. We are going to explore notemaking by making a case for it as a thinking process and part of your active learning. We put notemaking theory into practice immediately and ask you to explore a range of useful online resources designed to get you really proficient at notemaking.

1. Activity: Notemaking – what, why, how

Before you move on to the reading, spend a few minutes preparing yourself with a structured brainstorm on notemaking. Spend five minutes jotting down your responses to:

- Why do we make notes?
- When and where do we make notes?
- How do we make notes?

---

tip

When brainstorming, just look at the topic and write down anything that pops into your head – do not try to get things 'right', just try to capture your immediate responses.

Once you have jotted down some thoughts of your own, compare your responses with those of some other students:

- Why do we make notes?

  "To remember – I make shopping lists and lists of things to do."

  "To use the information, for example in my essays and exams."

  "To recall key points."

  "To understand what I am learning."

- When and where do we make notes?

  "I take notes at work, especially in meetings."

  "In lectures, seminars and tutorials"

  "When I'm reading – I'm not going to remember it all, am I?"

  "In the middle of the night in bed – no seriously. I often wake up and think of a really good point for my essay. So I keep a pad and pen by the bed so that I don't lose the thought."

- How do we make notes?

  "Well, I write my notes down – I know other people who tape theirs."

  "I take down too much information, I really hate my notes."

  "I take down key words, but I sometimes forget what they mean."

  "I make rough notes and do a shorter version later."

Query: Are these comments similar to your own? What else can you add to your own brainstorm after reading these?

Discussion: As with the prompts at the beginning of our chapters, the point of this brainstorm was to get you ready for the work that is to come. This happens in two ways: first, it quickly reminds you of what you do know on the subject (you are not empty). Second, it can indicate the gaps in your knowledge – thus it can tell you what you need to get from the chapter. We always learn more when we are reaching out for what we want and need.

 **tip**

Always brainstorm before a class, lecture, seminar – or any reading that you do. It acts as a goal setting, focusing device and you will get more out of what you subsequently do.

Notemaking – a dying art

Most people are aware that they are expected to make notes of some sort. They are aware that these notes would form some sort of record of their studies and that they will need this record to help them remember key points. Maybe they intend to use the information in the notes in their assignments and exams. So far so good.

Students are changing – before they took down every word I said, now they sit there and make no notes at all. They are not engaging – there in body, but not in mind! The old definition of a lecture was meant to be a joke: 'A lecture is where information passes from the tutor's notes to the students' notes without passing through the minds of either.'

Why notemaking?

A good notemaking system allows you to capture, re-order and understand information; coupled with an active revision cycle, notemaking allows us to actively select and remember useful information. Making notes puts you in control of your own learning; which is more engaging and powerful. Active notemaking is not just a study skill or an academic literacy, it is something that helps every student to take control of their own learning – and to gain a voice within their own education. **A good notemaking system also saves you TIME:**

" Taking notes – that you understand, so not just notes, but good clear notes – in class can actually save time. You are in class anyway so you are not wasting time doing them. If you combine class notes with doing 30 mins to an hour's research directed by the notes, you do not spend endless amounts of time looking down false trails, and you do get lots of relevant info quickly. "

A beginner's guide to ideal notes

There are different notemaking systems that people use, but they tend to break down into two main formats: some sort of linear (line by line) system or some sort of non-linear or pattern system. But whatever your system all good notes have:

- **Source** – if lecture, title, lecturer's name, date; if text, author, date, title, town, publisher
- **Headings** – capturing key sections
- **Key words** – key points, examples, illustrations, names, new ideas
- **Some structure** – things that make the notes easy to navigate: patterns, numbering, arrows, highlighting, etc. – things that link the notes to the course aims, outcomes and assignment
- **Mnemonic triggers** – things that make the notes memorable: cartoons, colour, illustrations (the Von Rostorff effect – we remember that which is bizarre, funny or bawdy (in Palmer and Pope, 1984))
- **Further reading** – people or articles to read – noted and highlighted
- **Links** – some indication of how the notes could be used in your assignment.

> **Query:** Do your notes usually appear like this? If not, read on.

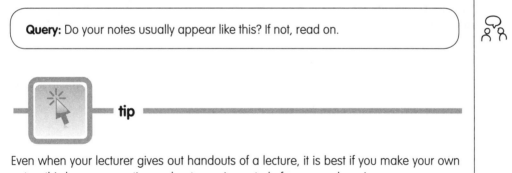

tip

Even when your lecturer gives out handouts of a lecture, it is best if you make your own notes: this keeps you active and puts you in control of your own learning.

Different types of notemaking – linear notes

Linear – line by line – notes are the most typical notemaking form adopted by students and university staff when they do make notes. Typically this notemaking form involves making lists, perhaps with bullets or numbers, with highlighting and underlining used to identify key or important topics.

This notemaking form is neat and has an instant logic and appeal. The danger is that it is very passive and you can be trapped into the argument and evidence used by the subject. This is the notemaking form most likely to promote conscious or unconscious plagiarism.

This is a linear presentation of notemaking advice:

Notes

What:

Bare bones
Record
Key words
For assignments/further research
Names & dates
Active
Organised
Patterns – see Buzan and Buzan (1999)
Linear – like this

Why:

Review & recall
Future reference
Research
Assignments
Exams
Active learning
Understanding

When:

Listening:

Lectures
Seminars
Tutorials
Discussion
Radio & TV

Reading:

Books
Journals
Websites

Thinking:

Planning:

Timetables
Assignments
(shopping etc.)

How:

Key points
Emphasis & highlighting
Structure & connections
Linear or pattern

The problem with linear notes

The 'old' student described above would feel that they had got 'really good' at notemaking if they always ended up with pages and pages of information. There would be a very reassuring feel to having captured everything. However, there are many problems with linear notes:

- You can take so many notes you feel swamped by them.
- You take so many notes that you never use them again.
- If you cannot write really fast, you feel left out of studying.
- If you don't capture something in a lecture, you panic and miss even more.
- If you leave things out you can feel like a failure.
- It is an exceedingly passive form of notemaking – you do not need to be able to think to make linear notes, but you do need to think to be able to learn.
- All the information looks the same, which makes it very difficult to recall specific points of information.
- It is a monotonous way of learning – it is boring and it only engages a small part of the brain, which is not a good thing.

tips

- If sticking with linear notes, use key points, structure the notes with headings, sub-headings, numbers or bullets, adding highlighting and mnemonics to make these notes as memorable as possible.
- Prepare charts and synthesise information from a range of sources – see 10 top tips on academic learning at the end of this chapter on pages 182–3.
- Try Cornell notes instead of straightforward linear notes and see how powerful these are.

Cornell notes

Cornell notes are similar to linear notes in that they too have a linear form. However, the Cornell system is intrinsically more active than the straight linear format, requiring the notemaker to engage both analytically and critically with the notes that they make. Typically in the Cornell system, the notemaker divides their page in three – one side is for the collection of notes and the other is for a summarising of the information into key words or phrases. The final part of the structure is for writing a brief summary of or critical commentary upon the notes. It is here that the notemaker can make reference to the course assignment or course aims and learning outcomes: a very active process.

The key benefit of this strategy is that it encourages students to understand why information is important and why they have noted it. It encourages critical reflection and the making of sense, meaning and connections. It puts the student's understanding and participation at the centre of the knowledge construction process.

Concept maps

The concept map, as with the mindmap, offers a graphical representation of key concepts organised hierarchically – and with relationships between concepts or sub-concepts indicated by links and connections. The foundations with respect to the use of concept maps are that: the material to be learned must be conceptually clear and stated in language relevant to the learner's

| Course: |
| Date: |

Main points	Notes
Summary	

FIGURE 11A Cornell notes template

Photocopiable:

Essential Study Skills, Third Edition © Tom Burns and Sandra Sinfield, 2012 (SAGE)

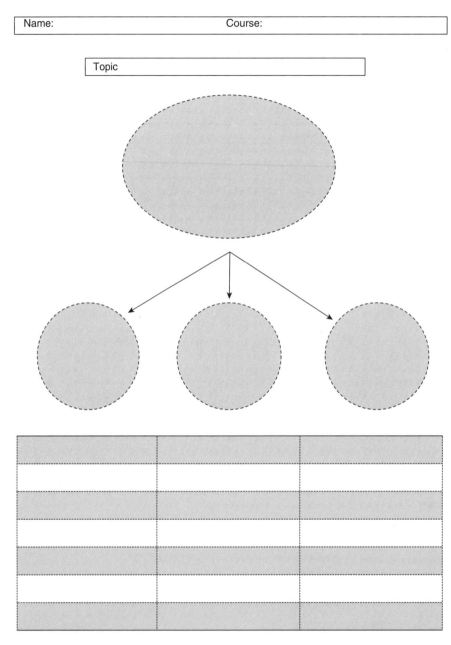

Name:		Course:

Topic

FIGURE 11B   Concept map template

 Photocopiable:

Essential Study Skills, Third Edition © Tom Burns and Sandra Sinfield, 2012 (SAGE)

prior knowledge; the learner must possess prior knowledge; and the learner must choose to learn meaningfully. This system sees the tutor as scaffolding the knowledge that the student interacts with.

Mindmaps

Mindmaps are perhaps the most familiar non-linear notemaking format. Also known as spidergrams or nuclear notes, these non-linear notes are encouraged by Buzan (Buzan and Buzan, 1999) as an active and creative way to both generate and capture ideas. The idea with the mindmap is to put the central topic in the centre of a diagram that the notemaker builds – by drawing out subsidiary lines with ideas linked to the main theme. The mindmap can be made memorable with colour and pictures, and the argument is that it is literally more engaging because it harnesses both halves of the brain, the logical left and the creative right. When working with students we have encountered resistance to using non-linear notemaking formats – but these are the formats proven to be the most powerful in promoting student learning and active engagement.

Pattern notes

Pattern notes are the name given to any non-linear format – and this is the one that we recommend most strongly. The pattern note format is more flexible than Buzan's strict one word per line mindmap – and when used it becomes both a notemaking and a learning tool. As with the mindmap, the idea is that students select and connect information for themselves. The argument is that this very selection/connection process is itself an active learning strategy. Pattern notemaking allows the formation of a set of unique pattern notes each time the student works. Typically when making pattern notes, it is important that students build in their own mnemonic triggers at the notemaking stage and thus each set of notes is unique and memorable. When making pattern notes, students have to dissect, engage with andre-structure complex concepts on their own terms – and they have to play with ideas as they do so; thus this is an extremely powerful, active notemaking system.

> As soon as one can no longer think things as one formerly thought them, transformation becomes both very urgent, very difficult and quite possible. (Foucault, 1988: 154)

Or, as our student might say:

❝ Also, I still say notemaking can save people time. Even if they do not follow through all the 'proper' processes, it will still help to narrow down the amount of research needed. All very useful for the student determined to maximise drinking time while minimising thinking time. But there is one caveat to that, the notes made in class must be clear and understandable. Otherwise, they won't save time, but they will get a sore wrist from all the notemaking, making holding pint glasses more difficult! ❞

Name:

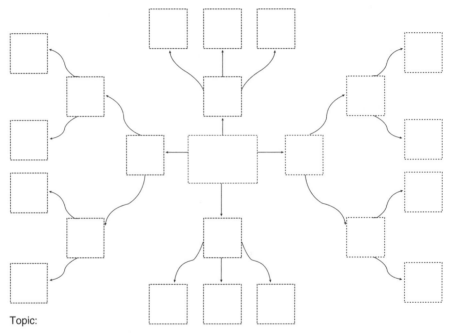

FIGURE 11C   Pattern note template

 Photocopiable:

Essential Study Skills, Third Edition © Tom Burns and Sandra Sinfield, 2012 (SAGE)

NoteMaker – our interactive resource

During our time with LearnHigher we worked with several learning technologists to put together an interactive online resource that gets users to think through the what, why and how of notemaking. We have called it the NoteMaker and you can find it via our Writing Groups site http://learning. londonmet.ac.uk/TLTC/connorj/WritingGroups/

Topic				
Name:				
Date:				

FIGURE 11D   Matrix notes template

Photocopiable:

Essential Study Skills, Third Edition © Tom Burns and Sandra Sinfield, 2012 (SAGE)

Patterns are best

Non-linear notes, patterns of some form, involve very active, interactive notemaking and require some practice to get used to. But when mastered, you will find that each time you make your notes you create distinctive patterns that not only record key points but also help you to learn those points.

The advantages of pattern notes are:

- Instead of taking down masses of possibly useless information, you select only that information that will be of use to you.
- They are short notes and you are inclined to re-use notes that are manageable.
- You do not need to be able to write quickly, you just need to practise selecting useful information (working in stages from rough draft to revised key word notes).
- Selecting and arranging useful information keeps you actively engaged with your information and hence you learn more.

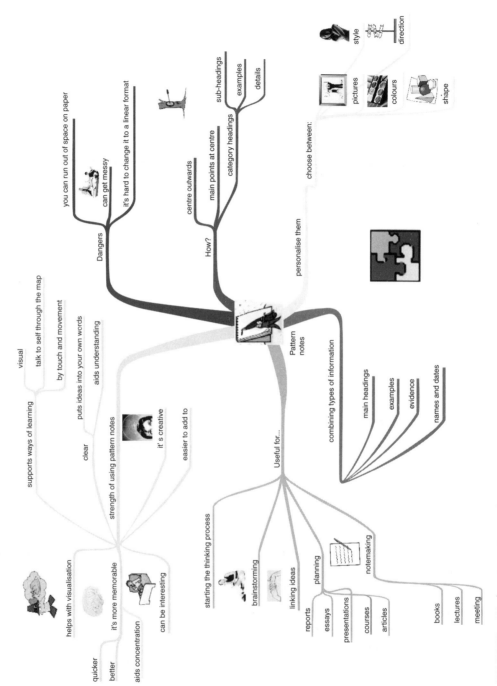

FIGURE 11E   Mindmap – pattern notes

- You can choose to make your notes interesting and memorable.
- Each set of notes looks unique – this also helps to make them memorable.
- Building colour, pictures, diagrams and unusual things (mnemonic triggers) into your notes engages the whole brain into your learning and therefore you learn more.

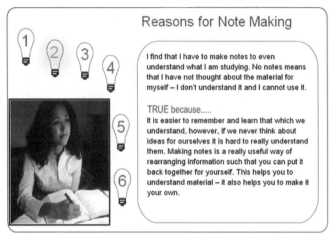

FIGURE 11F   Images from NoteMaker: Reasons for notemaking

FIGURE 11G   Pattern note example

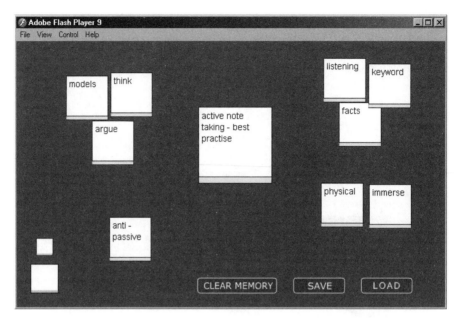

FIGURE 11H   Prototype of interactive section of NoteMaker

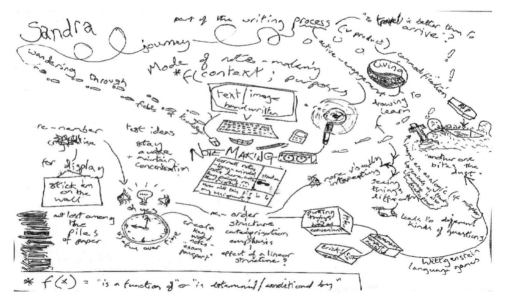

FIGURE 11I   A colleague's notes on one of our teaching sessions

Beginner's guide to pattern notes

To build creativity and activity into your notemaking develop a key word, pattern note-making system. 'Key words' means that instead of taking down every word that is said – or every word that you read – you devise your own key words that summarise or stand for the information that you have decided that you want to keep, because:

- They are easier to remember
- You have chosen them
- You should be using information for yourself, not rote learning a particular lecture or chapter from a book.

When making key word notes from lectures and from your reading there are several stages that you can go through – the trick is to remember that you can draft and re-draft notes. You do not need to get them right first go.

1 Prepare: Get an overview of the lecture or chapter before you start. With books, read the beginning and end of chapters. With lectures, you should get the sense of what the lecture is to be about from your syllabus or scheme of work.
2 Brainstorm: Once you know what the lecture or text is about then brainstorm. Identify what you know on the topic and what you need to find out (your assignment question will help you here).
3 Goal set: That is, work out the sort of information that you want to take away (an overview, key points, key names and dates, key quotes…). Remember to look at your assignment question to help you here.
4 Be active: With your goals in mind, engage with the lecture or the text in an active way – searching for and identifying key words, points, etc.
5 Draft: Put the key points down in a 'rough' way first. With a book, we have suggested that you make notes on the text itself. With a lecture, you might put the title in the centre of a piece of paper and draw points away from the title. If things connect directly to the central topic, branch them off. If they connect with each other, draw them off from the sub-branches.
6 Review your rough notes: Decide what you need to keep and what you do not need. Think about how to connect ideas with each other.
7 Construct your own key word pattern – adding colour, pictures and diagrams to illustrate points and to act as memory triggers.
8 Revise: Review your notes regularly to commit them to your long-term memory.

After: Talk about the lecture; compare notes with someone else; do not file your notes away – pin them on your wall; add to your wall notes every time you read – after every class; review your notes regularly; set action goals after notemaking.

The revision cycle

There is no point making notes if you do nothing with them or nothing about them. We forget 98% of what we encounter after just three weeks if we do not revise. This revision cycle builds memories in your brain and commits information to your long-term memory where you need it. After every lecture:

- Make a shorter more dynamic version of your notes. Put in pictures that are funny, bawdy or bizarre to stimulate your memory.
- A day later spend two minutes actively recalling your notes – plug memory gaps.
- Do this two-minute active recall again a week, a month and six months later.

tips

- Play with it: There are many, many different ways of arranging notes in patterns – from concept maps to mindmaps and beyond. Go to: http://www.visual-literacy.org/periodic_table/periodic_table.html#
- Buy an A1 pad and build up a pattern note of every module that you do. Add to your module pattern week by week.
- Paragraph patterns: When preparing for an essay (or other assignment) put key words from the assignment question onto different sheets of A1 paper, after every lecture or your reading add new points to the different paragraph patterns.
- Module walls: If you can, use the walls of your home to help you study. Put different module questions on different walls. When you come home from a class, when you have read something new, add notes of the information to the module pattern on the wall. You literally immerse yourself in your learning. More than that – when you look from one module wall to another, you can see the links between the different subjects you study. This is excellent, productive learning.

2. Activity: Practising pattern notes

Here we want you to practise your pattern notemaking techniques. Choose a lecture at university or a chapter from this or any book. Prepare yourself for making pattern notes on the piece:

- Have a piece of paper that you turn sideways, landscape fashion.
- Have plenty of coloured pens to hand.

- Remember your 'Beginner's guide to pattern notes', above, and our 'Active reading techniques' (Chapter 10).
- Question: What do you know? What do you need?
- Overview (course): Link your reading to your course: Overview your handbook or the assignment question.
- Overview (text): Read contents, introductions and conclusions first.
- Question: Think again: Why are you reading this… now?
- Read: Actively and interactively, marking up the text as you notice useful points.
- Re-read: Annotations and construct your key word, pattern notes.
- Review your notes and check that they are usable.

> **Query**: Have you made your pattern notes yet? If not, please attempt to do so before moving on. Do not be afraid of making mistakes. There are no mistakes, only rough drafts. The only way to avoid making mistakes is to do nothing at all – and that really is not an option if you want to be a successful student.

Once you have made your own notes, compare them to the different notes shown in this chapter – and the notes throughout the book. What do you think? Are you happy with your notes? We bet they are better than you thought they would be. What are you going to do now to improve? Make time in your diary for developing your notemaking.

tips

- Why not make pattern notes for each topic in this book? This will definitely give you the practice that you need to get started.
- Make pattern notes of television and radio programmes. More practice – without the stress of it being vital for success in your own subject.
- Visit other people's lectures and make pattern notes in those. Again there is no stress – just practice.

3. Activity: Exploring online resources (also on companion website)

Actively making your own notes is the best way to understand, learn and remember all the information that you will encounter when a student. In this activity we direct you to useful online and paper-based resources designed to help you make the best notes, learn the most – and get the best grades that you can.

➡️

Our NoteMaker – the what, why and how of making notes

Look at the website for information on why it is important to make notes – what sorts of notes you might like to make – and an opportunity to watch short videos and practise making notes: http://learning.londonmet.ac.uk/TLTC/learnhigher/notemaker/index.html

Now:

On your own or with a friend or study partner, review the following websites, resources and activities – consider their usefulness to you as a student. If completing some form of learning log or blog for reflective learning, or for one of your modules, make comments and/or a posting on what the resource is and why it is useful.

Strategies and tips

- Quick guide to keeping references: http://www.nottingham.ac.uk/nursing/sonet/rlos/studyskills/harvard/index.html
- Mini-notemaking lecture: http://www.youtube.com/watch?v=M1IHsPt_Nmg
- Mini Buzan lecture on mindmapping: http://www.youtube.com/watch?v=MlabrWv25qQ&feature=related
- Buzan's site – with 7-step guide: http://www.buzanworld.com/Mind_Maps.htm
- If you like making notes on video – try video ant: http://ant.umn.edu/
- Cornell notes – more structured and organised: http://coe.jmu.edu/learningtoolbox/cornellnotes.html
- 'Note book' site: online space for jottings, websites etc.: http://www.evernote.com/
- Concept map tools website: http://cmap.ihmc.us/
- Prezi: a tool for making creative notes (and preparing presentations): http://prezi.com/ NB: check out Playing to learn: http://prezi.com/rj_b-gw3u8xl/playing-to-learn/
- Visual Literacy site – check out different visual ways to represent information: http://www.visual-literacy.org/periodic_table/periodic_table.html
- Text to movie resource – capture key points in your own mini-animation note: http://www.xtranormal.com/
- Visual notemaking using your iPad: http://ninmah.be/2010/08/02/ipad-visual-movie/
- What to do in lectures: http://www.youtube.com/watch?v=Tiv9GG_Szll
- Draw-to-learn: http://www.brighton.ac.uk/visuallearning/drawing/
- Avoiding plagiarism – short tutorial: http://www.brighton.ac.uk/visuallearning/drawing/
- Don't forget to organise your desk: http://learning.londonmet.ac.uk/TLTC/learnhigher/desk/desk.html
- And remember that much reading is for our writing – check out our writing space: http://learning.londonmet.ac.uk/TLTC/connorj/WritingGroups/

Conclusion

We have examined notemaking as part of active learning and argued that a good notemaking strategy helps you both record and learn information. We have explored and illustrated different linear and pattern formats so that you can eventually choose the system that best suits you. We particularly wanted to make a good case for pattern notes so that you felt persuaded to develop them for yourself. In order to start this process off, we included an exercise on notemaking and an example of a pattern on the topic of notemaking itself. So now it is up to you.

Further reading

Buzan, T. (1989) *Use Your Head*. London: BBC Publications

Buzan, B. and Buzan, T. (1999) *The Mind Map Book*. London: BBC Publications

Gibbs, G. and Makeshaw, T. (1992) *53 Interesting Things To Do in Your Lectures*. Bristol: Technical and Educational Services

Palmer, R. and Pope, C. (1984) *Brain Train: Studying for Success*. Bristol: Arrowsmith

Rogers, C. (1992) *Freedom to Learn*. Upper Saddle River, NJ: Merrill

Rose, C. and Goll, L. (1992) *Accelerate Your Learning*. Aylesbury, UK: Accelerated Learning Systems Ltd

Review points

When reflecting on this chapter you might notice that:

- You realise the importance of notemaking and have decided to improve your notemaking strategies
- You have practised pattern notes – and it's a really useful strategy
- You have explored the online resources and blogged about your favourite one
- You have decided to construct module and/or paragraph patterns to improve your understanding of your studies and your preparation for assignments
- You are going to draw pattern notes of each chapter in this book...

10 Top Tips on Academic Learning

	Managing Your Time	Referencing	Presentations	Group Work	Critical Reading	Effective Reading	Successful Assignments	Getting the Most Out of Lectures
1	Keep your long-term goals in mind. They can motivate you	Be meticulous about publishing details. Accuracy is essential	Know who your audience is, what they know, & what their level of interest is	Meet with your group as soon as possible	Accurately record title, author(s), date & place of publication	Find a quiet, uninterrupted time & place to read	Read the question. Make sure you know what to do. If not, ask your tutor	Do the required readings before the lecture
2	Schedule due dates, work times, & social occasions on a semester planner	Decide the best way to cite your sources: quote directly, paraphrase, or summarise	Gather the material, find a focus, & structure it simply, clearly, & logically	Try not to be in a group with friends: working with friends can be harder than you think	Determine your reason(s) for reading the article. Is it for general background on a topic or supporting evidence?	Decide why you are reading the text	Schedule time for reading, note-taking, drafting, referencing, & editing	Download & read lecture notes & outlines before class
3	Prioritise tasks for the week & cross them off the list as you finish them	Quote if the exact words are really important	Frame your presentation with an introduction & conclusion	Decide on a timetable & exchange contact details at first meeting	Identify the author's purpose	Read for main idea first. This is found in the title, abstract, introduction, thesis statement, & conclusion	Read textbooks for general information before reading journals	Make note of important terminology before class
4	Break down large tasks into smaller tasks	Paraphrase when you want to support your argument	Hand out an outline to help the audience follow your points	Identify your strengths & say what you can contribute to the group	Ask yourself 'Does the author describe adequately the current knowledge on the topic?'	Look for organisational cues: sub-headings, graphs, & summaries	Plan the structure of your assignment – make an outline	Arrive before the lecture to get any handouts

	Managing Your Time	Referencing	Presentations	Group Work	Critical Reading	Effective Reading	Successful Assignments	Getting the Most Out of Lectures
5	Focus. Identify your time wasters (TV, surfing the net), & manage them	Summarise main ideas & conclusions	Signpost your presentation. Use phrases like 'Another important point is'	Brainstorm so that each person has a task to do before the next meeting	Find the evidence to support the author's argument	Read topic sentence (usually first) of each body paragraph	Start writing a draft as soon as you have something to say	Sit near the front of the room to help in your concentration
6	Schedule in breaks every hour	Use transition phrases to link your & others' ideas	Repeat important points	Turn up to ALL meetings	Take notes of key information. Write any questions you think of, as you read	Identify author's purpose, perspective, approach & orientation	Draft a thesis statement & write according to your plan	Be an active listener. Ask yourself questions, & make notes based on these questions
7	Plan to study at times when you are alert & motivated	Use the right referencing format for your school or department	Make eye contact, & use gestures & voice in a natural way	Be respectful to ALL group members & remain task-focused	After reading the text, ask yourself, 'What do I think of what I've just read?'	Evaluate the evidence	Revise, edit, revise, & proof read	Experiment with concept maps & other strategies to organise lecture material
8	Establish a nice, comfortable study place	Use Endnote or similar software	Don't rush. Speak slowly & clearly	Leave time to finalise assignment or rehearse together	Consider the argument in light of your other reading & experiences. Does it make sense?	Highlight, underline, & take notes during full reading of text	Follow guidelines regarding word limit, due dates, & submission requirements	Review your notes. Make a list of questions you need to ask about
9	Reward yourself when you finish a task	Avoid plagiarism. Acknowledge the original author	Never go over time. Allow time for questions	Communicate as much as possible – always gain consensus	Identify any weaknesses or limitations in the argument	Every 20 minutes, take a short break (e.g. roll shoulders, look at ceiling)	Submit on time	Record the lecture (with the lecturer's permission)
10	**Find out & attend workshops in your college or university**							

FIGURE 11J 10 top tips on academic learning

Photocopiable:

Essential Study Skills, Third Edition © Tom Burns and Sandra Sinfield, 2012 (SAGE)

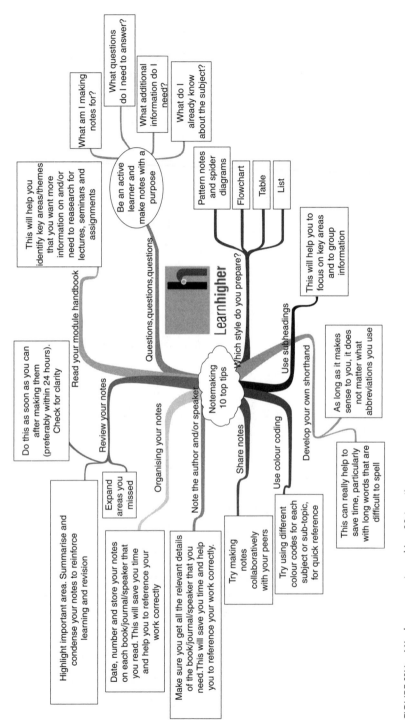

FIGURE 11K   Mindmap – notemaking 10 top tips

Before the lecture	During the lecture	After the lecture
Prepare:	Start on a new page	Check notes: compare; discuss; revise and reduce
• Read handbook	Write date and title	Plan your further reading – put a date in your diary
• Brainstorm		
• Preliminary question	Listen carefully	
• Review Assessment Question		
	Make legible notes	Bibliography details (Names – who to read)
	1. Headings ←	Page numbers
	keywords ←	Information and
	phrases ←	ideas
	2. Definitions	Observations in practical work
	3. Conclusions ←	
Prepare questions	Ask questions	Notes made in practical notebook
• Know what you know	Listen to discussion	
• Know what you need	Make additions in gaps in your notes	Think
		Learn
	Understand	Remember
Arrows represent additions to notes before and after lecture	Learn	Store notes in assessment folder; paste on wall

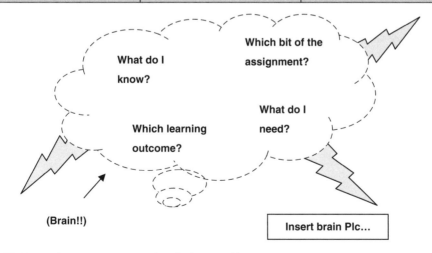

FIGURE 11L Making notes as an aid to thinking and learning

(Source: Marie Patvrel)

Section III

Creative Strategies and Learning Effectively

12

How to be Creative in Your Learning

Aims

Being organised is brilliant – but to really shine, to go that one step further, everyone also needs to build creativity into their learning. This chapter explores creative and visual approaches to study.

Learning outcomes

It is hoped that by the end of working through this chapter you will have:

- realised the importance of creative learning strategies
- been introduced to creative assignment preparation techniques
- been introduced to a variety of draw-to-learn techniques
- reflected on the usefulness of these techniques in terms of improving the quality of your learning – and your own engagement with and enjoyment of your studies.

Introduction

Study techniques can turn studying around so that your learning becomes effective, satisfying and successful. In this chapter we are taking this a step further. Logical strategies are fantastic, they will make all the difference in themselves – but to really shine, to go that one step further, everyone also needs to build creativity into their learning.

❝ I went to a volunteering conference where we were asked to solve the problem of trident nuclear missiles. In seeking alternatives I decided the cheapest option was to make papier mâché missiles. **❞**

❝ I went for a job and was asked to give as many uses of a pen as I could think of in 2 minutes. **❞**

Why should we be creative?

You will benefit from creative thinking: it can turn studying into something that you enjoy, not just something you endure. It makes life feel lighter and more fun. It stretches and develops another part of you and this is a good thing in itself.

We all have the capacity to be creative, but often this is not valued or developed by the education system. In this chapter we demonstrate how to develop creative approaches to studying, assignments – and your whole learning journey. We give examples of creative things to do to help that to happen.

We would like you to feel really positive about being creative when you study, so we have gathered a few arguments together. Read them through and see what you think.

Creative approaches: The assignment brainstorm

The idea behind the brainstorm is to open up the creative side of your mind. It involves the use of a word association process that operates without censorship and preconceptions. We have already used the brainstorming device as a focusing activity: the 'What do I already know on this topic? What do I need to know?' questions. Therefore, you should have started to familiarise your brain with this technique.

When using brainstorming on an assignment topic, the strategy is to brainstorm all the key words in the question and allow as many ideas as possible to float into your mind.

The trick is to respond immediately and not to censor your thoughts. Sometimes a thought might appear silly, irrelevant or frivolous. It may be that the thought seems odd, with no place in an academic context. Yet just that silly or odd thought could lead you on to a really bright or original idea.

Following up that idea is what will make your assignment clever, even unique. When our work has that spark of originality, when it is that bit different from all the other assignments that are dropping on to a tutor's desk, then we may gain the attention of the tutor – we may even gain a higher mark.

6 If you have not tried creative techniques before, we will be asking you to change or adapt your learning style. And, as always, you might find that change uncomfortable. No one likes to be uncomfortable, even more so perhaps in the educational context where for so many of us everything already feels so strange and uncomfortable. Try to reassure yourself that the discomfort will pass, and that the benefits in terms of improvements in your ability to study and learn – and in the grades that you will get for your work – will more than compensate you for the discomfort that you are experiencing.

Some people believe that you are either born creative or you are not – the same way that much of education is predicated upon the belief that you are either born a good student or you are not. But just as we argued that everyone can rehearse successful study techniques and thus learn how to be a successful student, so we argue that everyone can learn creative learning styles and with practice become more creative. A really influential voice in this area at the moment is Ken Robinson.

Robinson argues that the world needs people who can respond to complexity in adaptable, resilient and creative ways. He criticises much of the education system for actively stifling creativity; however, we can find and develop our own creative aspects. If we do this we move from enduring our lives to enjoying our lives; and, we argue that if you do this as a student, not only will you better enjoy your studies, you will be better fitted for the world of work when you gain your degree.

How can I be creative?

Why should we be creative?

5 If you become trapped into using information in the way that other people have used it, you are in danger of producing assignments that only give back to the tutor what s/he has said and what s/he has recommended that you read.

Obviously this is neither active nor significant learning. But it gets worse. Something that just passively parrots-back information to the tutor will at best only gain you an average grade. It is also really boring for the tutor. Imagine the tutor with 150 assignments to mark, all of them only giving back what s/he has used in the lectures? Only citing the books that the tutor recommended?

It is the essay that has gone somewhere different, that has found an original example or illustration, that has put ideas together in an original way that will catch the tutor's eye that will make them smile. And oh what a relief from reading those 149 other essays that all say the same thing! Thus at this very practical, common sense level, it is good to be creative.

Common sense.

One justification that we would like to offer for creative learning also touches on the notion of active learning – or the lack of it.

Carl Rogers, humanist, psychologist and teacher, addressed this by emphasising that significant learning takes' place when students reach out for what they want and need when learning.

Active and significant learning.

Without a creative approach the student is in danger of remaining a passive learner, only using information in the way that other people have used it. Because they have not used a creative notemaking system, but have passively recorded what others have said, and the way that they have said it, these students get trapped into other people's thought processes.

4 We argue that creative approaches can help you to identify what it is that you want and need from your course. Yes, you will still have to read those set texts – and you will still have to frame your answers in certain way: you will have to get to grips with academic practice. But getting an original angle on a question; seeking out original things to research and read; and then recording information in your own original and creative way – will help you to make the course your own.

FIGURE 12A Mindmap – why should we be creative?

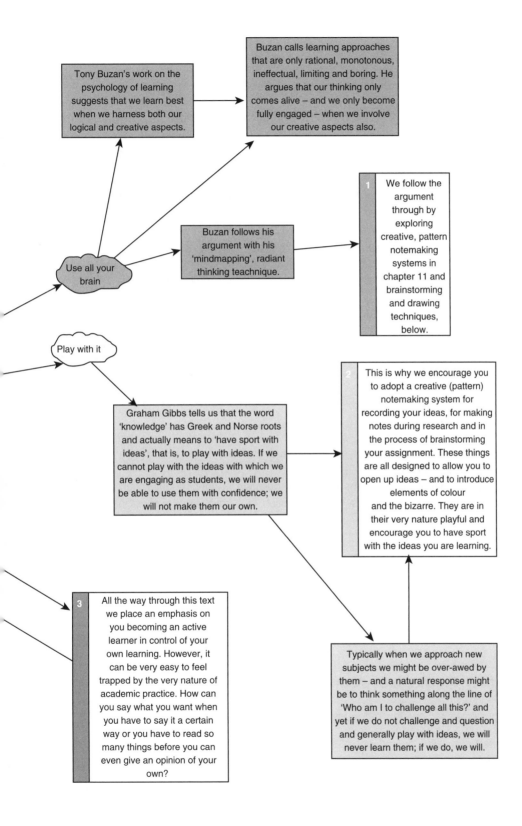

Tony Buzan's work on the psychology of learning suggests that we learn best when we harness both our logical and creative aspects.

Buzan calls learning approaches that are only rational, monotonous, ineffectual, limiting and boring. He argues that our thinking only comes alive – and we only become fully engaged – when we involve our creative aspects also.

1 We follow the argument through by exploring creative, pattern notemaking systems in chapter 11 and brainstorming and drawing techniques, below.

Buzan follows his argument with his 'mindmapping', radiant thinking teachnique.

Use all your brain

Play with it

Graham Gibbs tells us that the word 'knowledge' has Greek and Norse roots and actually means to 'have sport with ideas', that is, to play with ideas. If we cannot play with the ideas with which we are engaging as students, we will never be able to use them with confidence; we will not make them our own.

2 This is why we encourage you to adopt a creative (pattern) notemaking system for recording your ideas, for making notes during research and in the process of brainstorming your assignment. These things are all designed to allow you to open up ideas – and to introduce elements of colour and the bizarre. They are in their very nature playful and encourage you to have sport with the ideas you are learning.

3 All the way through this text we place an emphasis on you becoming an active learner in control of your own learning. However, it can be very easy to feel trapped by the very nature of academic practice. How can you say what you want when you have to say it a certain way or you have to read so many things before you can even give an opinion of your own?

Typically when we approach new subjects we might be over-awed by them – and a natural response might be to think something along the line of 'Who am I to challenge all this?' and yet if we do not challenge and question and generally play with ideas, we will never learn them; if we do, we will.

Beginner's guide to brainstorming the question

Try this brainstorming strategy with one of your assignments and see how well it works for you.

The trick with an assignment question is to brainstorm every single word in the question.

1   Write the whole question in the middle of a really large sheet of paper – A1 or flip chart paper is best.
2   Do not abbreviate the question. Any word that you do not write down is a research avenue that you do not explore – this could well mean marks that you have thrown away.
3   Look at all the words in the question. Circle or underline the key words.
4   Write anything and everything that comes to mind when you look at a word.
5   When you have finished, move on and do the same to another word. Keep this up until you have tackled all the words in the question.
6   Then go round again – even more ideas might pop out.

tips

- Do this with another student, a friend or a study partner.
- It gets easier with practice.
- Practise 10-minute brainstorms with every question in your module/course hand-book. Choose to actually answer the question that gave you the most interesting brainstorm.

Query: Is this how you would usually approach your assignments? If so, you are already using useful creative learning strategies. If not, why not move on to the brainstorming activity below?

1. Activity: Practice brainstorm

We have given you a very small study skills question to practise on:

- Write the question out for yourself – in the middle of a large sheet of paper.
- Underline the key words.

- Then brainstorm (jot down all those ideas) for about 10 minutes.
- When you have finished, compare your brainstorm with ours.

Remember two things:

1 There is no right or wrong when it comes to the brainstorm.
2 Brainstorming, like most other skills, gets easier with practice.

The question: Evaluate the usefulness of pattern notes to a student.

tip

Spend 10 minutes on this initial brainstorm – and then move on.

Queries:

- How do you feel it went for a first attempt?
- What will you do next?
- Now have a look at our example below, Figure 12B.

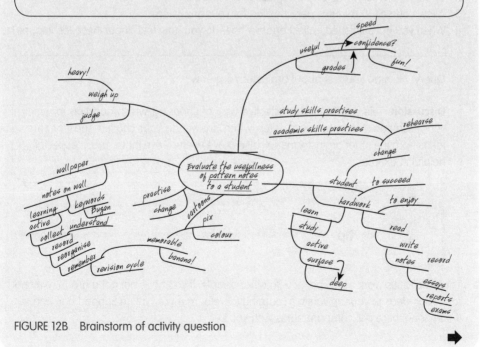

FIGURE 12B   Brainstorm of activity question

➡️

> **Discussion**: Was your brainstorm similar to or different from ours? Did looking at our one give you more ideas for your own? It would be great if that were so, since working with someone else gives you more ideas. If you were actually going to write an essay on this question you should now have ideas from both brainstorms and be in a very strong position to decide just what you would read in order to get your answer ready.

2. Activity: Keep practising!

We have argued that brainstorming gets easier with practice. The best thing that you can do now is to use these techniques a lot.

1 Go to one of your module/course handbooks – preferably one that offers a range of questions from which you have to choose an assignment to do.
2 Choose between three and six questions to work on.
3 Allow yourself 10 minutes per question for your brainstorm.
4 When you have finished, reflect again – how do you now feel about these techniques?

> **Query**: How do you feel about brainstorming now?
>
> **Discussion**: This can be a very effective way of choosing which question to write your essay on. More than that, often when answering your chosen question, the ideas from the other brainstorms will also prove useful – use them. This is especially helpful in exams.

 **tip**

These activities work much better with other people. If you have not got a group, why not take your ideas to your university's Learning Development or Writing Support unit and see if someone there will compare notes with you?

Creative approaches: Draw-to-learn

Drawing is one of the most under-used learning techniques or academic literacies. Perhaps because most of us stop drawing when we leave primary school, it becomes something that we do not do. Instead of being enjoyable, drawing makes us feel vulnerable, silly, inadequate or foolish. But drawing can be an intellectual activity that helps us analyse, reflect upon, investigate, explore and communicate about the world, our experiences and our studies.

Practical draw-to-learn activities

Here are some ways to use drawing in your studying and learning. As always, try the ideas out and see how useful they are to you in practice.

" When you told me what we'd have to do in your class, I wanted to leave – but it was too late … I'm so glad it was too late. The creative approaches were a revelation – and the assignment got me my best grade... **"**

Draw a journey – to success

Draw a story board or timeline that shows how you got to be at university. Put in pictures that represent key moments or turning points in your life. Reflect on your journey to university. Then draw a story board or timeline of how you see yourself succeeding at university. Make this as creative as possible – draw your goals and visions. Pin this picture over your desk to inspire you when you get frustrated or stuck.

Academic pictionary

Choose a word or term or concept from the course you are studying. Instead of explaining that concept to someone else in words, draw a diagram or picture that represents the word for you. Show it to another person and see if they can guess what you were trying to say. Then discuss it.

Draw your notes

After reading a chapter just draw a representation or diagram of all the information that was in there. Use one side of a piece of paper – make that paper any size that you want. Use as many colours as you like and be as imaginative as possible with your images. Reflect on how well you now understand that reading.

> **"** There was this group of students working with young people on a drawing project... and it was so cool because they all used their overalls as their learning logs! They would draw pictures on them. Write notes on them. Paste things onto them. I've been wanting to do that myself ever since. **"**

Picture your lecture

Go to your next class or lecture and make notes only in pictures – write no words at all. If worried that you will miss important information this way, pair up with a friend and make sure that you compare notes at the end. When we have experimented with this technique, these drawn notes are always the ones that we remember for the longest time.

Collage your project plan

If having trouble getting started on an essay or a project, use creative visualisation techniques. Make a habit of collecting pictures from newspapers and magazines so that you always have a store of images.

When you want to get started on a new project use the images to create a collage (a picture made from sticking other pictures on a surface together). With your topic or question in mind, choose pictures that seem to represent the question, parts of an answer, your own beliefs or thoughts on the topic at that time. Combine the images you have chosen by sticking them onto a large sheet of paper in a way that makes sense to you.

Reflect on the picture you have created and see if it gets you started on your assignment journey. To help here write out or say into a recorder a literal description of what is on the picture; what the collage represents; how the collage 'answers' the question.

These processes not only help to unblock you when stuck – they also help you to see things in fresh and energising ways.

Pictorial reflective journal

We have recommended that you keep a reading dossier (Chapter 10) that captures your reflections upon your reading. Either in that journal, or in a separate 'whole learning' journal, reflect very visually upon your learning by drawing a picture or creating a collage every day, or at least every week, whilst you study. Annotate with key words if you wish – but definitely form the pictures first. After a while, think about how this form of reflection has deepened and enriched your understanding of your course.

" At the end of our project we all had to produce one quilt piece that summed up the learning for us. We could sew on the piece – or make a collage on it... We were allowed to stick things on it – whatever we wanted. At the end all our pieces were sewn together into a friendship quilt of the module. It was a great experience – and the quilt is still hanging in the university hall. **"**

No, no, no – I really can't draw!

If your response to the visualising and drawing ideas suggested above is captured in our sub-heading: no, no, no... then try these one minute drawing tips proposed by Eileen Adams at an Access Art Sketchbook conference (accessart.org.uk, 2011). Remember – the idea is not to be a brilliant technical drawer – it is to liberate your drawing self and to harness that to liberate your creative self. Given that this will get easier with practice, why not try drawing regularly, say for five minutes a day or five minutes a week? You can do this in private if you are self-conscious; but we have found that doing these things with other people is more fun.

Five drawings in five minutes

Read the list below and draw a picture in response to five of the words for one minute each.
Asymmetric, beautiful, colourful, detailed, edge, far away, geometric, hidden, inside, joint, knot, look up, miniscule, number, opening, pattern, quirky, reflection, sensuous, texture, underneath, view through, wall, you choose.
Keep these drawings in a little exercise book and just enjoy them – or see how you can use the drawings in your notemaking, learning and revision practices.

Pauline Ridley from Brighton University and LearnHigher has put together *Drawing to Learn* booklets that can be downloaded from her website. Use these to help you to be more creative and more successful in your studies (or access via the LearnHigher website).

Conclusion

This chapter has explored how to bring creativity into your learning process. We learn when we can play with ideas – but perhaps need help to find and develop our creative selves. We explore how brainstorming and draw-to-learn techniques really help our approach to assignments and keep learning active, engaging and enriching. Many students have told us that these creative practices have changed their lives – and their grades – and that they actually enjoyed their learning for the first time.

Further reading

Buzan, T. (1989) *Use Your Head*. London: BBC Publications

Buzan, B. and Buzan, T. (1999) *The Mind Map Book*. London: BBC Publications

Gibbs, G. and Makeshaw, T. (1992) *53 Interesting Things To Do in Your Lectures*. Bristol: Technical and Educational Services

Palmer, R. and Pope, C. (1984) *Brain Train: Studying for Success*. Bristol: Arrowsmith

Ridley, P. *Drawing to Learn* booklets and Visual Learning website: http://www.brighton.ac.uk/visuallearning/drawing/

Robinson, K. (2006) Ken Robinson says schools kill creativity (speech). Available at: http://www.ted.com/talks/ken_robinson_says_schools_kill_creativity.html (accessed 10 December 2010)

Robinson, K. (2009) Changing Education Paradigms (speech). Available at: http://comment.rsablogs.org.uk/ (accessed 10December 2010)

Rogers, C. (1992) *Freedom to Learn*. Upper Saddle River, NJ: Merrill

Rose, C. and Goll, L. (1992) *Accelerate Your Learning*. Aylesbury, UK: Accelerated Learning Systems Ltd

Review points

When reflecting on this chapter you might notice that:

- You realise and are excited by the potential of creative learning strategies
- You have practised creative brainstorming techniques with your assignments and draw-to-learn techniques with your learning, and you will now use them on your assignments and throughout your time at university – and beyond.

Section III

Creative Strategies and Learning Effectively

13

How to Think Effectively: Analytical and Critical Thinking

Aims

University students are often frustrated by being told that their work is too descriptive – or that it is not analytical or critical enough... But what do these terms mean? This chapter explores analytical and critical thinking and suggests very practical strategies to adopt such that you become an effective and critical student.

Learning outcomes

After working through this chapter you will:

- understand the roles that analytical and critical thinking play in academic discourse
- have practised using the question matrix – an effective analytical and critical approach to tackling assignment questions.

Introduction

Critical thinking is often placed at the very heart of descriptions of what it means to be an academic, a student and a professional in the workplace. One of the key purposes of going to university, it is argued, is to develop critical

FIGURE 13A   Critical thinking Wordle™

and sceptical abilities: rational ways of viewing information, knowledge-claims and the world. The student is supposed to use their university time to develop their abilities to evaluate the arguments and evidence that they encounter – and to know the reasons why they have made the judgements that they have. This is not just about using our minds; it involves nurturing a critical *attitude*: a habit of approaching the world in a questioning and critical way; a desire to rid ourselves of purely instinctive, emotional or belief-based responses and develop the habit of analysis, interpretation and evaluation.

Well, you might say, that's all very well, but I just came here to learn business or history or science – what has this got to do with me? As an engaged learner in control of your own learning, you are not just consuming ideas – you are engaging with them. You have to evaluate and discriminate between different claims and make up your own mind about what you believe and think. Analytical and critical thinking offers you a strategy that enables you to do that well.

❝When I did my first sports management report in my second year – on the local tennis centre – I had all sorts of trouble identifying the theory at first. Later, when we had our results (I got an A, btw... shines nails on jeans, oh yeah!) the main feedback was exactly about that... I needed to use the theory more – and be more critical of it.❞

A beginner's guide to critical thinking

The journalism questions:

I keep six honest serving men

They taught me all I know

Their names are **what** and **where** and **when**

And **who** and **why** and **how**

(Kipling)

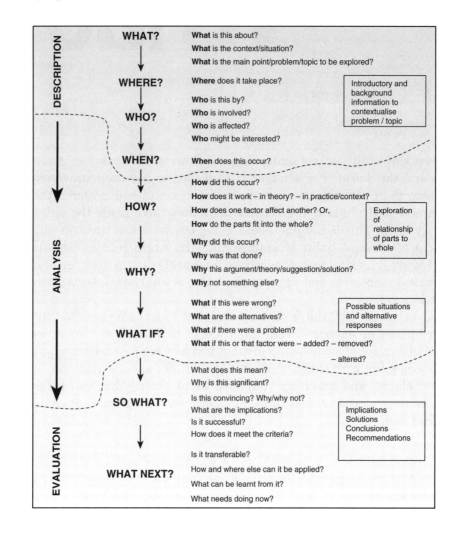

DESCRIPTION	WHAT?	**What** is this about? **What** is the context/situation? **What** is the main point/problem/topic to be explored?	
	WHERE?	**Where** does it take place?	Introductory and background information to contextualise problem / topic
	WHO?	**Who** is this by? **Who** is involved? **Who** is affected? **Who** might be interested?	
	WHEN?	**When** does this occur?	
ANALYSIS	HOW?	**How** did this occur? **How** does it work – in theory? – in practice/context? **How** does one factor affect another? Or, **How** do the parts fit into the whole?	Exploration of relationship of parts to whole
	WHY?	**Why** did this occur? **Why** was that done? **Why** this argument/theory/suggestion/solution? **Why** not something else?	
	WHAT IF?	**What** if this were wrong? **What** are the alternatives? **What** if there were a problem? **What** if this or that factor were – added? – removed? – altered?	Possible situations and alternative responses
EVALUATION	SO WHAT?	What does this mean? Why is this significant? Is this convincing? Why/why not? What are the implications? Is it successful? How does it meet the criteria?	Implications Solutions Conclusions Recommendations
	WHAT NEXT?	Is it transferable? How and where else can it be applied? What can be learnt from it? What needs doing now?	

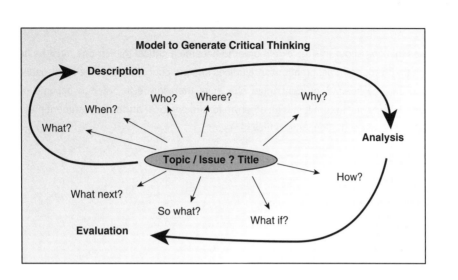

FIGURE 13B   A beginner's guide to critical thinking

Use the journalism questions when encountering new ideas, information and knowledge: who wrote it, why, when, where? How will it be useful or applied?

When encountering a new knowledge-claim, interrogate it: Who said that? When? Where could I use the information? What does it mean? Why is it true or valid? How is it relevant?

You can see from the diagrams in Figure 13B that our colleague John Hilsdon also recommends using three more questions: What if…? So what…? What next?.

- 'What if' suggests looking for alternatives or testing the theory in slightly different conditions.
- 'So what', asks us to judge the evidence and to sound out the implications.
- 'What next' suggests that we think about how to use the information – or to consider our next research step. We might decide that we need to find more evidence or an alternative point of view – and thus do more reading.

All these questions are designed to get us thinking around a subject, thinking in depth, thinking reflectively – and extending our understanding.

Use them when researching an assignment question. Do not rush to an opinion – ask more questions.

A big problem with assignment questions is that when we see them, we think we need to produce an answer, but what we need to do is generate more questions before we even begin to think of an answer.

Investigate, research and read around all the smaller questions you generate to get your brain working on the whole assignment.

A student's view:

➡

➡

❝ I was thinking about this topic … In order to become a critical thinker one must be honest and deal with your own assumptions, prejudices and pre-conceptions … The word 'challenge' popped into my head. A student must challenge themselves in order to become critical thinkers. I was trying to turn it into an acronym for the personal attributes a student may need to become a critical thinker. This is how far I got:

CHALLENGE

Critical analysis

Honestly appraise your own prejudices

Critical **A**ttitude

Creative **L**earner

Learning techniques

Engage…

K**N**owledge??…

Goals…

Evaluate what you are learning. ❞

Critical thinking and the question matrix

Using the question matrix with assignments is a good way of consciously developing an analytical and critical approach. Like the brainstorm (Chapter 12), the question matrix is designed to open up a question and expand our thinking and our research base. The matrix generates breadth and depth and extends our potential for creativity. Some people see it as another sort of brainstorm.

 **tip**

When generating our smaller questions it is quite useful to apply the journalism questions (five Ws and an H plus the extension, so what) to each part of the assignment:

- Who?
- When?
- What?
- Why?
- Where?
- How?
- What if…?
- So what?
- What next?

1. Activity: Prepare a question matrix

Use the Question Matrix (QM) questions to unpack the following question. Then compare your results with the example below. Note: the QM technique gets easier with practice.

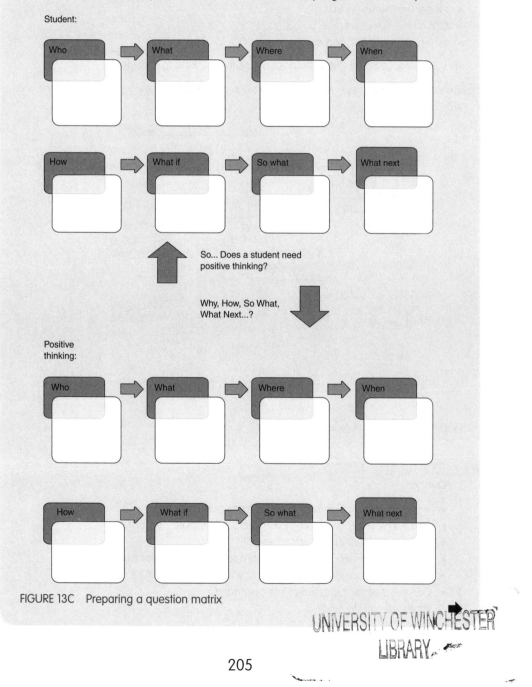

FIGURE 13C   Preparing a question matrix

UNIVERSITY OF WINCHESTER
LIBRARY

205

We have given a very small study skills question to practice on:

- Write the whole question out in the middle of a very large sheet of paper.
- Underline the key words.
- QM all the key words.
- When you have finished compare your QM to ours.

The question: Evaluate the usefulness of positive thinking to a student.

We suggest that you spend five or 10 minutes on this before moving on to compare your effort with ours.

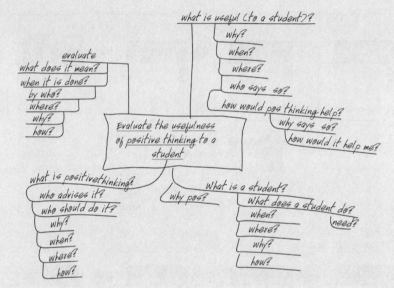

FIGURE 13D   Question matrix on the sample question

Query:

- Is your matrix similar to or different from ours?
- Can you see that there are no answers – just more questions?
- How do you feel after a first attempt?
- Is this how you would normally approach an assignment question?
- What do you do differently? What do you do that is similar?
- Can you see the potential of this approach?
- What will you do next?

Discussion: One thing that we can see is that a first matrix on a topic brings with it no answers at all; it opens the question up to more ideas and avenues of thought. This is a good thing. If our first thought when looking at a question is the whole answer, then we are usually doing something wrong. So if one of your worries about yourself as a student is that you do not know all the answers – relax. You are doing something very right.

tip

Using a matrix like the one here with its open boxes will prompt you to read. Do not wait to gather all your evidence before you start writing. Writing is also a thinking process and will help you to understand what you are reading.

Here's what another student has said:

❝I learnt when a certain question needs to be answered, that question needs to be broken into sub-questions. This is followed by free writing, which I do apply to my assignments but did not realise I was already applying this technique.❞

❝The writer must explode and question and apply various different resources to critically analyse the materials found. The writer must apply five 'W' and 'H' method which means an assignment should contain who, what, when, where, why and how reasoning.❞

❝As with any type of work, practice makes perfect as the saying goes. To be a good writer one must practice writing. I have learnt a valuable lesson in this session and I am now more aware of what is expected from me. I have come to appreciate how to analyse and be critical of the resources I use for my assignments.❞

2. Activity: If you are really interested in this topic, explore the following question

Evaluate the usefulness of critical thinking strategies to you as a student.

tip

To seed your research, look at the resources for Critical Thinking on the LearnHigher website. There is a great video of John Hilsdon talking through the critical thinking cycle.

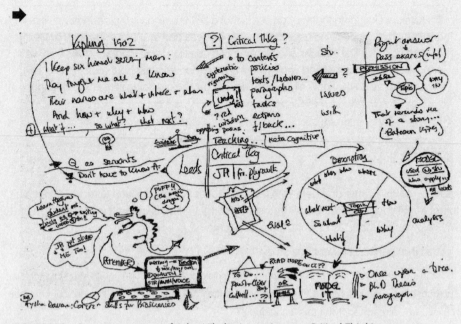

FIGURE 13E   Our notes on one of John Hilsdon's sessions on Critical Thinking

Conclusion

In this brief chapter we have linked analytical and critical thinking to the active learning strategies that we are developing throughout the book as a whole. We took you through the question matrix technique with respect to unpacking assignment questions: to generate avenues of research and to apply an analytical and critical framework to your research. We argued that you build in writing – drafting and re-drafting your work – as part of your critical *thinking*.

This chapter is deceptively short. Do not be fooled by that. These strategies will radically alter the quality of your research, your thinking and your writing. It is now up to you to try these things for yourself and see.

Review points

When reflecting on this section you might discover:

- That you now do have an appreciation of what analytical and critical thinking mean
- That you see the role of analytical and critical thinking in academic discourse – and for you as a student
- That you quite enjoyed using the question matrix technique – and you will apply it both to your preparation when tackling assignments and to your analysis of the new ideas you encounter when studying.

Section IV

Communicating Effectively in Assignments

Chapter 14 How to Write Better Assignments

14

How to Write Better Assignments

Aims

Academic writing can seem mysterious and daunting. In this chapter we aim to improve your confidence and success in academic writing with some very practical guidelines and advice.

Learning outcomes

After reading through this chapter, and engaging with the activities, you will have:

- thought about assessment – what, why and how
- explored your own writing strengths and weaknesses
- gained a snapshot of the key assessment forms in universities
- thought about writing as process – which is easier when you have something to say
- considered our 10 stages towards producing successful assignments
- explored useful online resources that focus on academic writing – and thought about how to use them in your own studies.

Introduction

Assessment is one of the most fraught areas in a student's life. Nobody really enjoys being assessed, it smacks of being judged, it means that we can fail;

we can make mistakes – mistakes that reveal us to be foolish or inadequate. Funnily enough, that is not really the point of assessment. In many ways tackling assessment is all part of becoming a graduate; and, practically, assessment procedures produce evidence that quality stamps your degree. This means that there are 'rules' to follow – and we will be covering them in the chapters in Part IV. Warning: these rules can make students feel that what they want to say won't be acceptable in a formal academic assessment. This can be very de-motivating. So whilst we want you to understand the 'rules' of assignments, we don't want you to lose your love of your subject – and your feeling that what you have to say is important.

What is assessment: A quick look at some assessment 'rules'

Essays, reports, presentations… all have their own structure and function. These are some of the major forms used in universities. As you read this, work out how knowing the information might help you to be a more successful student.

An **essay** (Chapter 17) is a *discursive* tool – you are supposed to argue for and against a topic using mainly theoretical evidence. The essay demonstrates your analytical and critical thinking. One of the most formal academic forms, essays are typically written in the third person, past tense with extensive accurate reference to supporting arguments and evidence taken from the key players in your discipline.

A **report** (Chapter 18) is a practical document where you write up the findings of your investigation into real-world problems – think scientific experiment or business report. Reports are written for specific readers, in the third person, past tense and are signposted with headings and sub-headings.

A **dissertation** (Chapter 19) is an extended piece of writing associated with Honours level projects or postgraduate study – Masters or PhD. The dissertation records the findings and conclusions of independent research into specific phenomena. The typical dissertation structure is like that of a formal report – with an extended Literature Review.

The **Literature Review** (Chapter 19): Can be part of a dissertation – though some courses set a Literature Review as an assignment in its own right. The Literature Review is written to record your exploration and understanding of the most up-to-date literature (research) in your subject – and the area that you are studying. The process of reading for and writing a Literature Review is designed to enable you to gain deep knowledge of your subject and its key issues and debates. Your Literature Review becomes your record of the most up-to-date and relevant knowledge-claims in your area – these seed your own research – and becomes a measuring stick against which you can compare your research findings.

➡

The LearnHigher website has a Literature Review on each area covered. If you want to see models before you write your own, go there.

A **presentation** (Chapter 20) is a talk of a set length, on a set topic – to a known audience. It is similar in structure to the essay – but is supported by audiovisual aids. The purpose of the presentation is usually to demonstrate the student's understanding and oral communication skills.

The **seminar** (Chapter 21) combines written and oral elements. The seminar giver has to write upon and present their research, normally to a group of fellow students. The goal is that research is discussed and new ideas or avenues of research are suggested – and this will be used to develop the work of the seminar giver.

The **exam** (Chapter 25) is designed to test learning so that students can use information learned on a course in new situations. Exams can be open or closed book, time or word length limited, or other variations. Always know what sort of exam you are preparing for.

A **reading record** is neither an essay or a report. It is designed to be an annotated account of the reading a student has undertaken on a particular course. The annotations are not supposed to be descriptive ('This book was about…') but analytical ('This text is a key text for this topic outlining the major theoretical perspectives of…'; 'This text could be used to support the arguments of...'; 'However, Y and Z would take issue with the following aspects of the major arguments…'). A tutor might set a reading record to test that students are reading in an active and analytical way (Chapters 10 and 13) – thus your annotations should demonstrate your understanding of the text and its relationship to the key debates in your subject.

An **annotated bibliography** is a condensed version of the reading record. A conventional bibliography records Author (date) *Title* location: Publisher, in alphabetical order, by author's surname. In an annotated one, you also note down information – on a text's strengths or weaknesses; how useful it was and why – in relation to the aims and learning outcomes of the module and the key theoretical debates of the discipline.

1. Activity: How does it feel? Writing questionnaire

We have said that assessment can be daunting, take just five or 10 minutes to answer the following questions on assessment – and to uncover your own responses to it.

1   What writing do you do at the moment (letters, notes, poetry, short stories, essays, articles, texts, tweets, blogs, websites...)?
2   What do you like about your approach to writing at the moment?

3   What do you dislike about your current writing strategies?

4   Are there any aspects of academic writing that make you uneasy?

5   What do you think would help you to become a successful academic writer?

Once you have completed your own questionnaire, please compare your points with these from other students:

1   What writing do you do at the moment (letters, notes, poetry, short stories, essays, articles, texts, tweets, blogs, websites...)?

> I actually do a lot of writing because I am working as a secretary to get me through university. It does not mean that I feel any good at it myself.

2   What do you like about your approach to writing at the moment?

> I enjoy writing and always have done, so research tasks are manageable for me and I am interested in much of what I read.

3   What do you dislike about your current writing strategies?

> Nearly everything! In fact when I faced my first assignment all I could think was: Would it be good enough? What was being good enough? Would I have read enough and taken enough notes to write a well researched piece of work?

> Having been out of education for over 10 years, I felt very anxious about undertaking my first piece of assessed work – I didn't want to be judged negatively, because it might over-whelm me and make me want to give up the course. I had a very fragile student identity.

4   Are there any aspects of academic writing that make you uneasy?

> Firstly, not knowing the level of learning required. By that I mean that it would have been really helpful to get examples of an A-paper, B-paper, etc. to get an idea of the sorts of knowledge which is valued within HE.

> I did not really know how to write in an academic tone. I picked up much of how to do this from reading the work of others and paying particular attention to the structure of the writing as well as the content. A lot of my writing skills were self learned and self developed so inevitably I made a lot of mistakes. My early writing was not good quality and certainly not good enough for the high standards set by my university. It was very much a matter of personal perseverance and motivation that enabled me to go on and succeed with some of my later writing.

> Referencing, as I really struggled with the whole concept of this. I could have used some general pointers on the level and detail of work at degree level. My last studying had

➡

➡

been 10 years earlier at GCSE level and it was impossible to know how high I had to jump from that to succeed at degree level. "

5 What do you think would help you to become a successful academic writer?

" More knowledge of what is expected of us and strategies of how we could reasonably achieve this. Small, manageable targets are better than masses of work with daunting deadlines. Some idea of the amount of time that should be spent on reading and making notes – this might have encouraged those with massive time pressures to get started, rather than leaving them to their own devices when they could easily become overwhelmed. "

" Try to build our confidence and make us take on a positive learner identity. Try to enable us to see that we can do it, we are good enough, but we just need to take a few risks, which inevitably leads to getting some things right and some things wrong. When mistakes are made, learn from them but don't be afraid to take a few risks again – it's one of the only ways to differentiate you from the crowd. "

" From early on it would have been useful to see example essays... During one of our lectures we were given four extracts from different essays and asked to mark them individually. We then had a group feedback session about what and why we had given the marks we had. We then did a show of hands to understand if we had marked similarly, which we had, although there were a few exceptions. Everyone found this a really useful task and we all learnt a lot about our own expectations and that of others. "

Query: Were these answers similar to or different from your own? What might you do now to answer some of your own questions?

Discussion: One thing we noted was the unhappiness and confusion: What is required in academic writing? How much work is enough?

---
tips

- If you want to see an example of a real student essay, run a web search for 'An Essay Evolves'. This essay was written over time – and the blog showed her thoughts and feelings as she wrote the essay.
- Read journal articles to show you how you might write in the future.
- Build your self-confidence (Chapter 22). Having confidence helps you succeed – low self-confidence can mean that you get defeated by problems rather than overcoming them.

> ## Writing = becoming a graduate
>
> Particular forms of writing – and reading and talking – may be seen as examples of the practices associated with the identity of an undergraduate, and also of a graduate. Academic writing encompasses a range of types, particularly papers written for an academic audience: for a conference or seminar, symposium, colloquium etc; for an academic journal, book etc. The purpose is or should be to present an argument in support of a knowledge-claim.
>
> The criteria for judging such an argument would include its location with respect to existing, broadly accepted and also contested knowledge-claims (the existing literature), the logical reasoning and the empirical evidence adduced. The style should be that which is generally accepted, including conventions for citations etc.
>
> … Above all, it requires the student to have something to say that is worth saying, their own voice with respect to the issues at hand. (Dr Leonard Holmes, Roehampton University, by email. If interested in Dr Holmes's points on graduate identity, you might like to visit his website: http://www.re-skill.org.uk/)

Struggle to write – write to learn

More than providing evidence of achievement, the *process* of preparing an assignment is heuristic – it brings about powerful active learning. That is, as you get to grips with a question and work out what you want to say about it, you must learn your subject. Typically this means that you revise your course material so that you develop a better understanding of it and you research the topic further so that you extend your knowledge.

As you study you will discover a whole range of differing arguments and opinions that you struggle to understand and synthesise. You shape your data to answer a specific question – and struggle to communicate effectively. These are the academic practices of a successful student.

It is in the 'struggle to write' that your learning happens. And we do mean struggle. As the typical writer says, '*Writing is easy – you just sit and stare at a blank piece of paper until your eyeballs bleed!*' Writing is hard for everyone. Not just you. Once you accept that, you realise that writing is difficult because it is difficult. There does not have to be anything wrong with you if you are finding it difficult also.

However, there are some successful planning and preparation strategies that can help you with your assignments – and we are going to explore those now. It is here that much of the advice that we have given elsewhere in this book comes together.

Why are we assessed: Formative and summative assessment

- **Formative** assessment is developmental. Designed to measure a student's progress at a particular moment in a subject, there should be an emphasis on tutor feedback where that feedback is designed to help you do better in the summative assessment.
- **Summative** assessment is final. Usually at the end of a programme of study, it is designed to measure the student's overall achievement in the unit, course or programme.
- **Process**: The best forms of assessment bring about learning in the student. That is, whilst there is a product – the essay, report or presentation – that can be assessed, the process of preparing and drafting the assignment brings about learning.

 **tips**

It helps if you view assessment in a positive light. Try to see assessment as a chance to:

- be dynamic and creative
- learn your material
- show what you know.

Remember:

- Writing and planning get easier with practice.
- Plan everything – even writing letters to friends.
- Write often – even if only for 15 or 20 minutes a day.
- Write a lot!

How to write better assignments – ten stages...

We have looked at the what and the why of assessment, so let's now move on to practical advice on *how* to prepare and write your assignments. We have broken this down into 10 key stages. There is a photocopiable checklist at the end of the chapter so that you can follow these 10 stages with all your assignments.

tip

Remember, studying is meant to be full time. Study for 35–40 hours each week. Read something every day. Write often.

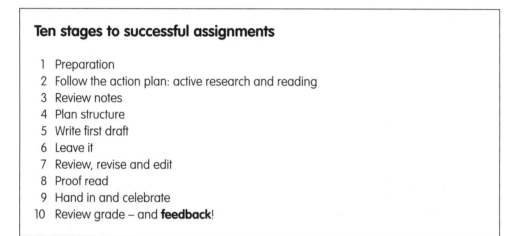

Ten stages to successful assignments

1 Preparation
2 Follow the action plan: active research and reading
3 Review notes
4 Plan structure
5 Write first draft
6 Leave it
7 Review, revise and edit
8 Proof read
9 Hand in and celebrate
10 Review grade – and **feedback**!

1: Prepare to research

This is a long section that reflects how important good preparation is. One trick with good preparation is to spend time on the *question*. Do not try to answer the question – think about it first. This is where it is important to manage your time (Chapter 6), as it takes a significant amount of time to prepare a good assignment.

tip

Start to work on an assignment as soon as possible: week one or two of your course would be good. Allow several weeks for reading and several more weeks to draft and re-draft your work. Work on it for half an hour a day and your academic life will be turned around.

Open a research folder

Have a folder for every assignment that you are doing. The folder becomes the place where you automatically put useful notes, press cuttings, thoughts and feelings on the assignment. Without a folder, your information can drift – and your thinking will too.

The research folder itself can be simple or elaborate – you can re-cycle old A4 envelopes or buy something really swish and attractive that will inspire you just by looking at it. The point is to have the folder so that you focus on the question early, and gather information throughout a programme of study – not in the couple of days before the deadline!

tip

Open a folder for every module that you do – and every question that you have to answer. Open the folder early and start collecting information from week one of your course. Put something in each folder every week.

Look at the question

Write the whole question on the outside of the folder or envelope. Do not abbreviate: if you miss a bit of the question you will definitely miss an important part of the answer. When this happens you are throwing marks away.

Examine the question: once you have written out the question (essay titles are often called questions, even when not phrased as such), analyse every word in it. Make sure that you understand exactly what and exactly how much the question is asking you to do.

Doing this early in a course of study tunes your brain into the course itself more effectively. In this way you 'hear' more in class and 'see' more in set texts; also you may hear and see more as you read the papers and watch television. Make notes of useful things you see, read and hear, and put the notes in your research folder. Record the source on the outside of the envelope; write: author, date, title, publisher... on the outside of the envelope and you will build up your bibliography as you go.

tips

- Write the whole question on the outside of your envelope.
- When trying to understand the question, put it in your own words and say it back to another student or a tutor.
- Underline every important word in the question – each is a research opportunity.
- Every word in a question is a gift – use them all. Each one is there to be investigated, questioned, challenged, argued for or against.
- Make sure that you do something about every word – don't leave any out.

Be creative

Consider every word in the question in a flexible, creative way. Don't forget to brainstorm and question matrix every word in the question (Chapters 12 and 13).

Performing a creative loosening up activity like this allows you to cover the question in more depth and breadth. Remember – you do not need to know the answer when you look at a question but you should know how to devise more questions.

tip

Put your brainstorm or matrix on the outside of your research folder. Look at it before you go to a lecture or seminar, before you start your reading.

Use the overview

Remember that when answering an assignment question, one brief comes from the question – the wider brief comes from the course itself: cross-reference the question with course aims and learning outcomes (Chapter 4). You must shape your essay so that it answers the question – and also so that it demonstrates that you have met the learning outcomes.

tip

Add key words from course aims and learning outcomes to your brainstorm or matrix. Brainstorm those words as well.

Rough plan

It can be useful here to look at your brainstorm and quickly sketch out the possible shape of your essay. What key arguments might you make? What evidence are you looking for?

tip

If stuck, don't write an introduction for your essay – write out a quick *conclusion*. This will show you where your thinking is going and should help you to make a rough plan of your essay.

Action plan

In the light of your brainstorming and planning, you then have to decide exactly what you will have to do to research and produce your assignment. Things to consider include:

- What do you now have to do?
- Who will you speak to (tutor, study partner, subject librarian…)?
- What will you read?
- When will you do these things?

tip

It can help to draw up a detailed list of everything that you will need to do and when you will do it. Allow a column for ticking off items as you complete them. Note:

- Which lecture notes to re-read
- Which essential texts to read
- Which additional texts to read
- Dates – when you will do the work
- Check off – space to TICK once you have completed the work.

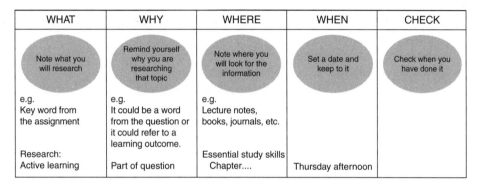

WHAT	WHY	WHERE	WHEN	CHECK
Note what you will research	Remind yourself why you are researching that topic	Note where you will look for the information	Set a date and keep to it	Check when you have done it
e.g. Key word from the assignment	e.g. It could be a word from the question or it could refer to a learning outcome.	e.g. Lecture notes, books, journals, etc.		
Research: Active learning	Part of question	Essential study skills Chapter....	Thursday afternoon	

FIGURE 14A   A sample action plan

2: Follow the action plan

Once you have devised your action plan, follow it through. Read actively and interactively, using your active reading technique (Chapter 10). Remember to get physical with the texts – mark them up, annotate, make comments and cross-references. You will get much more from your reading when you do this.

Read with a purpose

Don't look for the whole answer to the question in any one piece of reading. When reading, look for the answers to the questions generated by your question matrix; read around the words generated by your brainstorm.

tip

When reading to find the answers to an assignment question, read about one word or phrase at a time. Do not look for the whole answer to the question.

Paragraph patterns

- Use really large sheets of paper – A1 rather than A4.
- Put a key word or phrase from the question in the centre of each sheet.
- These are your PARAGRAPH pages – where you build your paragraph patterns.
- As you read put useful information on your different paragraph sheets. Thus, rather than having diverse information in your notes, you sort the information into paragraph topics as you collect it.
- Keep reading and adding notes, until each paragraph sheet has enough information on it to allow you to write a rounded paragraph.
- Remember to put Author (date) Title, town: publisher, and page numbers for quotes.

Creative notes

Remember to make your creative pattern notes (Chapter 11) on one side of the paper only: you do not want half of your information facing the table – you want it all facing you. Better still, write your notes on your paragraph patterns or on your walls – immerse yourself in your essay.

3: Review your notes

Once you have nearly finished your reading, look at the notes on your wall or the notes from your research folder set out in front of you. Look at what you have gathered for each paragraph: have you got a balanced perspective? Reflect on what you have discovered. Given all this information, what do you now think? Why?

 tips

- Notice the evidence for and against your topic.
- Think what your argument will be – given the evidence.
- Discuss your evidence. Remember, when other people write, they are not answering your question. When you use their points, you will have to work to build them into your arguments. This is why we always have to discuss our quotes. Relate the quote to your argument; relate it to the question.

- Index surf to brush up your paragraphs. Once you have completed your major research, and you are happy with it, you can just index surf to get little extra bits and pieces to take your work that little bit further.

4: Plan

After reviewing your information, make another plan for your assignment (essay, report, presentation). Think of the different ideas that will go to answer the whole question. Think about building a logical case and all the different ideas that you will have to cover to answer the whole question.

Remember that your reader will be thinking of the opposite evidence: do not just ignore inconvenient or contradictory evidence – know what it is and argue against it.

Once all the ideas are jotted down you can examine them again and number them according to where they should come in the body of your answer – order them so that you are building a logical case.

tip

Write ideas on separate pieces of paper. Move the pieces of paper around to discover the best structure for the answer. Remember a reader – who keeps saying, 'So what?' Make sure you answer the 'So whats'.

5: Write the first draft

Once you have the points (paragraph outlines) in a rough order – write the first draft of your answer.

Use the **paragraph questions** to prompt your writing.

Academic essays require one 'big idea' per paragraph... once you have your ideas, write about them by answering these questions:

- What is this paragraph about?
  - introduce topic (and claim)

➡

➡

- What exactly is that?
  - o define/clarify/explain
- What is your argument?
  - o give argument in relation to question
- What is the evidence? What does it mean?
  - o offer evidence and discuss it
- What is the opposing evidence? What does that mean?
  - o therefore…?
- What is your final point (in relation to the question)?
  - o tie what you have written to the question. It is not down to your reader to guess what you are trying to say – or to think 'I wonder how this relates to the question?' If your reader has to do that then something is missing from your answer.

Intros and outros

Write these last – but if you do them write early, remember to change them as the essay changes. An introduction can have some general remarks about the question – how important it is, how it touches upon key issues – and you must also give the agenda, that is, the order in which you will be presenting your points. In the conclusion you must re-state your main arguments and the points that you made.

tip

Write draft intros and outros – but change them when you have finished drafting your piece.

Go with the flow

As you write your first draft, try to build a flow into your writing – remember it is a first draft and does not have to be perfect. If you try to be perfect you will hit writing blocks (see Chapter 16).

So, when writing your first draft, do not try to answer all the paragraph questions at the first go. Leave gaps. Repeat yourself. Put in rough words rather than the 'best' words. Write messy sentences in poor English with no verbs. Write overlong sentences that hide the point you are trying to make. But remember also that you will be going back over this first draft several times.

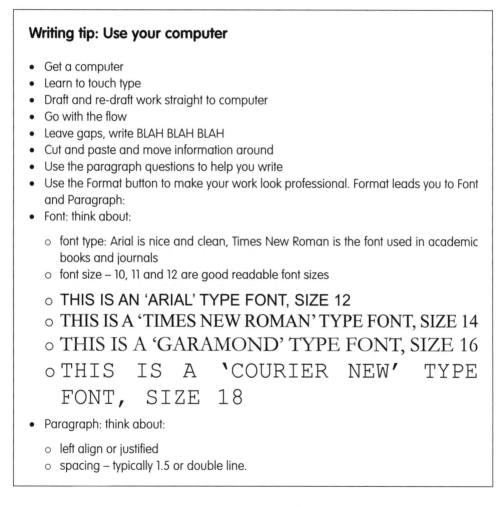

Writing tip: Use your computer

- Get a computer
- Learn to touch type
- Draft and re-draft work straight to computer
- Go with the flow
- Leave gaps, write BLAH BLAH BLAH
- Cut and paste and move information around
- Use the paragraph questions to help you write
- Use the Format button to make your work look professional. Format leads you to Font and Paragraph:
- Font: think about:
  - font type: Arial is nice and clean, Times New Roman is the font used in academic books and journals
  - font size – 10, 11 and 12 are good readable font sizes
  - THIS IS AN 'ARIAL' TYPE FONT, SIZE 12
  - THIS IS A 'TIMES NEW ROMAN' TYPE FONT, SIZE 14
  - THIS IS A 'GARAMOND' TYPE FONT, SIZE 16
  - THIS IS A 'COURIER NEW' TYPE FONT, SIZE 18
- Paragraph: think about:
  - left align or justified
  - spacing – typically 1.5 or double line.

6: Leave it!

Once you have written the first draft you feel great, your answer is great, your friends are great and life is great. Do not believe this! Put the work to one side and leave it for a while.

This will give you some distance and objectivity, but more than this: your unconscious mind will seek to close the gaps that you left. The brain likes closure. The brain will not be happy with all the gaps in your assignment. Thus your brain will struggle to close the gaps that you have left. If you allow a break in your writing process you are allowing the brain to close the gaps – you are working with your brain.

First draft tips

You are not looking for the one right answer that already exists – there are usually several ways of tackling a question. As long as you were creative with the whole question – and you cross-referenced with course aims and outcomes – you are probably on the right track.

- Write the first draft, following the plan.
- Or – write your 'favourite' paragraph first to get you started.
- Or – free write your conclusion to get an idea of where you want your answer to go – change the conclusion later.
- Do not even try for perfection – this will cause writing blocks.
- Be boring, repeat yourself – and, most importantly of all, leave gaps.
- When you get stuck for an idea put … (dot, dot, dot – this is an ellipsis) and write on.
- Academic writing is always tentative rather than definite. You will get very familiar with: 'typically', 'it could be argued that', 'thus this makes a case for…', or, 'this suggests that…'
- It can be difficult to be tentative when you do care passionately about what you are writing. Practise.
- If you write the first draft straight onto your computer, it is easier to revise and edit.
- As you play with the ideas – and possibly re-arrange them – you will need to re-write your introduction and conclusion to reflect the changes that you make; that is why it is usually good to leave these until last.
- Use the paragraph questions.
- At the end of each paragraph make a point.
- Remember to tie what you have written to the essay question. If your reader could say, 'So?' or 'So what?' after reading your paragraph – you have not said enough.

7: Review, revise and edit: Struggle to write

This is the stage where you go back over your work and struggle to make it the very best it can be. Here you have to re-read what you have written – and change it. Sometimes we have to change everything – and nothing of our first draft gets left. This does not matter.

We are writing to learn, so our thoughts *should* change as we write. Also, we would never get to a good version if we did not go through our rough versions. Be prepared to draft and re-draft your work.

Don't even try for perfection on a first draft – it is bad technique and it can actually stop you writing anything.

tip

Remember – once you have written something you have something to change but a blank page stays a blank page for an awfully long time.

Review in stages

On your first review, you might read from the beginning of your essay and improve, polish, as you go.

After that, try to concentrate on one paragraph at a time – and not always in the order it is written but in any order.

Polishing one paragraph at a time is much better than always going back to the start. If you always go back to the beginning, you may never polish the end – and you can quickly become very bored with what you are doing.

tips

- Review, revise and edit – this struggle is the assignment writing process.
- Allow plenty of time for this.
- Go through the whole answer when doing the first and last drafts – but in between, attack one paragraph at a time.
- This is where you go back and put in the 'best' word. This is where you put in the verbs. This is where you shorten long sentences so that you make clear, effective points.
- When you have finished polishing paragraphs, check the 'links' between paragraphs – make sure that they still connect with each other.

8: Proof read

Once you are happy with your assignment, you are ready to stop revising it and to say: 'This is the best I can do'. Sometimes we are never really 'happy' with our work, but there still comes a time to stop and move on to the next task. At this point you have to proof read the final version.

Proof reading is not editing: you are not looking to change what you have written, but here you are going through looking for mistakes, grammatical errors, tense problems, spelling mistakes or typographical errors.

Proof reading tips

You know that the brain likes closure – it will work to fill the gaps. This works against us when we are proof reading. Because the brain likes closure this can mean that our eyes will 'see' what should be there rather than what is there. To get over this we have to make our proof reading 'strange', which we can do by having breaks in between our proof reading.

 **tips**

- Read your assignment aloud (if it is a presentation, rehearse before a critical friend).
- Swap assignments with a friend – proof read each other's work.
- Cover the assignment with paper and proof read one sentence at a time.
- Proof read from back to front.
- Proof read from the bottom of the page to the top.
- Proof for one of 'your' mistakes at a time.
- Like everything else we do, proof reading gets better with practice.

9: Hand it in

You should now be ready to hand your work in on or before the deadline. And remember that deadline. On most university programmes a late submission is awarded an automatic fail. This is serious.

So once your assignment is done – congratulations! But before you rush off and celebrate remember to always keep copies of your work. Never hand in the only copy.

Obviously if you are writing on a computer it is okay – save your work to the hard drive and to a memory stick and email it to yourself and save in a 'cloud' – you can't be too careful!

If writing by hand – photocopy. And if the assessment unit loses your assignment, do not hand in your last copy – photocopy that. A student of ours came back and told us that the assessment unit lost her essay – the same one – three times!

10: Getting it back

When we get work back, we look at the grade, feel really happy or really unhappy, throw the work to one side and forget all about it. This is not a good idea.

What is a good idea is to review what you have written, and see if you still think it is good. As an active learner, you should try to take control of your own work and you have to learn how to judge it for yourself and not just rely on the tutor's opinions.

At the same time, you should also utilise the feedback that you get from the tutor. Be prepared to use that feedback to write a better essay next time. So a good thing to do is to perform a SWOT analysis of our own work, that is, look for the:

- Strengths
- Weaknesses
- Opportunities
- Threats.

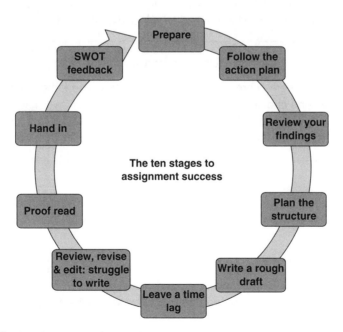

FIGURE 14B   The ten stages to assignment success

When you SWOT your work look for the things that you think you did well or not so well. Then look for the things that the tutor appears to be telling you that you did well or not so well. Resolve to do something about your strengths and your weaknesses.

Getting work back: A student response

It's hard to take feedback – it can feel like a personal attack or rejection. We have to learn how to use the feedback that we get. Here is how one student responded to some short sharp feedback.

" I feel that in this case (and in some others!) I slipped away from my main task which is usually identified by a thorough question analysis. Looking back, instead of presenting the strengths and weaknesses of Freud's theory of personality as measured against the yardstick of evidential science I decided at too early a point to become an advocate for it. I tried also to question the appropriateness of the paradigm often used to assess Freud when it might have profited me (in terms of more marks) to stick with it. It may have helped me achieve the stronger take-home message counselled by the assessor. And interestingly, in this case I carried out my question analysis belatedly. **"**

The assessor's final comment on the assignment:

…could be improved by having a clearer focus and a stronger take-home message, which could perhaps be achieved by interpreting the title in a narrower way…

Query: Would you have been able to respond to the tutor's comment like that?

Discussion: We were impressed by this student's response to her feedback. She had worked long and hard on the assignment and the mark was lower than she had hoped; however, she still managed to appreciate the tutor's comments and to take something away from the experience that will help her in future assignments.

──────── **tip** ────────────────────────

For more of this student's essay, find 'An Essay Evolves' (http://evolvingessay.pbworks.com/w/page/19387227/FrontPage) and read the essay as it developed – and the student's blog about her thoughts and feelings when writing the essay.

2. Activity: How to use writing resources

Reproduced below – and available as an activity sheet from our Sage website – are a list of useful online sites designed to help you with all aspects of your academic writing. We have also put Work Packs there to help you with the production of real assignments.

For this activity we want you to explore some or all of the sites listed below. Check them out – see what they offer you and how easy they are to use – and think about when and where you will actually use them.

If completing some sort of learning journal or blog as part of your course post comments about these sites and why other students would use them.

Don't forget to use the assignment preparation checklist at the end of the chapter, as well as the resources indicated here.

- Our resources are available through the **Reading and Notemaking** pages on **LearnHigher** – see particularly, Organise your Desk: http://learning.londonmet.ac.uk/TLTC/learnhigher/desk/desk.html and **our writing space**: a range of writing resources to support you, which includes a link to the **Preventing plagiarism** tutorial: http://learning.londonmet.ac.uk/TLTC/connorj/WritingGroups/
- Explore generally – and have a particular look at **Academic Writing** and **Assessment** on the **LearnHigher** site – see what resources are there for you to use.
- **An Essay Evolves**: This site contains a whole essay that a real student wrote over time. She also kept a blog of her thoughts whilst writing the essay. Really useful if you want to see what academic writing looks like – and what it feels like to do: http://evolvingessay.pbworks.com/w/page/19387227/FrontPage
- **Essay planning animation**: One way to plan an essay from Portsmouth University: http://ondemand.port.ac.uk/central/One_way_to_write_an_essay.wmv
- **Getting your writing right**: **AWE** = Academic Writing in English: http://slb-ltsu.hull.ac.uk/awe/index.php?title=Main_Page
- **Shared writing space**: This link goes to several shared writing spaces – some supported by Google. Consider how you might use these spaces to work collaboratively with other students – especially if preparing GROUP projects: http://etherpad.com
- **Shared thinking space**: This space is designed to support group work in more creative ways: http://www.sharedthinking.info/
- Excellent site for phrases to use in academic writing: http://www.phrasebank.manchester.ac.uk/
- Practising writing (for international students): http://www2.actden.com/writ_den/index.htm

➡

➡

- **Referencing**: http://www.lib.monash.edu.au/tutorials/citing/harvard.html
- Worried about grammar? http://www.dartmouth.edu/~writing/materials/student/ac_paper/grammar.shtml
- Detailed explanations and examples of Harvard: http://www.coventry.ac.uk/cu/caw/harvard
- **Proof reading tips** – try the following:
  - ○ http://www.indiana.edu/~wts/pamphlets/proofing_grammar.shtml
  - ○ http://businessmajors.about.com/od/collegeessaywriting/ht/EssayEdit.htm
  - ○ http://www.scribblepad.co.uk/HowToProofreadYourWriting.html

Conclusion: Becoming a successful writer

We have considered the what, why and how of assessment. 'What' argued that assessment is part of becoming a graduate whilst providing tangible evidence that you have engaged with your course. With 'Why' we stressed the active learning aspects of assessment; that whilst the product can be marked, your process, all the reading, thinking, discussing and struggling that you do to produce an assignment, is part of active learning. With 'How' we looked at assignment success and we broke the process into 10 manageable stages. We followed this with an activity designed to get you exploring and evaluating some online writing resources. We hope that you now feel in a better position to approach your assignments.

Review points

When reviewing your notes on this chapter and thinking about how to become a more confident writer, you might realise that:

- You can now look at assessment in a more positive light
- You are prepared to engage in writing to learn and having something to say
- You are ready for the 'struggle to write' – it does not mean that there is anything wrong with you
- You realise the importance of the 10-stage plan, prepare and review strategy
- You will use the checklist on page 234 – and the paragraph questions – to help you prepare and produce assignments.

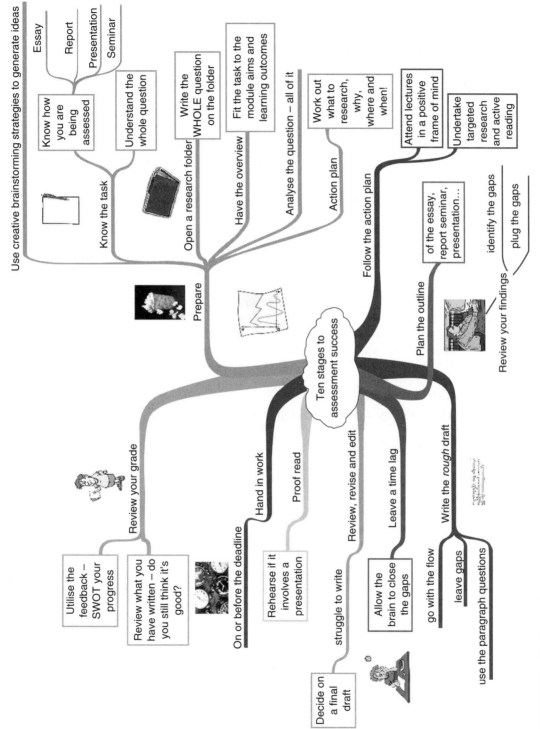

FIGURE 14C   Mindmap – ten stages to assessment success

Ten stages to assessment success

Photocopy this assessment preparation checklist – and complete one for every assignment that you undertake.

☐ Prepare:

- Know the task (the whole question) and the form (essay, report, presentation, seminar etc)
- Open a research folder – write the WHOLE question on the folder
- Have the overview – fit the task to the module aims and learning outcomes
- Analyse the question – all of it
- Use creative brainstorming strategies to generate ideas
- Action plan – work out what to research, why, where and when!

☐ Follow the action plan: Attend lectures and seminars in a positive frame of mind – undertake targeted research and active reading

☐ Review your findings – identify gaps – plug the gaps

☐ Plan the outline – of the essay, report, seminar, presentation…

☐ Write the *rough* draft – go with the flow – leave gaps – use the paragraph questions

☐ Leave a time lag – allow the brain to close the gaps

☐ Review, revise and edit – struggle to write – decide on a final draft

☐ Proof read – or rehearse if it involves a presentation

☐ Hand in work – on or before a deadline

☐ SWOT your progress

Photocopiable:

Essential Study Skills, Third Edition © Tom Burns and Sandra Sinfield, 2012 (SAGE)

Section IV

Communicating Effectively in Assignments

15

How to Prevent Plagiarism

Aims

Plagiarism is a serious academic offence – but many students stumble into it by accident. The aim of this chapter is to prevent plagiarism by introducing the concept of academic integrity and the requirement to reference and give bibliographic information in your work.

Learning outcomes

It is intended that after reading through this chapter and engaging with the activities, you will have:

- understood the concept of academic integrity and the need for recording and giving sources
- explored how to record source details from paper-based and online texts
- undertaken our online Preventing Plagiarism tutorial – and its exit test – to check whether or not you have fully grasped plagiarism and how to avoid it.

Introduction

The English university system is based on research and independent learning: you are not just taught your degree, but are expected to read for it. The fact that you are acquiring ideas, arguments and evidence from other people means that academic integrity is paramount: you must acknowledge your sources – you must credit the work of other people.

The reading that you do to prepare for your assignments provides you with ideas, knowledge-claims, arguments and evidence to seed your thinking and your writing. You are supposed to do this reading to gain an understanding of the guiding principles of your discipline and knowledge of the key ideas, concepts and theories that make up the subject you are studying. You are not supposed to be making it up as you go along – nor are you expected to have all the ideas and all the answers before you start your degree. Studying for your degree is a learning process and a process of exploration. After you have studied for a while, you move on to explore the more radical ideas, questions and debates that are in existence – and all this is evidenced in the references you put IN your assignments – and the bibliography that you write at the END of your assignment.

As an assignment is evidence of your engagement with your course, so your references are evidence of your engagement with the knowledge base of your subject. If studying is exploration, your references are your maps – recording your footsteps through the subject as it already exists.

tip

When you read, record your sources as you go – and in the correct format for your discipline's referencing system. Use **index cards** to keep a record of everything that you read – as you read it.

Use your index cards

Every time you read – keep a record: Author (date) *Title* location: publisher
  Author(s):
  Date:
  Title:
  Place published:
  Publisher:
  Key quotes (and page numbers):

➡

➡

Always note these essential details so you can cite them correctly in assignments – and in your bibliographies.

Record details of your reading on your index cards. Note the information above on one side of the card.

Experiment with the reverse: you could note what essay you used the book for; you could note the chapter or paragraph headings – so that you have an outline of the book… The trick is to make this process as useful to you as possible.

1. Activity: Some reasons for plagiarising

- Read through the examples of plagiarising given by other students below.
- Think about how you could avoid making the mistakes that they made.
- Make notes for yourself.

❝We were working on the assignment together. It was a group project – but we were supposed to write individual reports. Somehow, I couldn't write a different report to my mate – so I copied her version and handed it in as my own. I was punished for plagiarism and got zero for that module.❞

❝I had done the reading for that assignment ages ago. When I finally wrote it up, I couldn't remember what was my work and what I'd read. I really didn't know that this was plagiarism…❞

❝I found an essay on the web that was exactly on my topic. I did write my own introduction and conclusion – but it was still plagiarism. I'm lucky I didn't get suspended.❞

❝Well I did read that stuff – but it was what I was thinking anyway – so I didn't think I had to give any sources. Turns out I was wrong…❞

❝I just thought I had to write a bibliography at the end. No! You have to mention your reading as you write. You have to give the name and date of the source if you refer to it – and you have to give the page number as well if you actually quote it. Then you have to give the full author, date, title, town, publisher in the bibliography as well.❞

❝I thought I was doing well. I put all the good quotes down on the page – and just wrote little bits of essay around them. But that didn't work. You have to put it in your own words – still giving a reference – and discuss it. The tutor said I'd just handed in my notes rather than an essay. She said I was lucky not to be accused of plagiarism – and to digest my reading first next time. It's quite hard getting this bit right – harder than I thought it would be.❞

Query: What were your responses to the reasons – or excuses – given above? What do you plan to do to avoid making the same mistakes that those students did?

Discussion: We can see several different themes emerging from the justifications or explanations offered above.

One theme to emerge here seems to be about poor use of time: students did not allow themselves enough time to read and understand the material, so when they used it, they did not do it well. Too many long quotes in a piece reveal a lack of knowledge and understanding – give yourself time to read and understand.

Another theme seems to be about lack of organisation: students did the reading but obviously did not record enough SOURCE information. You must get in the habit of recording your sources every time you make notes. Remember to record the page numbers too in case you want to quote.

A third theme seems to be about not understanding the referencing tradition. You are supposed to note where ideas come from – and where they exist in the debate. So even when a writer agrees with you – or when you agree with the writer – you still need to record the source.

Referencing and avoiding plagiarism

2. Activity: Preventing plagiarism

Take our online Preventing Plagiarism course which you can find via the LearnHigher website (or do a web search).

View the separate units in the course – from the Introduction through to the Students' Views on Plagiarism to the 'Don't Cheat Yourself' tutorial and the exit test.

In the Learning Resources section there are small animations that show you how to reference correctly – from a range of sources. Look at these animations and make sure you see and understand what is going on.

Reflect on the tutorial after you have finished – and note three things that you can do right now to make sure that you do not plagiarise in the future.

Query: How did you find the Preventing Plagiarism course? Did you get all the questions right in the 'Don't Cheat Yourself' tutorial? Most people don't get them all right at first – in fact we know many lecturers who struggle a bit with these.

Discussion: Academic integrity and plagiarism are significant issues in university life. We frequently find students who get it wrong by mistake: don't let that be you. Studying is not about you having to make it all up as you go – or to know everything before you start… It is about joining an academic conversation – and showing evidence of what you have read and done.

Get into the habit of recording your sources every time you read – and you are going in the right direction.

tip

If you forget how to reference or how to record something in your bibliography re-visit the Learning Resources section of Preventing Plagiarism and the animations will remind you simply and elegantly.

Should I reference?

Still in doubt? Check out these additional resources:

- Plagiarism and academic integrity: http://www.scc.rutgers.edu/douglass/sal/plagiarism/intro.html
- Crossing the line: http://www.usask.ca/university_secretary/honesty/crossing_the_line.php
- Academic integrity: http://www.uoit.ca/EN/academicintegritystudent/main/225483/ai_module.html
- Academic integrity: http://www.ryerson.ca/academicintegrity/episodes/index.html

You can also use the flow chart in Figure 15A.

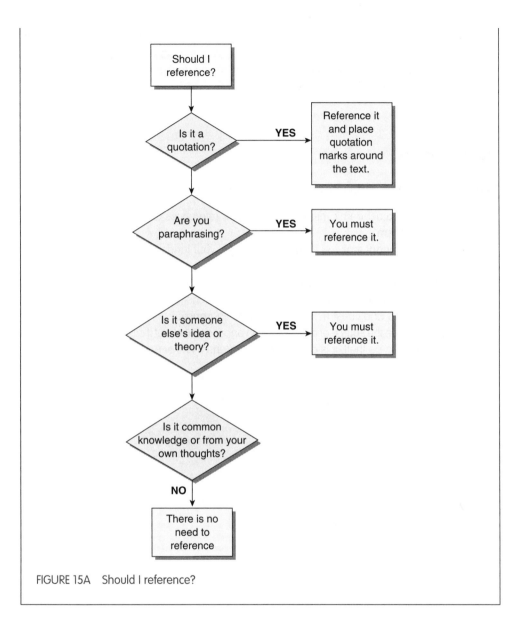

FIGURE 15A   Should I reference?

Conclusion

We hope that you can see that giving references reveals that you are a focused student who has done the reading, who has understood their subject and who can use sources well in their writing. Do not plagiarise by mistake or by laziness or through poor time management. Give yourself time to read and digest information. Keep good records of your sources and make sure you understand how to reference correctly – both in your writing and in your Bibliographies. Plagiarism is a serious academic offence – even when you do it in ignorance or by mistake. If in doubt, revisit the Preventing Plagiarism tutorial.

Review points

When reflecting on this chapter you may decide that:

- You understand academic integrity, the need for references and how to avoid even accidental plagiarism
- It is really important that you note where you got your ideas from when you use them in your writing
- You are not supposed to be generating new knowledge – you are supposed to be using the knowledge that is already out there, and demonstrating this by citing sources correctly in the text and constructing complete bibliographies
- If you do not give the source of an idea – even once you have put it into your own words – this is considered to be theft, it is called plagiarism and it is a serious academic offence.

Section IV

Communicating Effectively in Assignments

16

How to Overcome Writing Blocks and Become a Confident Writer

Aims

To explore how to overcome writing blocks to become a more confident writer.

Learning outcomes

After reading through this chapter, and engaging with the activities, you will have:

- considered the nature of writing blocks and how to overcome them
- practised overcoming writing blocks and begun the process of applying lessons learned to your academic writing
- considered the value of writing to learn as opposed to learning to write
- explored some free writing techniques to help with writing practice and development.

Introduction

Writing for assessment can be fraught with tension, stress and fear of failure; because of this we tend to approach academic writing in strange and unhelpful ways. For example, if we wanted to get better at cooking, driving or playing a musical instrument we would know that we would need to practise – a lot – in order to do so. However, there is something about academic writing that makes it special and different in the minds of most people: rather than practise, practise, practise, academic writing tends to be done in a rush and at the last minute. Academic writing is done under the most stressful of conditions and, strangely enough, when engaged with in this way, academic writing continues to be stressful.

In this chapter we are going to explore how to develop confidence in writing and how to practise your writing. It is designed to complement the 10-stage approach to assignment success covered in Chapter 14.

Writing development tips

- **Group writing**: Form a group with some friends that you trust. Brainstorm and plan 'perfect' answers to your assignments together. This is especially useful when preparing for exams.
- **Practise brainstorming**: Sit down with a list of questions. Give yourselves 10 minutes to brainstorm and plan each answer. Choose the question that you like the most – but use ideas from the other brainstorms in your answer. Remember – brainstorming and planning get quicker with practice.
- **Speed write paragraphs**: Once you have an assignment plan, sit down and use the paragraph questions to prompt your paragraph writing. Write quickly – put in lots of BLAH BLAH or 'I need to find a source here'… Use the first rough drafts to help you choose more material to read. Plug those gaps.
- **Do not aim for perfection**: Write something, anything… then change it.
- **Practise writing**: Do not just write for assessment – get into the habit of writing something every week, every day.

" When I was helping in the Students' Union, I used to get loads of students talking about their council tax – or their TV licence… Once we'd got that out of the way – they'd suddenly talk about their essays, asking for help. All those little problems become big when you're trying to write. Sometimes overcoming writing blocks means getting all that stuff out of the way first. **"**

Free writing

Free writing is a bit like brainstorming; however, rather than looking at a title and jotting down all the random thoughts that occur to you, in free writing you read the title and then write briefly, but in a really focused way to the title. Write in a 'stream of consciousness' – capturing everything that pops into your mind when you respond to the title.

In free writing you are not trying to be right, you are plumbing your unconscious to see what comes out that might be valuable in your preparation for writing the subsequent essay. As with other advice on writing a first draft, the free write is best if you just write. You do not check spellings, tense or grammar. You do not try to get the 'right' order. You just let everything out as quickly as possible on to your page. After some little time has elapsed you can look at your free write to see if you have captured anything useful to use in the essay proper.

Free writing can really surprise you, often revealing that you know much more about a topic than you previously thought – and also revealing that you can communicate really effectively when you do not get in your own way. Some of our favourite chapters in this textbook started as free writing where we just sat down and poured out everything that we thought and felt on a topic. Later we revised, shaped and otherwise improved what we captured the first go round. We ended up with what looked and felt like a proper chapter, but the writing itself was more joyful.

Useful things to do when free writing

Free write on your assignment questions as soon as you get them. Just sit down and write something when you see the question. Do not try to get it right, just write. Use the free write to help you understand your course – and your reading.

Free write after every lecture: sum up the main points; note how the ideas in the lecture will help with your assignment; put the main arguments in your own words.

Go to our Sage website and find our additional writing activities – including the Two Brothers PowerPoint. Use this to seed your creative writing – and to help you feel more confident about writing overall.

Search YouTube for Peter Elbow videos on writing and spelling, punctuation and grammar.

Search for 'An Essay Evolves' to see how the writer of the online Freud essay used free writing to approach the assignment. Have a look at the free write that this student did on the Freud essay question and consider the editing strategies she used to start her Freud essay journey.

 **tip**

Use free writing as one of your repertoire of academic writing techniques.

❝ When we did that free writing every week, I got the best mark I've ever got for an essay. ❞

❝ All the free writing helped me to take control of the module. I think it helped me be more creative. ❞

❝ I finally understood why I was reading! ❞

Free write your way to success

Included below are several free writing activities that are designed to help you to review your own approaches to writing – and in the process to build your own writing confidence.

1. Activity: Overcoming writing blocks

This is an activity you can try on your own – or with other people. Each person will need two pieces of paper plus pens or pencils.

1 Find a space in which you think that you would be able to write.
2 Settle down with two pieces of paper in front of you – and all the pens and pencils that you could want. Label one piece of paper – *writing*. Label the other piece of paper – *commentary*.
3 Give yourself a set time to write – at least 15 minutes and up to 30 minutes.
4 Settle down to write about anything that you can hear, see, feel or smell at the time of writing – **or** – write on your assignment question. Write continuously. Do not stop.

 **tip**

Do not worry about this… just write. Do not put the exercise off – do it!

5 Every time you do stop writing, put the reason for stopping on the commentary sheet of paper. No matter what the reason is – how silly, or small or trivial – make a note of it.
6 After your set writing time, stop writing.
7 Review all the different reasons you gave for stopping. Notice what your reasons for stopping are.
8 If you have been working with other people, discuss all the different reasons given for stopping writing.
9 Work out what to 'do' about some of your different reasons for stopping.

➡

➡

Here are some are reasons that other students have given for stopping:

❝Stopping to search for the right word.❞

❝Checking my spelling.❞

❝Wondering whether I've got the sentence right.❞

❝Checking my grammar and tenses.❞

❝I kept checking the time.❞

❝Thinking of a new idea.❞

❝I was trying to think of a better idea.❞

❝It was too hot.❞

❝I felt too cold.❞

❝I was uncomfortable; I kept wriggling in my chair.❞

❝I was thirsty.❞

❝I was hungry.❞

❝I heard a noise.❞

❝Someone left the room and I wondered what they were doing.❞

❝I could not see the point of this activity – I felt stupid and wanted to stop.❞

Query: Do you notice anything about these points? Are they anything like your reasons for stopping?

Discussion: There appear to be certain 'sets' of reasons for stopping work:

1 Searching for words and spellings, checking that the work is correct.
2 Thinking of new or better ideas.
3 Feeling uncomfortable physically – hungry or thirsty or too hot or cold or uncomfortable – or mentally – hating the task, wondering what people are doing.

Query: Is there anything we can 'do' about these things? Think about it first – then move on to our suggestions.

1: Thinking of words and spellings and generally getting it 'right'

We have mentioned above that you should be prepared to draft and re-draft your work. In first drafts *you should not even try for perfection*. Put in the wrong word, do not worry about getting the spellings and tenses right. When stuck for a word put in an ellipsis (dot dot dot) or BLAH or a note to yourself – and move on. The trick with getting a first draft down is to keep the 'flow' going. Definitely do not interrupt your flow of ideas, for in doing that you will lose the thread of your thinking.

tip

Practise using the ellipsis (…) to keep your flow going. Accept the notion of drafting and re-drafting work.

2: Searching for ideas

We've mentioned that it is a good idea to brainstorm before you write. Even with a task like this, it is typically a good idea to jot a few ideas down before you start. At least brainstorm a few key ideas to get a rough shape to your work. Once you have a plan, write to your plan.

tip

Practise brainstorming and planning.

3: General feelings of discomfort

This could mean that you have not yet sorted out 'where to write' or perhaps 'why' you are writing or studying.

Where: Perhaps you need to do a bit more work on your organisation – plan when, where and how you will study (Chapter 6). Or perhaps you need to explore your own individual learning style (Chapter 5). Remember there is no one correct way of working. Some people like quiet, some like noise. Some like bright lights, some definitely do not. Some people like to sit still,

249

some like to move around. Discover where you want to study and what learning conditions suit you. Next time you write, write in your study space.

Why: If you are feeling really resentful about the writing that you have to do on your course or more generally about all the time that being a student is 'costing' you, perhaps you have not fully accepted that you are a student – or perhaps you have not chosen the right course or the right module? Being a student should be taking about 35–40 hours per week of your time – every week. You will not want to give this much time to something you are not interested in or motivated about. Have a look at Chapter 5 that explores how to be a successful learner. If you really want to get your degree you have to convince yourself that it is worth it – at the very least you have to fake it to make it and *act* like an interested student.

tip

Complete a Learning Contract for the course that you are currently undertaking (Chapter 5). If you think you have chosen the wrong course after all and that you will never be able to put in the effort that is required, make an appointment to see Careers or the Student Counsellors at your institution as soon as possible to discuss this.

After reflecting on these topics – plan what you need to do next, and when you need to do it.

2. Activity: Prompted writing – paper prompts

As with the Overcoming Writing Blocks activity, above, this is an activity you can try on your own – or with other people. Each person will need paper plus pens and pencils. Before you start to write you need to collect together photographs from magazines or newspapers or old cards – birthday, Christmas, old postcards; you could write quotes from philosophers or people you are studying on large index cards. The pictures and cards need to be mixed up and placed face down on a table so that no one can see what is on them.

1 Find a space in which you think that you would be able to write.
2 Settle down with your paper in front of you – and all the pens and pencils that you could want. Everybody chooses one 'prompt' picture or card at random.

3 Give yourself a set time to write – at least 15 minutes and up to 30 minutes.
4 Settle down to write about anything that pops into your head when viewing the prompt card. Write continuously. Do not stop.

 **tip**

Do not worry about this... just write. Do not put the exercise off – do it!

5 After your set writing time, stop writing.
6 Review this writing process – how similar to or different from your academic writing process was it? Notice what was good about writing in this way. Notice if there was anything that you did not like about writing in this way.
7 If you have been working with other people, discuss what you liked and disliked about writing in this way.
8 Work out how you can learn about what encourages you to write from this activity – and build what you learn into ways of approaching your academic writing.

What other people have said:

❝I just loved having other people in the room working at the same time as me. I did not know that about myself. I will work in the library more often now, that will encourage me.❞

❝I started to write, then thought that everybody else had chosen a better card than me. I was convinced I'd chosen a bad card... This IS the way I am on a course. I keep thinking I've made a bad choice and this gets in the way of me getting anything done at all. **I have to believe I've made a good choice and then just get on with it.**❞

❝I found that I wanted to write about two different things at once. So I just got two sheets of paper and did that. I do get like this with my essays too – I feel blocked because I really want to say something, but I know it's not really what the question wants. I think next time that happens I will just write out what I want to get off my chest – and then dump it.❞

➡

➡️

> **Query**: Are these comments anything like your own? Can you also 'learn' from these points and your own? What will you do with this information?
>
> **Discussion**: All sorts of little things can get in the way of our writing: we do or do not like having other people around us; we do or do not like the question that we have been set; we do or do not have something to say – or, worse, we know that what we really want to say is not what the question wants from us. Notice how the other students, above, plan to deal with their issues, and think of some tips or tricks of your own that you think will help you with your writing in the future.

tip

Have a look at the draw-to-learn activities in Chapter 12; use these also to help overcome writing blocks and start assignments.

3. Activity: Prompted writing – physical prompts

As with the activities, above, this is an activity you can try on your own – or with other people. Each person will again need paper plus pens and pencils. Before you start to write you need to collect together physical objects that you will then use to prompt your writing: candles, pieces of wood, rock or machinery, statues or other interesting objects. Place all the objects in a sack. Everybody then chooses an object at random and uses this to prompt free writing, as above.

Reflect on the writing you produced and the writing process itself when you have finished the activity.

Again the writing and reflection on that writing can be used to help you understand what helps or hinders you with respect to writing. Plan how to use what you have learned to help you overcome any writing blocks of your own.

tip

This activity is especially useful if you are a kinaesthetic learner (Chapter 5) or if you want to develop your creative side (Chapter 12).

Conclusion

This chapter has been very activity focused, giving you lots of free writing activities to trial and to reflect upon. We hope that you now feel less apprehensive and more confident about writing generally. Yes, writing is a struggle – but that is because it is meant to be an active learning process – so it takes effort. At the same time, this process gets easier if we can overcome our fears and other blocks and get into a writing habit. Your academic writing will get easier with practise – so practise it. Look out for more free writing resources on our Sage website.

Review points

When reviewing your notes on this chapter, you might realise that:

- You have appreciated the importance of practising writing – and of writing often
- You have enjoyed these free writing activities and you will attempt free writing with your next assignment
- You have learned more about your own approaches to both studying and writing and you have noted some strategies to put into place immediately to help you become more confident as a writer and more successful as a student.

Section IV

Communicating Effectively in Assignments

17

How to Write Great Essays

Aims

To prepare you for successful academic writing focusing on how to write great essays.

Learning outcomes

After reading through this chapter and engaging with the activities, you will:

- understand the what, why and how of the academic essay
- have explored your own approaches to essay writing and considered how to use your successful strategies in future writing
- have reviewed advice on successful approaches to essay writing
- have explored the essay as dialogue – and essay instruction words
- have thought about how to prepare your first academic essay.

How to plan, prepare and draft great essays

The essay is the great analytical and critical thinking form. It is where we write about our research in a way that is designed to answer a set question. It is also about learning to communicate effectively in concise, targeted writing: if we can communicate our ideas effectively we will get better marks. The trouble is that people are often so stressed about being assessed when they write their essays, they forget that a real human being will have to read, understand – and enjoy it: that we will have to *communicate* with real people. What helps good communication can help you to produce better assignments. In this chapter we are going to look at the what, why and how of the academic essay.

Communication tips:

- on essay writing – look out for 'the paragraph questions'
- on report writing – look for the sections on 'the reader'
- on presentations – look for information on the audience, body language and the use of prompts rather than scripts.

What is an essay?

The word 'essay' comes from the Latin word exagium, which means the presentation of a case. When building an essay, think like a lawyer prosecuting or defending a client. When defending a client, it is not enough for the defence to say, 'He didn't do it, your honour!' The defence has to look for evidence to prove their client's innocence. They have to predict what the other side will say – and look for evidence to counter it. They have to make a case. That is what the academic essay is all about.

The essay – legal precedent model

The defence might open thus:

> The defence will prove that the case against our client is utterly mistaken. In particular we will prove that he could not have been identified as being at the scene of the crime for it was too dark to make a definite identification. We will tell you that the so-called witness suffers from poor vision and therefore could not identify our client. Finally, we will conclusively prove that our client was somewhere else at the time.

Do you see how all the points have been separated out? And how they are all flagged up here in the introduction? The listeners are not left wondering, 'Where is all this going?' This is the same in an essay – and with an essay introduction.

➡

257

The defence then elaborates upon those three key points:

1   The alley was too dark blah blah
3   The witness was not wearing his glasses blah blah
3   My client has an alibi for the time blah blah

The defence might conclude:

> In conclusion, we argue that despite everything that the prosecution has said, you must find our client innocent because we have conclusively proven his innocence. He definitely could not have been identified as being at the scene of the crime. Firstly, it was too dark to positively identify anyone, further the witness was too short sighted to have any value placed upon his testimony and finally we proved beyond a shadow of a doubt that our client was somewhere else at the time of the incident.

Here in the conclusion all the main arguments are re-visited; all the main points are re-stated.

tips

When it comes to searching for the answer to academic essay questions, use the legal model and:

- break the whole question down into mini-points that can be covered one at a time
- think of a case that you want to make
- think of the separate arguments that would go to making your case
- search for evidence for and against your arguments
- make sure you have evidence for each argument.

And you would have to do this within the academic 'rules' of your subject – that is the arguments you construct must build upon and use the arguments and evidence that already exist in your subject. So you will have to:

- re-read your lecture or class notes to get a starting point for your research
- read further – read around the topics looking for 'evidence'
- present your arguments in the correct way for your subject.

See the essay structures shown in Figures 17A and 17B.

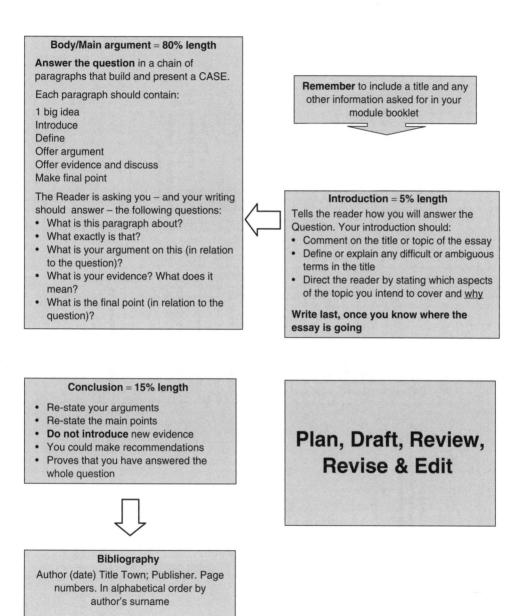

Body/Main argument = 80% length

Answer the question in a chain of paragraphs that build and present a CASE.

Each paragraph should contain:

1 big idea
Introduce
Define
Offer argument
Offer evidence and discuss
Make final point

The Reader is asking you – and your writing should answer – the following questions:
- What is this paragraph about?
- What exactly is that?
- What is your argument on this (in relation to the question)?
- What is your evidence? What does it mean?
- What is the final point (in relation to the question)?

Remember to include a title and any other information asked for in your module booklet

Introduction = 5% length

Tells the reader how you will answer the Question. Your introduction should:
- Comment on the title or topic of the essay
- Define or explain any difficult or ambiguous terms in the title
- Direct the reader by stating which aspects of the topic you intend to cover and <u>why</u>

Write last, once you know where the essay is going

Conclusion = 15% length

- Re-state your arguments
- Re-state the main points
- **Do not introduce** new evidence
- You could make recommendations
- Proves that you have answered the whole question

Plan, Draft, Review, Revise & Edit

Bibliography

Author (date) Title Town; Publisher. Page numbers. In alphabetical order by author's surname

FIGURE 17A   Developing a plan or structure for your essay

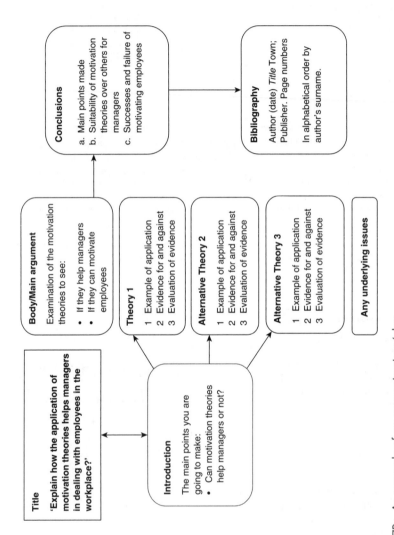

Title

'Explain how the application of motivation theories helps managers in dealing with employees in the workplace?'

Introduction

The main points you are going to make:
• Can motivation theories help managers or not?

Body/Main argument

Examination of the motivation theories to see:
• If they help managers
• If they can motivate employees

Theory 1

1 Example of application
2 Evidence for and against
3 Evaluation of evidence

Alternative Theory 2

1 Example of application
2 Evidence for and against
3 Evaluation of evidence

Alternative Theory 3

1 Example of application
2 Evidence for and against
3 Evaluation of evidence

Any underlying issues

Conclusions

a. Main points made
b. Suitability of motivation theories over others for managers
c. Successes and failure of motivating employees

Bibliography

Author (date) *Title* Town; Publisher. Page numbers

In alphabetical order by author's surname.

FIGURE 17B   An example of an essay structure/plan

The essay explained

An essay has a formal convention – a set style to which it must conform or it is not an essay. The convention is as follows:

The body

This is the section of the essay *where you answer the question* that you have been set. It can be 80% of the total length. You answer the question in a chain of paragraphs that you have organised to build a well-argued case. **Note**: Typically written in the third person, past tense. That is: *It can be argued that…* NOT *I think this…*

Paragraph structure

Each paragraph also has a set convention: introduction; definition; argument; evidence plus discussion; final point. This is where it is useful to remember that you are communicating with a **reader**. When writing, imagine your reader asking you questions and make sure that your writing answers them.

Paragraph as dialogue

- What is this paragraph about?
  - Introduce your topic
- What exactly is that?
  - Define, explain or clarify
- What is the argument – in relation to the question?
  - Say something about your topic
- What is the evidence? What does it mean?
  - Say who or what supports your argument. Give evidence. Say what the evidence means
- What is your final point? (How does this paragraph relate to the question as a whole?)
  - Take the paragraph back to the question.

 **tip**

Write these questions out on an index card and stick them on your computer screen. Look at them when you write.

➡

The introduction

This is the first part of the essay. It can be between 5% and 15% of the total length. In the introduction you tell the reader how you are going to answer the question. You write some remarks that acknowledge the importance of the topic and then give the **agenda** of the essay.

— **tip** —

Write the introduction last, when you know where the essay is going. Writing it too soon will give you a writing block.

The conclusion

This is the last, often long, paragraph of the essay. It can be 10–15% of the length. In the conclusion you restate your main arguments and points in a way that proves that you have answered the whole question. You do not include new information or evidence, but you may make recommendations if appropriate.

— **tip** —

Use the words from the question in your conclusion to prove that you have answered the whole question. Write a rough conclusion first to see where you want the essay to go.

Bibliography

Literally a book list, it is now a record of all the sources you have used to construct your essay.

— **tips** —

- Harvard System: author (date) Title, town; publisher
- British Standard System: author, Title, publisher, date
- Alphabetical order by author's surname.

Why write essays?

The essay is perhaps the most theoretical of the assessment forms. It is the assessment mode that invites you to read, understand and then use for yourself the major theories, knowledge-claims, arguments and evidence of your subject. If all assignment production is designed to be heuristic, to bring about active learning, then the essay is the form that is designed to get you to undertake *deep* learning of your subject. Indeed, there are many who say that students cannot be said to really understand their discipline until they can write subject essays.

tip

Make the most of your essay writing opportunities. Read the key books and journal articles. Make notes that you can use again and again as you study your subject. Summarise your essays to prepare for your exams.

How to prepare and write an essay

1. Activity: Thinking about your approach to writing essays

On the website 'An Essay Evolves' (http://evolvingessay.pbworks.com/w/page/19387227/FrontPage), a student volunteer undertook to read for, plan, draft and revise an essay on the topic of Freud's theory of the personality. Visit that site to see how the whole essay evolved through to the final draft of the essay and the mark and feedback that the essay received. The site gives fascinating insights into how a real person has approached an assignment task.

This activity is designed to help you understand and develop your own writing strategies and approaches. For this activity, we want you to read the student's response to the essay question, below, and then to answer the questions we have set at the end.

Question: *Evaluate Freud's theory of personality.*

263

➡

❝I only have 1500 words in which to do this, so I will not be able to go into a long explanation of the ins and outs of the theory. How to reduce a life's work to 1500 words, though? Plus, I do not want to do the obvious thing where I explain all the theory and then evaluate it. Boring. Boring. I want to give a flavour of evaluation, of opinion, right from the off, as in take a critical view of the concept of personality. I also do not want to stick to purely scientific evaluation. There is not really enough of it.

Evaluate to me suggests be even handed in my assessment. Look at pros and cons, with evidence for both, and come to an opinion. OK, I already feel that Freud's ideas are unfairly and unreasonably dismissed. I need to limit myself to areas of theory that have something to say for and against. Also the essentials: dynamic unconscious, psychological defences, id and ego, we develop through psychosexual stages. Personality quirks can arise from fixation. So also a discussion of libido. I notice in my argument list I mention libido late, and do not explain it. I need to get it in early, with the id. Then I need to finish by saying that contemporary scientists have seen fit to take Freudian theory and subject it to systematic appraisal. What is more, it has not been found as wanting as the hype would have us believe.❞

Now think about and answer the following questions. Take your time – this is not a race. Give yourself space to reflect on your own writing practices.

1   How has this student approached the question? What has she done? What initial thinking can you see?
2   How do you usually approach a question? List your successful strategies.
3   Discuss your successful strategies with a partner. List five things to do before you start reading up on any assignment question.
4   Take a real assignment question. Analyse the question. Make a list of – and then DO – the five essential things that you need to do before you start to read.

> **Discussion**: When we have undertaken this activity with students in class they all noticed that this student was *having fun* with her assignment. For most of them this was a revelation; they understood that assignments were hard work, they had not realised that you could enjoy that work.

As always – make sure that you have identified things for you to do right now to put what you have learned from doing this exercise into practice.

(Our thanks go to 'An Essay Evolves' for the content – and to Lisa Clughen from Nottingham Trent University for sharing this activity.)

How to write an essay: Big essay writing tips

In this section we have collected some of the most popular questions about essay writing and some of the best advice on tackling essays. Read through and make notes of the advice that will be of the most use to you.

SOCCER

First remember the full range of SOCCER activities:

- **S**tudy techniques: plan and use your time well
- **O**verview – remember you course aims and learning outcomes
- Be **C**reative – brainstorm and question matrix
- **C**ommunicate effectively – in the right form
- **E**motionally – want to do well
- **R**eflect on your practice and your progress – also follow the 10 stages to success.

How much should I read?

Dip into between three to five textbooks, five to ten journal articles and a couple of peer-reviewed websites when reading for an assignment.

Read for one word from the question at a time

Use the reading from one assignment in another: often reading is transferable across several modules so a canny student chooses to read texts that can be re-used in this way.

When planning:

- Write the whole question out in the middle of a large sheet of paper.
- Circle key words or phrases in the question – and draw a line from each word. Note key points from your reading against the key words or phrases in the question.
- Number the different sections of your rough plan in the order in which you think you will mention them in your essay.
- Write all the ideas you have generated onto separate pieces of paper. Move the pieces of paper around to discover the best structure for the essay. Now number the points on your plan.
- Use your notes.
- Write on the walls!
- Make paragraph patterns.

- Spread your notes on the floor (only write on one side of the paper!).
- Go with the flow – how to write the first draft.

Once you have your plan ready, sit down at your computer with your plan in front of you. Write straight from the plan as quickly as possible.

Do not try to be perfect – just write. If you cannot think of a word or phrase, if you get stuck in any way – do not search for the right word/spelling/tense. Put an ellipsis (three dots) or write something like BLAH BLAH then move on.

Continue like this until you have a first draft of your essay written. Once you have something written – no matter how bad – you have something to work upon and change.

Worried about your grammar?

Just 20 typical errors account for 91.5% of all grammar mistakes. See http://www.dartmouth.edu/~writing/materials/faculty/methods/grammar.shtml to find out what these errors are, or buy a really simple grammar book to help you get better – Lynne Truss's book, *Eats Shoots and Leaves* is still really popular.

What should it look like?

One way to know what your final essay should look like is to read journal articles to see how they are written:

❝So I learned how to write and I learned how to structure from my reading. Sometimes I used to copy from the book to see the way they just write it down ... then through that experience I started knowing how to structure my phrases and my writing. It just ... I don't know, it just got better through practising. That's the main thing.❞

Practise, practise, practise

Don't just write for an assignment, write little and often and you will see that your writing really does improve with practice. It is very similar to learning to play a musical instrument; you only get better if you practise.

Free write! When you get your module handbook go straight to the assignments. Give yourself 10 minutes to start writing an answer to any of the questions that look interesting. Do not worry about getting the answer 'right', just write and see what comes out. When you have finished you should be able to see what you already know about the subject – and what you need to find out. This will help you make more sense of the course – and it will help you to make more sense of the reading you have to do.

One worry at a time

Learn how to concentrate on one thing at a time. Typically, you will be studying several courses or modules at the same time. Each course will have several assignments and often hand-in dates will be the same or very nearly so. In any one assessment week you may have to hand in two or more different assignments. So, if you are writing essay A, you need to be able to not worry about essays B, C and D; you need to be able to put the other essays on a mental shelf and only take them down one at a time when you are going to concentrate on them. This is a trick that gets easier with practice.

Get a receipt

When handing your work in always get and keep a receipt so that you have proof that you handed work in on or before a deadline. Never miss a deadline, even to improve your work, because a missed deadline tends to mean the work will be awarded a fail grade.

Use proof reading symbols

Proof reading can be easier if you use the proof reading symbols that publishers use when you go through various drafts of your work. So try using the following:

⊔⊓	TRS transpose words
≡	UC upper case
≢	LC lower case
⋏	Insert word or letter
⌒	Delete word/section
⋏	Close gap
Y	Insert gap
...	Stet leave as it is

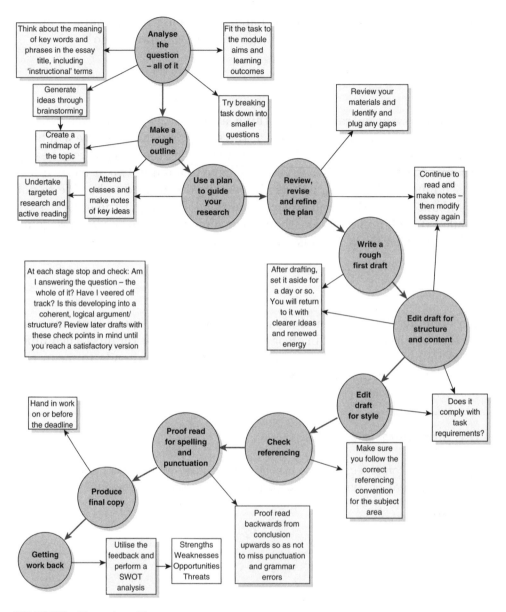

FIGURE 17C   Stages to writing your essay

How to write: Use the paragraph questions

One way of writing a paragraph is to imagine a conversation between you and your reader. Imagine your reader's questions and write to answer them.

268

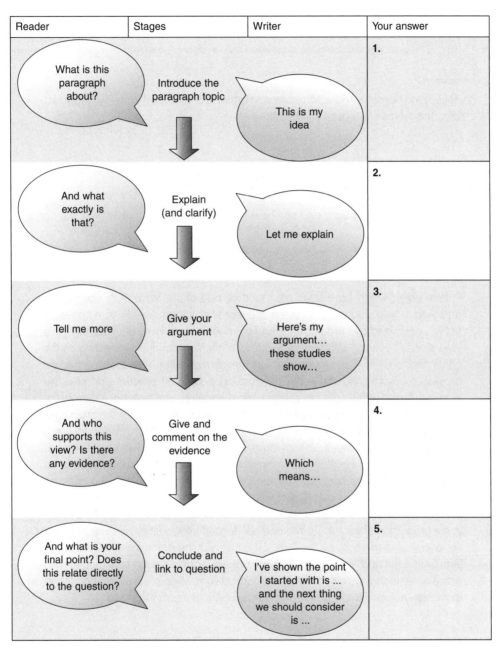

FIGURE 17D   The paragraph conversation

 **Photocopiable:**

Essential Study Skills, Third Edition © Tom Burns and Sandra Sinfield, 2012 (SAGE)

tip

Photocopy the paragraph diagram shown in Figure 17D and use it when writing your real essays. This works if you put it into practice.

2. Activity: The paragraph as dialogue in action

Explore the paragraph below and see how it has been written in answer to the paragraph questions.

This simple paragraph could be from an essay entitled *'Evaluate the usefulness of pattern notes to you as a student'*.

Pattern notes, which have been an important part of our Study Skills course, are designed to help students both select and learn key information. Pattern notes are actively generated by the notemaker and are non-linear in form, often having a key idea placed centrally, with subsidiary ideas branching out and connecting as the notemaker sees fit. It is argued that it is the very selection/reduction/connection processes involved that make this notemaking system an effective part of active learning. Buzan (1989) calls this process 'mindmapping', positing that it mirrors the lateral way that the brain actually works, engaging both halves of the brain, creative right and logical left, in the creation of successful notes. Whilst traditional linear notes are said to be literally monotonous, monotone, only involving half the brain in one's learning, the pattern notemaking process engages the learner in more productive and more successful whole brain learning. Buzan recommends an active revision system in conjunction with the notemaking to firmly fix the information gathered in the long-term memory. In effect, pattern notes engage the student in the production of very structured and condensed information, with less in quantity to learn, but more in quality. Thus, if it is true that the more active we are in our learning (Burns and Sinfield, 2004), the more we learn, it seems logical to use an active notemaking system, coupled with an active revision process, to record and learn material, and to become more effective and successful students.

Now:

1 Mark the different parts of the paragraph in different coloured highlighters.
2 Find another source, apart from Buzan, who would support the arguments in this paragraph.

270

3 Find one or more sources that might counter or disagree with the arguments in this paragraph.
4 Re-write the paragraph to build in the additional supporting sources and/or to take account of the counter evidence.

Re-write the paragraph here:

Query: What do you now understand about academic writing?

Discussion: When using the paragraph questions ourselves, we have found that they remind us to search for evidence and to *discuss* that evidence in our writing. We also really like being reminded that we need to make a point at the end of the paragraph. It is all too easy to leave a paragraph dangling, to not tie it back to the essay question… and thus to throw away marks. Use the paragraph questions in your own essay writing and see how they help you.

Using the question

Essay questions never ask you to write all you know on a topic – they always tell you *how* you are supposed to go about answering the question. It just takes a little practice to understand what the question is asking us to do.

All assignment questions can be broken up into the following components:

- **Instruction words**: Tell you what to do – assess, discuss, evaluate – it is important to interpret these words properly
- **Topic words**: Tell you what the essay is about
- **Aspect words – reveal topic focus**: Once you know the topic you need to know which aspect of it to focus on
- **Restriction words – reveal topic boundaries**: A question is never: 'Write all you know about…'. The *restrictions* will limit your discussion and help you shape your essay.

Here is an example to demonstrate what we mean:

- **Essay question**: 'Assess the importance of free writing for student academic success'
- **Instruction**: Assess

- **Topic**: Free writing
- **Aspect**: Importance
- **Restriction 1**: Academic success
- **Restriction 2**: Student

In this example you are not asked to write all you know about free writing, but you are expected to assess its usefulness in promoting academic success for students.

You would have to define free writing – and say what it can do – but you have to show how a student might benefit from using that to enhance their *academic* success.

Knowing what the essay is asking you to do prevents you from *describing* – and moves you on to finding and evaluating information – and then to *using* that information analytically and critically to answer the question. It diverts you from seeing one key word in a question and writing about that, to seeing the whole question. There are several instruction words used in essay questions. The list below gives advice on how to approach them in your thinking.

Common instruction words	Definition
Account for	Give reasons for; explain why something happens.
Analyse	Break up into parts; investigate.
Assess	Decide the importance of and give reasons for.
Comment on	Identify and write about the main issues; give your reactions based on what you've read/heard in lectures. Avoid just personal opinion.
Compare	Look for the similarities between two things. Show the relevance or consequences of these similarities. Perhaps conclude which is preferable.
Contrast	Bring out the differences between two items or arguments. Show whether the differences are significant. Perhaps give reasons why one is preferable.
Critically evaluate	Weigh arguments for and against something, assessing the strength of the evidence on both sides. Use criteria to guide your assessment of which opinions, theories, models or items are preferable.

Criticise	Requires an answer that points out mistakes or weaknesses, and which also indicates any favourable aspects of the subject of the question. It requires a balanced answer.
Define	Give the exact meaning of. Where relevant, show you understand how the definition may be problematic.
Describe	Give the exact meaning of. Where relevant, show you understand how the definition may be problematic.
Discuss	Investigate or examine by argument; sift and debate; give reasons for and against; examine the implications of.
Distinguish between	Bring out the differences between.
Evaluate	Assess and give your judgement about the merit, importance or usefulness of something. Back your judgement with evidence.
Examine	Look closely into something.
Explain	Make clear why something happens, or is the way it is; interpret and account for; give reasons for.
Explore	Examine thoroughly; consider from a variety of viewpoints.
Illustrate	Make something clear and explicit, giving examples of evidence.
Interpret	Show the meaning and relevance of data or other material presented.
Justify	Give evidence which supports an argument or idea; show why a decision or conclusions were made; answer the main objections which might be made.
Narrate	Outline what happened.
Outline	Give the main points/features/general principles; show the main structure and interrelations; omit details and examples.
Prove/disprove	Both of these require answers which demonstrate the logical arguments and/or evidence connected with a proposition: prove requires the 'pro' points, and disprove requires the 'contra' points.
Relate	(a) Narrate (b) Show similarities and connections between.
State	Give the main features briefly and clearly.
Summarise/outline	Draw out the main points only; omit details and examples.

➡

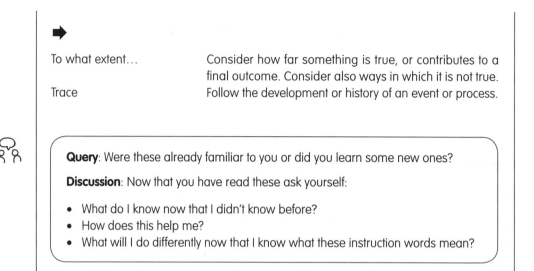

| To what extent... | Consider how far something is true, or contributes to a final outcome. Consider also ways in which it is not true. |
| Trace | Follow the development or history of an event or process. |

Query: Were these already familiar to you or did you learn some new ones?

Discussion: Now that you have read these ask yourself:

- What do I know now that I didn't know before?
- How does this help me?
- What will I do differently now that I know what these instruction words mean?

How to write an essay: Putting it into practice

If you are writing an essay right now, use the simple questionnaire in Activity 3 to help you use the above information in approaching your question.

3. Activity: How to write an essay: prepare to research

Once you have used the task words to think about the assignment that you are currently working on consider the following:

1 Write down in your own words what you think the assignment is asking you to do.

2 What do you already know about the subject matter of the essay?

3 What background information do you need to help you to complete this essay?

4 How do you think this essay differs from or is similar to other assignments that you are working on at the moment?

5 What are you going to read – and why?

6 As you begin to read for your assignment, read and make notes with the essay in mind.

Query: How do you feel now? What are you going to do next?

Discussion: Once you have done that… don't forget the 10 stages to essay success, below.

tip

Use our online Sage assignment packs to help you with future essays. Check out our LearnHigher pages on Reading and Notemaking – including the links to our essay writing resources. Also look at other LearnHigher information on Academic writing and Assignments.

➡

10 stages...

- **Prepare**: Analyse the question (as above) and devise an action plan: note what you are going to do and read to get the essay ready. When will you do these things?
- **Follow the action plan**: Photocopy chapters from books and print journal articles. Read actively and interactively, marking the texts as you go and always keeping the question in mind. Make active notes focusing on one Q word or phrase at a time.
- **Review your findings**: Review your notes – analyse your information. If you have not already done so, make paragraph patterns. Collect together all the information for each potential paragraph.
- **Plan the essay**: The structure to the essay may be obvious; sometimes it is not clear at all. Move the paragraph patterns around until you have a structure that makes the best case or the most sense.
- **Write a rough draft**: Follow the rough structure you have found. Write quickly and without correcting yourself. Go with the flow. Use the paragraph questions. Make sure you leave gaps – and write BLAH BLAH rather than struggling for a perfect draft first go. Highlight gaps and prompts in a bright colour so your brain knows your writing is incomplete.
- **Leave a time lag**: Put the work to one side, think about something else. Let your unconscious continue working on the essay.
- **Review, revise and edit**: Struggle to draft and re-draft your essay. Make sure each paragraph does answer all the paragraph questions. Make sure the essay is in the best 'shape'.
- **Proof read**: At some point you have to stop writing and decide that the essay is finished. Proof read the final draft. Correct your mistakes. Keep copies on different devices.
- **Submit**: Hand in on or before the deadline – and get and keep your receipt. Go and celebrate – be happy – be proud.
- **SWOT your progress**: Get your essay back and do not just look at the grade – look at the feedback you received and work out how to build on your strengths, correct your weaknesses and write a better essay next time.

WiiFM: Getting work back

Always make the effort to go and get your work back – yes, you only care about your grade, but there is so much to learn from the thing itself, especially if you have a tutor who likes to scribble all over your assignments: SWOT your essay.

- **Strengths**: Go through the essay very carefully; look at all the ticks and positive comments. These indicate that you have done something well. Check out the good things you have done – make a note to do them again.
- **Weaknesses**: Look at all the passages without ticks or with comments suggesting that something is missing or incorrect. Note these: make a note to do something about them. Go and find the missing information – correct errors.
- **Opportunities**: Think what you can do now to learn the subject better or improve your grades. Think how to write a better essay in your next module.
- **Threats**: Ask yourself if anything is stopping you from doing better work. Find out what it is and do something about it. Sometimes we can be frightened of success just as much as of failure – is this you? What are you going to do about it?

 **tips**

- If you can answer an exam question on a topic previously covered in an assignment, put the assignment in your revision folder.
- If you improve the essay then the exam answer will be even better. This is a good thing.
- Share it. Read each other's work, discover different writing styles and other ways to answer a question – this stretches our thinking.

Conclusion

We have considered the what, why and how of the essay. What: we looked at the structure of the essay and at building a logical case using argument and evidence. Why: we emphasised the 'struggle to write' as a learning process – we write to learn rather than learn to write. How: we gave tips and tricks and activities to do to take you through the planning and drafting of a real essay. We referred you to useful websites such as 'An Essay Evolves' so that you can see how other students have gone through the process from beginning to end. We also directed you to our assignment packs on the Sage website which are designed to help you to prepare real assignments in the future. We hope that you now feel in a better position to approach your assignment essays.

Review points

When reviewing your notes on this chapter, you might realise that:

- You are prepared to engage in 'writing to learn' as opposed to writing up what you know
- You are ready for the 'struggle to write': you know that you should draft and re-draft your work
- You now think of communicating successfully in your essays, using the paragraph questions (in reports you will think of reaching real readers and in presentations you will consider the audience)
- You now feel ready to tackle the most theoretical assessment form – the essay
- You realise the importance of the 10-stage plan, prepare and review strategy
- You have realised that preparing for an essay can be 'fun' and stimulating as well as an assessment activity.

Essay checklist

For every essay check:

- ☐ Have you answered the whole question?
- ☐ Have you addressed the aims and learning outcomes?
- ☐ Is there an introduction that acknowledges the significance of the question and gives the agenda of the essay?
- ☐ Would that agenda actually answer the question set?
- ☐ Are the paragraphs in the best possible order?
- ☐ Does each paragraph have its own introduction, definition, argument, evidence and final point?
- ☐ Have you referenced your evidence?
- ☐ Have you discussed your evidence?
- ☐ Is there a conclusion re-stating the main arguments and points?
- ☐ Do you use all the words from the question to prove that you have answered the whole question?
- ☐ Is there a comprehensive bibliography (referring to every source you have mentioned in the essay)?
- ☐ Is it in alphabetical order by author's surname?
- ☐ Have you proof read and made corrections?

tips

- Print your essay. Cut up the paragraphs. Mix them up. Put them in the best order.
- Allow time between writing and reviewing your essay.
- Use a computer – even for your first draft – it is easier to cut and paste and rewrite an essay that has been drafted on a computer.

Section IV

Communicating Effectively in Assignments

18

How to Produce Excellent Reports

Aims

To enable you to plan, prepare and produce excellent reports.

Learning outcomes

After reading through this chapter, and engaging with the activities, you will have:

- considered the what, why and how of the academic report
- made links between preparing the report and other successful assessment strategies (especially the 10 stages, Chapter 14)
- reviewed a report drafted by another student
- reviewed additional, online, resources.

Introducing how to write excellent reports

Report writing is becoming an increasingly popular academic assessment, especially on business and science courses. In this chapter we will be looking at the what, why and how of reports. We will also be referring back to the basic 10-stage approach to assessment (Chapter 14) which works with all your assignments – and setting you the task of reviewing a report drafted by another student.

What is a report?

The essence of the report is that it is a document designed to deal with the real world. Specifically, a report is a practical document that describes, details or analyses a situation in the real world such that the reader can make decisions or take specific actions about that situation.

1. Activity: Thinking about reports

Think about other reports you might have seen – school, surveyor's or a *Which?* magazine report – and how they worked:

- **School report**: Gives information on academic progress. The carer can use the information to assess the child's progress. If unhappy, the information in the report should help those concerned make decisions about what needs to be done to make a difference.
- **Surveyor's report**: Gives factual information on the status of a property. The buyer uses that to decide on purchase (structural integrity of the building versus price).
- ***Which?* report**: Information given allows readers to judge different items against disclosed criteria. They can then decide on what to buy depending on their own criteria (cheapest, best value, best quality, best price for a certain level of quality).

> **Query**: What do the reports have in common?

It could be argued that these reports have the following in common:

- Each report is designed to give specific information to specific readers.
- Each writer of a report knows what sort of reader they are writing for.
- The writer will expect the reader to act on the information in the report.
- The reader knows what to look for in the report – and how to use the report to make decisions.

> **Query**: How might knowing this help you to write better reports?

What is a report – well it depends... take a look of Figure 18A.

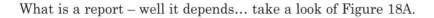

	Literature Review	General Scientific Report	Chemistry Report	Laboratory Report	Non-scientific Report	Standard Business Report	Research Report
1	Title page	Title page	Title page	Title page	Title page	Title page	Title page
2	Abstract	Abstract	Abstract	Introduction	Introduction	Executive summary	Executive summary
3	Introduction	Abbreviations	Abbreviations	Materials and methods	Main body of text	Acknowledgements	Introduction
4	Main body of text	Introduction	Introduction	Discussion	Conclusion	Table of contents	Method/methodology
5	Conclusion	Materials and methods	Results	Conclusion		Main body of text	Results/findings
6	References	Results	Discussion			Conclusion	Discussion
7		Discussion	Materials and methods			Recommendation	Conclusion
8		Acknowledgements	Acknowledgements			Bibliography/ References	Recommendation
9		References	References			Appendices	Appendices
10						Glossary	Bibliography

FIGURE 18A   Types of report

Photocopiable:

Essential Study Skills, Third Edition © Tom Burns and Sandra Sinfield, 2012 (SAGE)

What reports should have and do

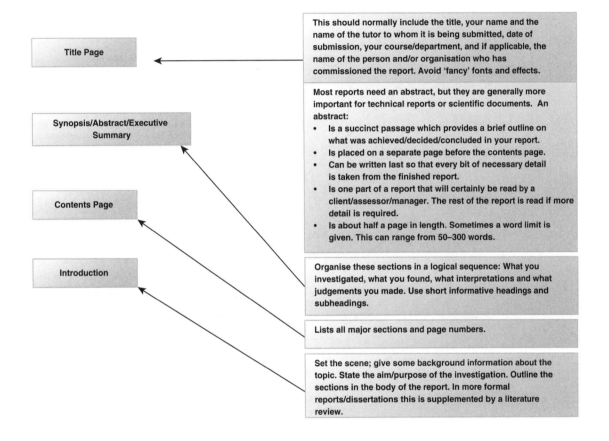

Title Page

This should normally include the title, your name and the name of the tutor to whom it is being submitted, date of submission, your course/department, and if applicable, the name of the person and/or organisation who has commissioned the report. Avoid 'fancy' fonts and effects.

Synopsis/Abstract/Executive Summary

Most reports need an abstract, but they are generally more important for technical reports or scientific documents. An abstract:
- Is a succinct passage which provides a brief outline on what was achieved/decided/concluded in your report.
- Is placed on a separate page before the contents page.
- Can be written last so that every bit of necessary detail is taken from the finished report.
- Is one part of a report that will certainly be read by a client/assessor/manager. The rest of the report is read if more detail is required.
- Is about half a page in length. Sometimes a word limit is given. This can range from 50–300 words.

Organise these sections in a logical sequence: What you investigated, what you found, what interpretations and what judgements you made. Use short informative headings and subheadings.

Contents Page

Lists all major sections and page numbers.

Introduction

Set the scene; give some background information about the topic. State the aim/purpose of the investigation. Outline the sections in the body of the report. In more formal reports/dissertations this is supplemented by a literature review.

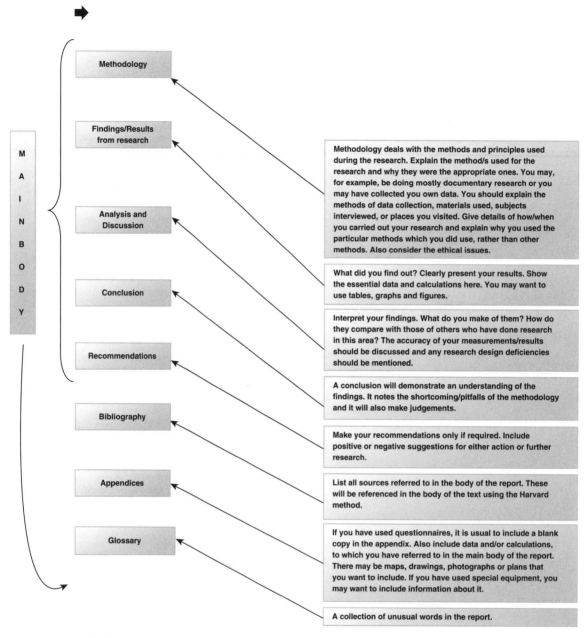

FIGURE 18B   What reports should have and do

Photocopiable:

Essential Study Skills, Third Edition © Tom Burns and Sandra Sinfield, 2012 (SAGE)

Title page

This is the front sheet of the report. This should include: title, sub-title; date; author's name and position; distribution list (reader(s) name(s) and positions(s)); reference number/course details/statements of confidentiality:

- **Title and sub-title**: Usually divided by a colon. The title gives the big picture of the report – the sub-title narrows this down. Thus the title gives a focus of the report and the sub-title indicates the scope of the report – the 'terms of reference' of the report.
- **Date**: Places the report in real time.
- **Author's name and position**: When you write a college report you are often told to assume a position – public relations expert, tax consultant… You have to write the report as though you were that person. Revealing who you 'are' tells the reader where the report is 'coming from' – and thus it reveals what angle you might be expected to adopt on the topic.
- **Distribution list**: As your position as writer might be revealing with respect to the report, so might the list of readers and their positions. You would write a different report for the bank manager than for the trade union rep.

Abstract

(Not always necessary – check with tutor.)
The abstract – synopsis or summary – is the essence or gist of your report. The abstract might include:

- overall aims
- specific objectives
- problem or task
- methodology or procedures
- key findings
- main conclusions
- key recommendations.

tips

- Journal articles typically begin with an abstract – read the journals and see how they do it.
- Check with your tutors to see what they expect.
- The abstract refers to the whole report – write it last!

Contents page

The contents page lists all the major sections of the report, including subsections and appendices – with page numbers.

The contents page allows the reader to navigate your report. Use detailed, clear headings in the report – and put them all in the contents.

tip

Check out the contents pages of books. Do they help you as a reader? How? Make yours just as useful.

Introduction

The introduction should help the reader understand the what, why and how of your report. It needs:

- Background to the report: Either why you were interested in the topic or why the report was necessary.
- Terms of reference: The focus, aims and scope of the investigation – its purpose or goal, any specific limitations.
- The methodology: The research methods you used to put the report together – Literature Review or something more practical: Interviews, questionnaires…

Findings (the body of the report)

This small word refers to the major part of your report. You sometimes do call this section findings, but you *do not* call this section 'the body'. The different sections of this part of the report need clear headings.

If using a number system, each section gets its own large number, and each sub-section gets its decimal point.

Note: When writing reports, as with essays, we have to use clear but formal English – there is no room for abbreviations or slang.

The conclusion

Each finding should have a conclusion. Conclusions point out the implications of your findings, that is, you tell your reader what they mean – tactfully.

Recommendations

Each conclusion should lead to a recommendation. Whilst the conclusions tell us what the findings mean, the recommendations tell the reader what to do about them (or more tactfully, suggests a range of things that might be possible).

Appendices

An appendix is something added on or attached to something. 'Appendices' is the plural of this.

In this section you can show your reader some of the things that you have used to compile your report. For example, if you used interviews, you would place the interview questions there. If you circulated a questionnaire, you would place a sample questionnaire there.

 **tip**

Appendices do not count in the word limit for your report – but this does not mean that you can just put everything in there. You must mention appendix items in the main parts of your report, otherwise they should not be there.

Bibliography

As with the essay:

- Harvard System: Author (date) Title, town of publication: publisher
- British Standard System: Author, Title, publisher, date.

Glossary

A glossary is literally a list of unusual words. This is especially useful in a report accessible to more than one reader: For example, a technical report that will also have to be read by a layperson (member of the public).

Presentation and style

Make sure this is:

- Neat and easy to read
- Word processed
- Consistent style: Simple basic layout used consistently throughout your whole report.

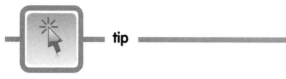

tip

Decide where you will number, underline, embolden, italicise. Save a template (pattern) and use every time you start work; check for a department style – use that.

Why write reports?

Whilst essays are theoretical and discursive, reports are designed to be practical, evaluative and analytical. Reports give you practice at developing different aspects of your written communication skills. More importantly perhaps, there are two characteristics to reports that make them significant for you:

- Reports on courses *model the reports we will write in our jobs*. Writing reports at university therefore prepares us for the work we will do.
- Reports also *model academic journal articles*. Writing reports at university can be academically challenging and may prepare us for publishing our own research.

The 'why' of individual reports

Each report that we write at university is designed to investigate a particular topic – to be read by a particular reader – and to achieve a particular purpose. If we focus on these things we can see some other 'whys' to writing each specific report that we write, and this gives us two useful questions to keep in mind when we write:

- Why am I writing this report – what am I trying to achieve?
- Why am I writing this report – what do I want my reader to think and do after reading my report?

Why write reports: Explain the world or change it?

There are three main forms of reports: Factual, instructional and persuasive; each has a different purpose and will require different arguments and evidence to achieve that purpose. It will help you write good reports if you know what you are trying to achieve before you start your report.

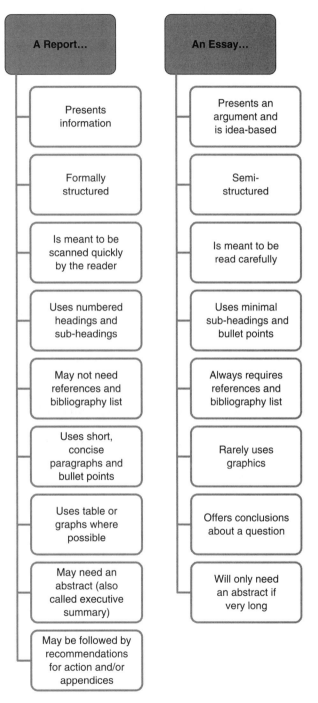

A Report...

Presents information

Formally structured

Is meant to be scanned quickly by the reader

Uses numbered headings and sub-headings

May not need references and bibliography list

Uses short, concise paragraphs and bullet points

Uses table or graphs where possible

May need an abstract (also called executive summary)

May be followed by recommendations for action and/or appendices

An Essay...

Presents an argument and is idea-based

Semi-structured

Is meant to be read carefully

Uses minimal sub-headings and bullet points

Always requires references and bibliography list

Rarely uses graphics

Offers conclusions about a question

Will only need an abstract if very long

FIGURE 18C   Reports vs. essays

- **Factual**: The factual or informative report is expected to define or establish a current situation. The school report might fall into this category.
- **Instructional**: The instructional, explanatory, report is supposed to explore a situation and suggest a range of options for further action. The *Which?* report might fall into this category.
- **Persuasive**: The persuasive or leading report is supposed to investigate a problem and suggest a specific course of action. A surveyor's report might fall into this category.

The line between these reports is blurred; but do try to set your goals before you start your own report.

Query: Are you writing a report right now? Is it factual, instructional, persuasive? Will this affect you in any way?

tips

- If your report is factual, you will be gathering information to fully explain or define a situation.
- If your report is instructional, you will be gathering the information to explain a problem and offer a range of solutions.
- If your report is persuasive, you will be gathering the information to explain a problem and recommend just one solution.

Why write the report? What I want my reader to think and do...

Unlike an essay, which is often written as though for an intelligent, interested member of the public, a report is written for a specific reader or readers. These are real people. The thing with real people is that they have wants, needs and beliefs; a head of Human Resources will be influenced by different arguments from those that interest the Union representative, for example. Therefore, if you want to influence a real reader, and make them think and do what you want, you must consider the reader when planning and writing your report.

Key questions to consider here might be:

- Who is my reader?
- What can I expect my reader to already know about this topic?
- How can I deal with this in my report?
- What can I expect my reader to believe about my topic?
- How can I deal with this in my report?
- What can I expect my reader to want from this report?
- How can I deal with this in my report?
- What will I want my reader to think and do after reading my report?
- What language, tone and style will my reader respond to?

 **tip**

When drafting reports, think of the language, evidence and examples that will influence your real readers.

How to plan and prepare a report

When writing reports, don't forget the 10 stages to assignment success – they work with reports as well:

1 Prepare
2 Follow the action plan
3 Review your findings
4 Plan the structure
5 Write a rough draft
6 Leave a time lag
7 Review, revise and edit: Struggle to write
8 Proof read
9 Hand in
10 SWOT feedback.

If this is the first chapter in the book that you are reading, you might like to read through Chapter 14 before proceeding. That chapter looks at *How to...* strategies that will work with all your assignments.

Questions to ask yourself when planning your report

- Why is this report necessary? What is the background, situation or problem that needs to be tackled?
- What am I trying to achieve with this report?
- Am I *describing* a situation or trying to find a *solution*? Am I offering just one solution or several? Will I be factual/instructional/persuasive?
- Who is my reader?
  - What might they know on the topic?
  - What might be their beliefs/attitudes?
  - What might they want from my report?

- What do I want my reader to think and do?
  - How will I make that happen?

- What am I going to have to do to gather information to prepare my report?
- How much reading will I have to do?
- How much primary research will I have to do – and what sort (interviews/question-naires/focus groups)?
- How will I justify my methodology – what can I say about interviews/questionnaires/focus groups?

 **tip**

Read relevant journal articles and see how they justify their methodological approaches.

- If using interviews, questionnaires or focus groups to gather information:
  - How will I design my questionnaire? How will I keep the questions open and useful? Who will I get to fill them in? How will I make this happen?
  - How will I design my interview questions? How will I conduct interviews and make sure I do not influence the outcomes – but get real information?
  - Should I try to run a focus group? Who would I get to take part? How can I get real opinions?
  - How will I critically analyse the data that I collect?
- What sections will my report need?

tips

- Think of clear titles – headings and sub-headings that you can use. Make sure that they reveal what is going on to your reader.
- Think of the language, tone and style that will impress your potential reader.
- Make sure that there is a conclusion for each section of the body of your report.
- Write a recommendation for each conclusion.
- When proof reading: Do not look for all your mistakes at once. Keep a record of all the mistakes that you commonly make. Look for one of 'your' mistakes at a time.

LearnHigher

For useful resources explore LearnHigher especially their pages on Report Writing, Doing Research and Listening and Interpersonal Skills.

2. Activity: Review this student report

The report is a practical document. It is designed to get you to analyse a real-world situation, to draw conclusions based on your analysis and make recommendations based on your conclusions.

One way to engage with report writing is to review a report yourself. Therefore, the activity that we recommend here is that you read through this student report – and evaluate it.

Report: An evaluation of the impact of the Study Skills course on a first year student

For: The University Management Team
By: XXXX, First year student
Date: July 2011

Contents:

Introduction
Terms of Reference
Methodology

Introduction

This report will describe and discuss some of my most valuable learning experiences and skills that I have learnt while on the Study Skills module. Study Skills are techniques developed to aid the student to become successful, they encourage learning and help establish certain routines or ways of studying (Northedge, 1997).

Terms of Reference

The skills that the report will investigate are Active Learning, Reflective Learning, the Learning Contract, and Active Research and Reading.

Methodology

This is a personal report using my own experiences as a case study. Thus the method is that I will reflect on my own development as I learned and practised the study skills that appear to have made the most difference to me.

Findings: Study Skills and Student Success

These skills are supposed to give students means to gain knowledge by being active in their research, setting goals, being more critical in their approach and their way of thinking, making the essential links between the learning overview and the coursework, and also understanding what is being asked and how best to achieve that. This ultimately leads to being in control of your studies which boosts confidence.

Active Learning

The most valuable learning experience that I have had while on this Study Skills module is the talks on active learning. Active learning is about taking responsibility for your learning, being accountable and getting involved with your studies (Burns and Sinfield, 2012). It is planning ahead, thinking critically, producing solutions and understanding what it is that you are studying, which gives you a stronger foundation to build upon and take your learning to the next level.

Everything that we did on the module involved active learning – active reading, note-making, discussing, and so on. Beginning with a close scrutiny of the course handbook set the ground for this. We examined the aims and learning outcomes of the module as a whole. We examined the syllabus and considered what we would be doing and why; this all helped to develop an overview of our studies. Finally, we all drew up individual Learning Contracts in the light of what we had learned. Thus, each student was encouraged to understand the form and content of the module and to set personal goals; which was very much an exercise in taking that responsibility for our own learning. By being active in your studies you take the initiative to become a more capable student in control of your learning and therefore more fulfilled generally. I have always believed in taking responsibility for oneself but it has never occurred to me (until now) to apply this to my studies.

Reflective Learning

The learning log has been an important skill that I have learnt through the Study Skills module. It is a reflective daily or weekly diary of your studies and progress (Burns and Sinfield, 2012). At the end of each day or week you ask yourself a series of questions regarding each class/seminar/lecture/book, etc. studied in that period – questions such as: What was it about (the main points and meanings)? Why is it important? What have I learnt from it? and What is my reaction or feeling to it? These questions in a log or diary encourage the student to become an active learner and take responsibility for their studies. Being active via the learning log helps to make links between the class, book work, the learning outcomes in the handbook and your own experiences; you are able to interpret information and think critically about your day or week. This gives you a much deeper understanding of what is being asked of you (Cottrell, 1999); ultimately gaining the confidence needed to become an effective student and take control of your studies. I believe this tool will be of great importance to me, not only as a reference guide, but also it will be the foundation for my future studies.

Learning Contract

Another tool, which will be of great value to me, is the Learning Contract. The Learning Contract is a personal affirmation which answers a series of probing questions; such as what you want from your studies or course, the possible difficulties you may come across, what you are prepared to do in order to achieve your goals and the changes to your life once you have accomplished those goals. By answering these questions, the student

➡

➡

becomes conscious of what it is they want from their studies (O'Dell, 2001). They take ownership of their goals (Burns and Sinfield, 2012) and realise what realistic goals or targets can be set and how best to achieve them (O'Dell, 2001); in this way the Learning Contract then becomes an indispensable motivational tool (Burns and Sinfield, 2012). Further, by reviewing past (and present) contracts the student can reflect on what has been accomplished and what can still be achieved in their studies. In my own experience I have found that by setting goals, working towards those goals and then achieving them, I can take control of my future studies/work, etc. and subsequently gain confidence and accelerate in those areas.

Active Research and Reading

The QOOQRRR active research and reading tool has been a revelation for me. By scanning, questioning, reading, re-reading and reviewing your work, you become much more effective, efficient and active within research by being more selective in your approach to it. It teaches you to think critically and to question what it is you are researching (Burns and Sinfield, 2012). This has been discussed by many people, one being Edward Glaser (1941, lost page number …); he said:

> 'Critical thinking calls for a persistent effort to examine any belief or supposed form of knowledge in the light of the evidence that supports it and the further conclusions to which it tends.'

By being critical in your approach and making the necessary links through research, you have a much greater understanding of the area or topic – and what is being asked of you. This ultimately leads you to produce a better outcome … **[I need more here …]** thus gaining confidence. This tool will become invaluable to my future learning as it can be applied to all aspects of study, including essays, presentations, reports, etc.; it gives me the knowledge needed to accelerate and become a successful student.

Conclusions

Good Study Skills are all about active, critical and reflective learning. They occur when students take control of their learning – and this report focused on several ways to do this.

Active Learning

Active Learning was the focus – and it involved actively doing things: reading, note-making, discussing – but also thinking actively as well: Planning ahead, thinking critically, taking the initiative, producing solutions. This laid the foundation for success in future studies.

Reflective Learning

We used a daily learning log to actively reflect on what we did, why we did it – and what we learned in the process. This active reflection became part of our active learning – leaving a record of all that we had done on the course. Without this we would not have felt that we learned anything.

Learning Contract

The Learning Contract was of value to me and to all students. They take ownership of their goals and the Learning Contract becomes an indispensable motivational tool.

Active Research and Reading

The QOOQRRR active research and reading tool was a revelation. This tool will become invaluable to my future learning as it can be applied to all aspects of study, including essays, presentations, reports, etc.; it helps me find the knowledge needed to become a successful student.

Recommendations

The Study Skills course was one of the best things I have done. I saw how active you have to be to be a successful student. I would recommend that other students do a course like this, but even if not on a course like this they should definitely take control of their studies, think critically and reflectively, set their own goals in a Learning Contract and review their own learning in a learning log.

Bibliography

Burns, T. and Sinfield. S. (2012) *Essential Study Skills: The Complete Guide To Success at University.* London: Sage
Cottrell (1999) *The Study Skills Handbook* [where?]: Palgrave
Edward Glaser (1941) (forgotten where I got this – back to library!)
Northedge (1997) *The Good Study Guide* (publisher?)
O'Dell (2001) (forgotten where I got this – back to library!)

Now answer these questions:

- How good do you think the report is and why?
- Does it make a difference knowing this is the first assignment written by this student – and it is her second draft?
- What advice would you give this student in order to write a better report?

➡

299

Query: What did you gain from this activity? Did you review any parts of the chapter – or any additional resources – to help you critique this report? (You might find the resources on the LearnHigher site useful.)

Discussion: We are often asked by students for models of the academic writing that they have to undertake. It is always difficult – do you show a brilliant piece of work in order to inspire – and end up intimidating? Do you show something of poor quality that they can improve upon…?

Well, here we hoped to show something that a real student has cared about and invested real time in. They have not dashed this off in a few minutes. They have tried to do the best they could – and they have worked hard. At the same time, it is not the most brilliant piece of work.

Think about the sort of feedback that would help you to improve if this had been your first report… and write that down.

We have included a report checklist at the end of this chapter – it is designed to help you to review your own future reports. It may help you to review the student report above.

3. Activity: Optional – write your own report

One way to make reading effective and meaningful is to have a specific assignment question in mind when you read. Moreover, we have been looking at report writing – and reports are practical documents designed to investigate real-world situations. So, to help you review online resources designed to help with report writing, write a report on the following:

A report on the usefulness to new students of online resources on report writing

Advice:

- Go to the LearnHigher pages on Doing Research, Report Writing and Listening and Interpersonal Skills.
- Explore the resources and see how they can help you as a student and as a report writer.

The Report Writing site covers much of what we have highlighted here – including offering report structure information and checklists. It also has a useful section on using graphical data and a discussion comparing the report to a dissertation.

The Doing Research site will also be useful to you when preparing your dissertation, with a section on: 'What is research?' and tutorials on collecting data ('Collect this'); data analysis ('Analyse this'); getting started with SPSS; and a link to 'Engage in Research', an interactive resource for bioscience students.

Listening and Interpersonal skills offers information, video tutorials and interactive resources on body language, open and closed questions, and more.

And finally – check out this interactive site for scientific reports. Initially, it may seem a bit complicated, but it's quite easy to follow once you have read the guide they provide: http://www.ncsu.edu/labwrite/

tips

- Analyse the usefulness of the various resources to you as a student. If you are really into the swing of this activity prepare a brief report on the question set above.
- At the very least, blog your findings or make a note in your learning log about the usefulness of those resources – especially to a new student.
- Make sure you actually do something with the information.

Conclusion

We have looked in some detail at the academic report, making links to the strategies necessary for any successful academic assignment. As always, we recommend that you reflect on everything that you have read and done, and what you have learned about the report. Make brief, pattern notes to remind yourself of all the things that you will now follow up and do to plan for, research and write a really great report.

Review points

When reviewing your notes on this chapter, you might realise that:

- You can now look at report writing in a more positive light
- You now feel ready to tackle your academic report
- You have read and 'marked' a real student report
- You have started exploring online tutorials to develop your approaches to report writing, data collection and analysis.

Report checklist

Photocopy this checklist and use it with every report that you write.

- ☐ What was my aim in writing this report?
- ☐ Have I achieved my goals?
- ☐ Is the title page adequate: title and sub-title; author and position; reader and position? Date?
- ☐ Is the title/sub-title appropriate?
- ☐ Was an abstract necessary? Is there one? Is it clear?
- ☐ Is there a contents page? Is it clear?
- ☐ Is there an introduction?
- ☐ Are there sub-sections on:

    - Background?
    - Terms of reference?
    - Methodology?

- ☐ Are the sections and sub-sections of the findings clearly labelled?
- ☐ Does the reader get sufficient information to make the decisions I desire?
- ☐ Is all the information necessary or have I written too much?
- ☐ Can the reader follow the development of my ideas? Are they laid out logically?
- ☐ Is the layout simple and consistent?
- ☐ Are the language and tone suitable for the actual reader?
- ☐ Is the style appropriate to the subject and reader?
- ☐ Do I offer sufficient evidence to 'prove' my points?
- ☐ Do I discuss my evidence/data?
- ☐ Does my conclusion follow logically from my arguments?
- ☐ Is there a 'conclusion' for every section of the body?
- ☐ Have I really laid the groundwork for my recommendations?
- ☐ Is there a recommendation for each conclusion?
- ☐ Should there be a glossary? If there is one, is it comprehensive?
- ☐ Are the appendices clearly labelled? Is the reader directed to each appendix in the body of the report?
- ☐ Is the bibliography adequate? Is it laid out in the correct way? (Remember, alphabetical order by author's surname.)

Obviously if the answer to any of these questions is 'No' then you must make the necessary changes.

Photocopiable:

Essential Study Skills, Third Edition © Tom Burns and Sandra Sinfield, 2012 (SAGE)

Section IV

Communicating Effectively in Assignments

19

How to Write a
Brilliant Dissertation

Aims

To help you prepare and write a brilliant dissertation that has followed your research interests and captured your own voice.

Learning outcomes

After reading through this chapter, and engaging with the activities, you will have:

- considered the what, why and how of the academic dissertation
- started the process of organising yourself to plan, prepare and draft your dissertation
- been guided towards the processes of setting your research project in motion.

Brilliant dissertations and research projects

A dissertation or major project is increasingly becoming a requirement for all Honours degrees. These normally equate to a double credit module and therefore account for a substantial part of your third year coursework and degree grade. Your dissertation can be a vehicle for enhancing career opportunities, further research that you might want to do, enable access to other courses – MA, PGCE, MPhil, TEFL – or any other activity that you see as enhancing your life and/or career.

Your whole course should be feeding into your dissertation research question. If you were passive in your studies up until now (and readers of this book would not have been!), this is the opportunity to change and become active: demonstrate independent choice, research and analytical skills.

Why undertake research projects?

The project allows you to discover an area of your subject that really interests you. It is designed to help you to take forward research into that area such that you develop deep and intimate knowledge of that subject – and of how to undertake research in your field.

You are supposed to read the existing literature to discover the most up-to-date knowledge-claims on the topic. This review of the literature should reveal to you areas that are contemporary or contentious; these would be the areas that you could follow up in your own research.

I want to change the world…

A typical first stumbling block for most students is choosing their research question. They want to change the world – but are not quite sure how to phrase the question.

A quick tip here is to relax – you are unlikely to change the world with your undergraduate dissertation – but it can change things for you. So, if you want to do well think first: 'What am I actually interested in?', and, if being strategic: 'What topic might help me get that job… or that place on the postgraduate course that I'm interested in?'

Be realistic – we may not revolutionise knowledge construction in one third-year dissertation, but it is not a bad place to start.

 **tip**

Ask 'Does the question allow me to show how clever I am?' and 'Does the question facilitate do-able data collection and analysis?'

What is a dissertation?

Here we outline the basic dissertation structure but do remember your department will have their own guidelines.

tip

Make notes of your own in the table below – make this your own.

Sections of a report

Section	Features	Comments and Tips
Title page	Title of dissertation Your name Organisation/Course Date	
Abstract	Summary of every part.	Write it last.
Contents page	The sections of the dissertation clearly labelled. Page numbers.	
Introduction	Acknowledges significance of the area under research. May give the background or context to this project (why it was undertaken). Gives the terms of reference, the aims & scope of the project.	
Literature Review	A significant section critiquing the relevant literature on the theory/ies being explored in the research project. Relates the literature to your research objectives. Typically, you will utilise similar methodological approaches to those used by the theorists that you cite – or give reasons why you are using different approaches: then you may critique the methods used in the literature reviewed – if this can be used to justify your own methods.	See www.learnhigher.ac.uk for a range of Literature Reviews. Structure the Literature Review around your research objectives.
Methodology	Justifies the approach that you took in your research – whether you used quantitative or qualitative data and why.	PhD theses in your subject area will typically have justified their methodological approaches – note how they did this.
Results/Findings	Presentation of the data acquired during the research phase.	Go to the web addresses on data suggested in the 'Resources for the presentation and interpretation of data' box below.
Discussion	Interprets and evaluates your findings and reveals the significance of your analysis.	Go to journal articles/PhD theses to see how academics in your field discuss their findings.

Conclusion	This lays out the conclusions that can be drawn from the research undertaken, the findings and your discussion.
Recommendations	Lays out the recommendations that can be drawn from the conclusions if appropriate.
Glossary	List of terms, e.g. acronyms used.
Bibliography	List of all references in the correct format.
Appendices	Attachments, e.g. questionnaires and surveys used.

Additional resources: For a comprehensive web textbook on undertaking research projects, including major issues in research and evaluation; ethics; sampling; measurement; design; analysis; and write up – go to: http://www. socialresearchmethods.net/kb/

Thinking about time

You need to be especially strategic with your use of time when undertaking a long project like a dissertation for you will have several key time-consuming stages to work through:

- Think of research angle
- Research the literature to discover the key theories and developments that you are going to explore in practice
- Draft Literature Review
- Decide on methods – justify
- Write methods
- Put research methods into practice and gather data
- Analyse data
- Reflect on data – plug gaps…
- Write findings – with reference to the points identified in the Literature Review
- Discuss findings
- Draw conclusions…
- Review, revise and edit…
- Proof read
- Bind
- Hand in.

This complex and lengthy process requires even more systematic and strategic organisation of your time than usual.

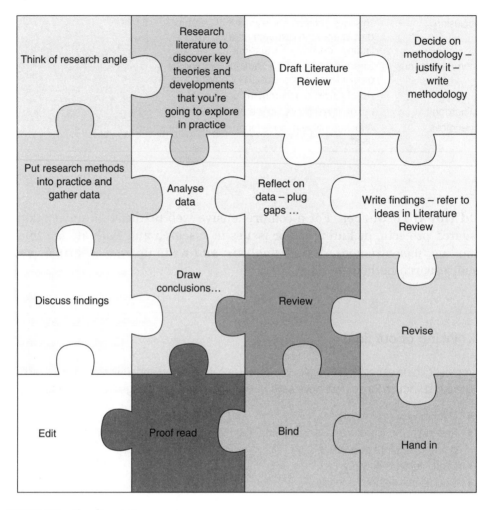

FIGURE 19A   The dissertation process

How to prepare and write your dissertation

It starts with the question

❝ I did my dissertation on the value of new media to actors, directors, camera operators and everybody technical in the film industry. When I applied for work in the business, I really did have information that made me stand out! **❞**

We have included a dissertation pattern note at the end of the chapter – follow it and it will help you generate your dissertation proposal.

tips

Look back over the reading that you have already undertaken on your degree – especially in the modules that have introduced you to the key theoretical concepts in your subject – and key research methods. Ask yourself:

- What are the key issues?
- What interests you?
- What would you like to explore in some depth?

Research question and objectives

To decide on your question, think about your course: Which modules were the most interesting and which topics sparked the most debate in class? Which did you think about long after the class was over? The trick is to find something that you are really interested in and try to get a question from that.

tips

- If you don't know what to research or why... Make sure you keep a notebook in your pocket everyday on placement or at work. Make notes of interesting things that happen – especially things that relate to the theories covered on modules that you enjoyed and that you might like to research further. Annotate these notes later to kick start your reflective thinking.
- If you will be researching an aspect of your work that happens already, make sure that you do make notes that record what has already happened. What interests you about this topic? Why?
- What sort of research can you undertake in your workplace? Are there any ethical considerations?

- Can you undertake action research? When turning theory into action in your workplace think about setting up an action research project. You will need to agree this with your line manager – and make sure that all the correct ethical procedures have been followed.

Once you have a question: Examine it asking yourself two sets of questions:

- **Theory**: Which theory will I be drawing on here? What have I already covered on this or a related topic? What additional reading will I be doing? What aspect of my practice relates to the theories I am exploring? Am I already engaged in relevant activities at work – or will I have to set up some specific activity to allow me to investigate the theories in practice?
- **Methods**: What reading will I have to do to justify my methods?

Doing the research: Make sure that you plan what has to happen – and when it will happen. Consider the following: When will you undertake the activity? What will you need to do before the activity? What resources will be necessary? How will you set it up? How will you make sure people engage? How will you evaluate your findings?

If you cannot undertake your project or dissertation research in your own workplace – where are you going to do it – and how are you going to arrange it? What sort of permissions will you need? Are there any specific ethical considerations?

What will you have to do to set your research in motion? What resources are necessary? How will you set it up? How will you make sure people engage? How will you get participants…? What follow-up action might be necessary or ethical?

Ethics and legal constraints

It is a requirement of all dissertations that they have clear ethical statements indicating that the research was conducted without harm, that anonymity was maintained, that participants gave informed consent and retained the right to withdraw from your research at any time – and that the research was carried out within the frameworks of the institution and the profession, and within the laws of the United Kingdom. You must find and use the appropriate statements for your subject, department and professional body or association.

Scary bit: Your question can be the point things can go wrong – not least because of potential ethical considerations about who or what we want to investigate and how we think we are going to gather data. This is where academia intersects with the real world, real people and professional bodies. It is not that the question itself is the problem but how it will be tackled. Things to think about: 'Am I researching vulnerable people or people under 18 years of age?'. Here there are extra legal and professional constraints that must be adhered to as this is where a career can be ended. Your institution will have guidelines: you must use them.

Literature Review

Your Literature Review is where you locate your dissertation in your academic discipline, in its epistemology – and into the conversation that your subject is having with and about the world. It is where you conduct research into the current literature in the area that you are interested in.

A Literature Review is not an annotated bibliography – where you just write notes on everything that you read. You have to select your reading with care – with a view to how the people before you covered your topic, how they researched it – and the conclusions they drew. You then have to write a long essay drawing their ideas together – in a way that launches your own research. A good Literature Review gives focus and shape to the dissertation that is to come.

tips

- Read upwards of 30 sources – of these you may focus on one, two or five or more key textbooks. You might review 10 or more journal articles – perhaps articles written recently by the people who wrote the chapters in the textbooks. This keeps your theory up to date.
- Know whether your subject requires more of an empirical or more of a theoretical approach.

Methods

All dissertations require you to justify your methods – how you researched the topic – and how you gathered and analysed your data. You will also be expected to critique your research methods. Be aware that the methods that you choose will also signpost a philosophical and ideological position. That is, they fall into different camps: Positivist, postmodernist, interpretivist, ethnographic – and you may be expected to consciously place your work within those paradigms and justify your decision. For the most part, the main issue is not contradicting yourself: For example a postmodernist is unlikely to rely on quantitative data.

Quantitative research: Encompasses a group of methods focusing on quantities, on numbers. It is argued that the larger the scale, the greater the reliability. This method includes randomised controlled trials, cohort studies and controlled studies. Generally falling within the positivist, normative paradigms, it is seen as more scientific, objective and rational than qualitative research because it is not supposed to involve personal or subjective judgements but objective, accurate noting of facts – of realities. Critics argue that it tells us the what – but not the why of phenomena.

Qualitative research: Located within the social sciences and the humanities – dealing with social phenomena – beliefs and experiences – that have reference to the wider contexts of lived lives. Researchers in this paradigm utilise interviews, focus groups and participant observation, arguing that it generates deeper and richer data. This approach is criticised for being non-factual, subjective and unreliable.

Although specific types of methods are associated with particular paradigms, they are not exclusive and it is argued that by mixing methods we increase the internal validity of the research project. Note – not by reducing bias but by supplying more data – from another angle or place.

To do this, we could be conducting a survey or a questionnaire to flag up particular issues – this would then feed into our interview design for the next stage of our research. Here we are gathering statistical data to capture a snapshot of issues of concern to follow up in our qualitative research rather than claiming any statistical relevance.

Equally, when we have conducted interviews to gain personal responses we could then code those responses, for example by pulling out how many times a female respondent expressed one thing – and a male respondent expressed something different. This could be represented in a table or a pie chart. Thus a qualitative method can be expressed in a quantitative way.

tips

- For interactive quantitative/qualitative research methods tutorials, with explanation, quizzes and resources, see: http://www.nottingham.ac.uk/nursing/sonet/rlos/ebp/qvq/index.html

- See LearnHigher for: Doing research: What is research; Collect This – tutorial on the principles of data collection; Analyse this – analysis of quantitative and qualitative data; Survey Design; Getting Started with SPSS
- Follow up the Wikipedia entries on quantitative and qualitative research methods. Whilst tutors often dislike Wikipedia as a source of information, following the links will take you to peer-reviewed material that tutors will like:

  o http://en.wikipedia.org/wiki/Qualitative_research
  o http://en.wikipedia.org/wiki/Quantitative

Resources for the presentation and interpretation of data

- Probability associated with inferential statistics tutorial – with explanation, quizzes and resources: http://www.nottingham.ac.uk/nursing/sonet/rlos/statistics/probability/3.html
- Descriptive statistics for interval and ratio scale: Includes mean, mode, median, measures of dispersion and standard deviation – with explanation, quizzes and resources: http://www.nottingham.ac.uk/nursing/sonet/rlos/statistics/descriptive_stats/index.html
- Real datasets combined with worksheets to create authentic scenario-based learning activities around the analysis of data. Examples relate the subject areas of Business, Health and Psychology: http://stars.ac.uk/
- Animated resource demonstrates how to convert survey or experimental data into cross-tabular data and the steps involved in this process: http://www.ucel.ac.uk/rlos/cross_tab_data/main.html

---

Findings/Analysis

Findings/Analysis is where you present the data you have gathered via your primary research which may be accompanied with tables or graphs. You sum everything up – but show, emphasise and say what your significant findings are. This is where many students do not do justice to their research – they just present all the data without identifying the most significant aspect. You need to say what is the most important and why.

Discussion/Conclusions

This is where you link the findings and what was found to be significant back to the Literature Review – point by point. It can feel like you have already said what needs to be said; but this is where we are pulling it all together, spelling out to the reader what is important and why. Linking this to the Literature Review and research question can feel repetitious but needs to be done.

It is here that we can also bring in new sources to support our analysis. It is worth noting that if the additional source is going to have a major impact on the analysis and not just act as an additional point it may be worth going back and adding a new section on them to the Literature Review.

tip

Read many different dissertations and read many different journal articles. See how people write about their methods and see how they present and discuss their findings. You need to become familiar with how others present this information. There is not one model – there will be many different ways to do this, but you must discover a way to present your ideas and you must feel confident that you are doing it well.

Recommendations

Some dissertations invite you to end with a recommendations section. This can indicate the necessity for further research that needs to be undertaken, especially where that research could overcome any limitations or problems that you have identified with your own data collection. Certain research in professional fields might flag up the need to revise policy or practice.

Each recommendation should flow from a conclusion. Each conclusion should flow from a Finding/Discussion Point – and this should all be supported in the Literature Review.

Conclusion

In this chapter we have tried to encourage you to see your dissertation as an opportunity – not a problem. It is your chance to explore something that you are really interested in. To give yourself time to focus on something that you think is significant or relevant and to conduct research using a method that is appropriate – but also of interest to you. Do use the dissertation pattern note at the chapter end to help you think about your own ideas – and generate your dissertation proposal. We have given an introduction to all the things you need to think about to plan for and undertake your dissertation and we have provided links to online resources – including interactive tutorials – that you might like to take to develop areas that you are having particular issues with.

Review points

When reviewing your notes on this chapter, you might realise that:

- You can now look at the dissertation in a positive light; it is a chance to follow your own interests, to research something that you find interesting or meaningful – and to present your findings in an academic mode but in your own voice

1. Activity: Review online resources – keep a record in your journal

We have gathered together some links to online resources designed to help you with your research and your whole dissertation process. There are also specific sites for Science, Education and postgraduate students. There will be more resources online from our Sage website – including a very user-friendly PowerPoint on the Literature Review.

As always, we recommend that you engage with these sites and note what they have to offer and what you will be using – why and when… If keeping a learning log or dissertation journal – or for your own study blog or PDP file – make a note of how useful they have been to you as a student.

On-line Literature Review (on student reading): http://litreview.pbwiki.com/
LearnHigher pages on research: http://www.learnhigher.ac.uk/resourcepages/doing research/doingresearch.html
Cornell University site: http://www.socialresearchmethods.net/kb/
CETL-AURS: Interactive research site for science students – how to conduct Literature Reviews and improve scientific writing: http://www.engageinresearch.ac.uk/
Education Studies – Action Research website – with links to BERA: http://www.jeanmcniff.com/index.html
Publisher's forum on Research Methods: http://www.methodspace.com/
Postgraduate – Managing your research project: http://www.vitae.ac.uk/1220/Managing-your-research-project.html and: http://www.unisa.edu.au/ltu/students/research/default.asp

Use Figure 19B to help clarify your thinking and to help you write your own Dissertation Proposal.

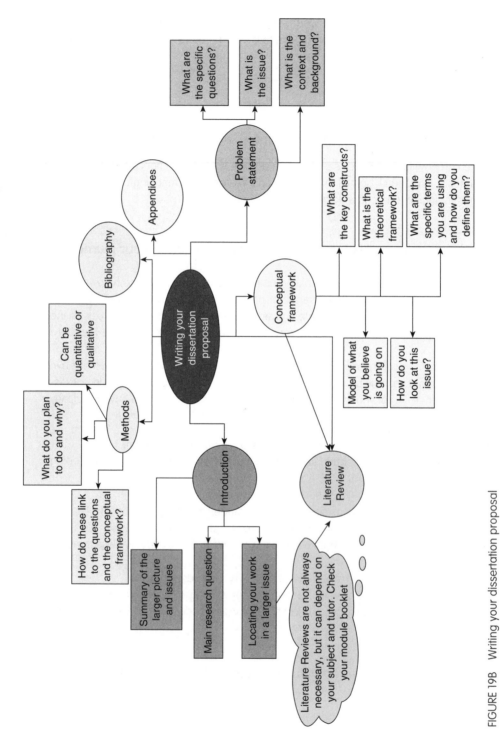

FIGURE 19B   Writing your dissertation proposal

(Adapted from Golde, C. (1997) *Some Thoughts on Dissertation and Proposal Writing*)

Section IV

Communicating Effectively in Assignments

20

How to Deliver Excellent Presentations

Aims

To enable you to prepare and deliver excellent presentations.

Learning outcomes

After reading through this chapter, and engaging with the activities, you will have:

- considered the what, why and how of presentations
- considered the nature of oral communication and issues surrounding communicating effectively, especially in presentations
- started the process of organising yourself for successful presentations
- made links between preparing a presentation and other activities covered in this text: organisation and time management; using the overview; being creative; notemaking; targeted research; and active reading.

Oral communications: The presentation

Typically introduced onto academic programmes to acknowledge that most of us are much better at speaking than we are at writing, presentations are becoming an increasingly popular assessment tool with tutors. Of course, what this glosses over is that students, alongside every normal human being on the planet, tend to be terrified of public speaking, of presentations. We cannot make all the fear go away, but we can help you to realise that you can get really good at presentations – you might even get to enjoy them.

❝ I really hated the thought of presentations, but once they were over I felt so good about myself. In the end I wanted more of them. **❞**

What is a presentation?

There are several 'whats' to a presentation that we are going to cover here – they are all true. The trick for you, as always, is to think 'How will knowing this help me to give better presentations?'

It's just talking, isn't it?

A presentation is a formal talk of a set length on a set topic given to a set, knowable, audience. When preparing your presentation you have to think about all these factors: time, topic, audience. That is, you have to fit the topic into the time you have been given – there is no point saying that it could not fit into five minutes. If that was the task, then that is what you have to do.

You also have to pitch the topic at your actual audience. Again, as with the report, these are real people with real knowledge, thoughts and feelings. You have to make sure that your language, style and tone are just right for the real people that you are going to address. Finally, you have to make sure that any audiovisual aids (AVA), your supporting material – handouts, PowerPoint, websites, photographs, posters – are appropriate and will connect with your actual audience.

❝ I remember this presentation, it was on breast cancer, a really frightening topic, and the students had left all the funny noises on their PowerPoint. So there they were giving life and death statistics and scaring everyone silly, and all the while there are explosions, and whistles, flying noises and breaking glass! **❞**

It's all an act

No matter what anyone else tells you, remember that a presentation is a *performance*. You are standing in front of people and talking to them: they are looking at and listening to you – this is a performance. Therefore you are a performer. Use this knowledge. Like any performance a presentation is an act. To make it work for you, *act* happy, confident and interested – even if you are bored silly or scared witless. If you are happy, your audience can be happy, if you are not, they cannot. If you are bored – your audience will be too… and if your audience is not interested, then this fails as oral communication. So act your socks off.

It's an act – positive body language

Remember the performance aspect of the presentation and resolve to use positive body language:

- do face the audience
- do not only look at the whiteboard behind you
- do stand or sit straight
- do not hold anything in front of your face
- do smile
- do not tap your foot or hand or make chopping motions with your hands
- do draw people calmly into your presentation with brief welcoming gestures
- do not hold your arms defensively in front of your body
- do stand in a relaxed manner
- do not stand there with clenched fists or looking as if you want to be somewhere else
- do dress for success
- (in a group presentation) do not act as if you hate everybody else on the team
- do ACT calm, confident and in control.

It's communication

As a performer, you will have to build a rapport with your audience and create a relationship with them. You will also have to communicate and interact with them. This means that you will need to *look at them*. You will have to make eye contact with everybody in your audience.

So ignore those who advise you to look at the ceiling at the back of the room. That may be okay if you have an audience of 1,000 or more people, but in a small group it looks weird, and not in a good way. You will need to look at people to draw them into your talk and take them with you. You will also need to check that they are following and understanding what you say. This will tell you when you have to repeat or explain something. You will never discover this if you do not look at your audience.

Further, to be a successful performer, just like an actor on the stage, *you must never, ever speak from a script*. You must not read a presentation. You must learn your presentation and then deliver it fresh, as though for the first time. Reading a presentation is the quickest way to lose your audience and lose marks.

The formal convention

The presentation has the same form (formal convention) as the essay – and it has the same need to address real audiences as the report. Therefore, you should have a sense of the presentation already from what you now know about essays and reports.

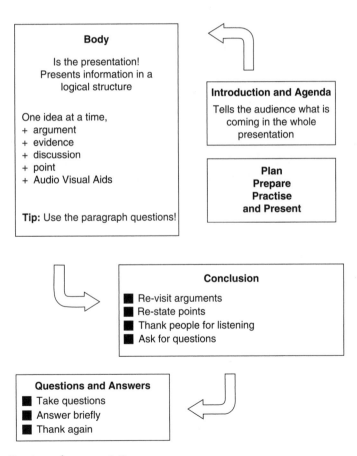

FIGURE 20A   Structure of a presentation

Presentation explanations

Introduction

The Introduction should include a clear agenda:

- Introduce yourself
- Give the topic title
- Make opening remarks
- Give the agenda of the talk.

The Introduction is where you acknowledge the question and hook the audience; tell them why they should be listening to you. Are you going to be interesting, useful or funny? Will it help them pass an exam or get better grades? Will it save them time or effort? Think of something.

The agenda is where you tell the audience exactly what is coming in your presentation. Without an agenda the audience does not know where the talk is going. This is unsettling – and confusing. A confused audience is not a happy audience. Tell them what is coming... and this simple technique will dramatically improve the presentation itself and your marks.

Body

This is the presentation. This is where you answer the question that you were set.

As with the essay, think about one big idea at a time – supported by argument and evidence – and AVA. Think about building a logical case.

tip

Use the paragraph questions to structure the sections of your presentation:

- What is this section about?
- What exactly is that?
- Tell me more?
- What is your evidence? What does it mean?
- How does this relate back to the question as a whole?

There are two main purposes of using AVAs:

- To help the audience follow and make sense of your presentation, e.g. an outline of the whole presentation, a poster or pattern note of the whole presentation
- To illustrate, emphasise or underline your points, e.g. a quote, a picture, an example, a physical object.

Conclusion

As with the essay conclusion, this is where you draw the whole presentation together. Re-visit your main arguments, re-emphasise your main points – and use all the words from the question to prove that you have answered the whole question.

 **tips**

- Write introductions and conclusions last.
- Accept this is a repetitive structure: tell them what is coming; tell them; tell them what you told them. This can feel silly, obvious or uncomfortable, especially in a short presentation. But this is what is required, so bite the bullet and do it!

The question and answer session

It's over – you want to rush out screaming! Don't.

You now have to thank the audience for listening and ask them for questions.

 **tips**

- Do re-phrase difficult questions – check that you have understood.
- Do keep answers short.
- Do keep answers good-natured.
- Do notice when people put their hands up – take questions in order.
- Do not start fighting your audience.
- Do not try to make everyone agree with you.
- Do not think that you have to know everything (unless it is a job interview or an oral exam).

- If you cannot answer why not try: 'That is a very good question – what does everyone else think?' If no one else knows, 'Well, that has given us all something to think about. Thank you again for listening!'
- Do bring the question and answer session to a firm end. The audience likes to know when it is all over safely.

Why do we set presentations?

As with planning and preparing any assignment, the process of preparing a presentation is designed to be an active learning process. As you plan, prepare, practise, perform and finally reflect on your presentation you are really getting to grips with and learning the material. As you think about how to communicate a topic effectively to your audience you are synthesising and using information. Effective communication of what you have learned leads you to develop an understanding of the way your subject actually works; you become familiar with the academic practices of your subject.

It's an opportunity

And, yes, presentations really do extend the range of assessment opportunities open to you. Before you have successfully delivered and survived your first presentation you may find this hard to believe, but once you have done this, you may find that given the choice between an essay and a presentation, you would choose the presentation every time. Once you have cracked how to do presentations well, you will realise that it is easier to get good grades for a presentation than for a piece of writing.

“I did everything you said and practised again and again. The tutor said I was a natural – if only she knew.**”**

And a job skill

Further, good oral communication skills are definitely required by employers – some even require a formal presentation as part of the interview. Developing good presentation skills whilst at university can make the difference between getting that job you want – or not.

What a gas – self-esteem rises

Finally, once you can do presentations, your self-esteem really improves. From the very first one that you plan, prepare, practise and present, you start to feel better about yourself as a student. This is not just something that we are telling you here to make you feel better – this is something that all our students have told us: succeeding in presentations is one of the best confidence boosters they have ever had. In addition, an increase in self-confidence in one area enriches all your studies.

How to succeed in presentations

Here we will be looking at the four presentation Ps: plan, prepare, practise and present.

P1 – Plan

Think about your time limit, your topic and your audience:

- **Time limit**: How can you fit the topic in the time you have been allowed? What will you have to put in – what will you have to leave out?
- **Topic and audience**: Remember – an audience is made up of real people with real knowledge and expectations of their own. They will not want to be patronised – they will want to learn something.

Some things to think about

- What can I expect my audience to know about this topic before I start?
- What will I want them to know when I have finished (= the aim of your presentation)?
- How will I get them from where they are to where I want them to be (= a logical structure to your presentation)?
- What language, tone and style will be right for this audience?
- What arguments and evidence will they understand – and relate to?
- What audiovisual aids will help – and will work with this audience?

  o think of visual aids to illustrate the topic – photographs, charts, diagrams, key quotes, posters

➡️

➡

     o think of visual aids that will help people follow your presentation – have the agenda on a handout or write it on the board, make a large pattern note of your presentation, and display it.

- How will my audience react to this topic? Will they be resistant, happy, frightened, interested? What will I have to do to get them to respond positively?
- What questions might they ask me? What answers will I give?

Action plan: Now that you have considered all these things: what will you do, read, find and make to get your presentation ready?

"I must stress the research and preparation!! When I've participated in presentations, either on my own or in groups, confidence came from how well we had worked together and how much research we (thought we) had done.**"**

P2 – Prepare

Preparing a presentation requires the same research and hard work that an essay does, and then you have to make audiovisual aids as well.

Here are some preparation tips:

- Remember the 10 stages: Brainstorm the topic, link to the learning outcomes…
- Read actively and interactively – gather all the information you need to answer the question.
- Plan the presentation – give it the shape that will take your audience from where they are to where you want them to be.

 **tip**

Be interesting! Never tell the audience everything from A to B to C. This is boring. Choose an interesting aspect of the topic – focus on, elaborate and illustrate that.

- Remember to make your AVA – with backups (e.g. handouts of PowerPoint slides).

    "I knew a postgraduate student who went all the way to Japan to deliver a presentation based on a video. The technologies were incompatible, they couldn't show the video. The whole thing was a huge and expensive disaster!**"**

- Convince yourself first. If you can act as though you believe it, it will help the audience to believe you.
- Prepare a script. Once you have collected all your data and understood and shaped it, you may wish to prepare a script for the presentation. A script can give you a sense that you have taken control of your presentation and organised your material to your satisfaction. That is okay – if you remember that you must not read from your script. So at some point you should destroy your script.
- Prepare your prompts. Make cue cards or prompt sheets to guide you through the presentation itself. This could include:

  o key words or pictures instead of words
  o key examples and quotes
  o key names and dates
  o notes of the key AVA.

- Number your cue cards and your points.
- You must destroy your script – no really!

 **tips**

- You must not read from a script – you will be boring and dull and you will lose your audience.
- Re-create your presentation from the key words on your cue cards.
- It does not matter if you forget something – the audience won't know. Better to be lively and miss a bit – than dull and say everything.

P3 – Practise: rehearse, rehearse, rehearse

Once you have a shape to your presentation, with your prompts prepared, you are now ready to review, revise, edit and learn your presentation – and this comes through practising or rehearsing your presentation. You must not say the presentation for the first time in front of an audience – the words will sound extremely strange to you. You will confuse and upset yourself. This is not a good thing. You must learn and be comfortable with your presentation.

There are several key stages to your rehearsal:

1: Change the presentation – refine and polish it

Tidy it: Your first rehearsal allows you to review, refine and finish your presentation. This is very similar to going over your essay so that all the gaps are closed, the boring bits are tidied up and the overlong sentences are shortened so that they become clear and effective.

Change it: Then you need to move from a script – a *written* communication form – to spoken words – an *oral* communication form. What works in writing rarely works in speaking. Therefore, you need to hear your presentation and shape it again so that it works as spoken rather than written communication. This can take time. It can help to refine your presentation if you rehearse in front of a critical friend who will give you useful feedback.

tip

Do not rehearse in front of your children. Our mature students always say that their children tend to say 'it's boring, it's silly'… leaving them feeling really discouraged.

Improve it: A critical friend can tell you what is good about your presentation. They can tell you what is working, what is easy to follow and understand. But they can also tell you what is not working. Where they do not follow you or your meaning is unclear.

tip

Listen to this feedback. Do not argue with your critical friend. Do not just shout louder so that they understand better. If they cannot understand, neither will your audience. You are not yet communicating effectively. Change your presentation until it can be understood.

2: Learn the presentation

Once your presentation is as good as it can be you need to rehearse to learn it. Practise with your cue cards and your AVA. Do this until you know your presentation really well – until you could do it in your sleep.

tip

Walk around your home delivering the presentation to your cat or a chair. Make yourself feel comfortable speaking those words out loud.

"The success of the group presentation relied very heavily on how well we had got on before the day and the solo presentation relied very heavily on how much effort I had put into the preparation and research. There were very few students who could 'wing' it and often those that tried fell short when questions were put to them.**"**

3: Give your presentation life

Once you are comfortable with speaking out loud and you know your presentation by heart, then you need to practise some more until you can say it every time as though you are saying it for the first time. This will keep your presentation fresh and alive and it will appeal to and grip your audience.

 **tip**

Video it. For really important presentations, assessed ones that carry a high percentage of your course marks – oral exams, vivas – and for job interviews, videotape your rehearsals and check how good you are.

"I think one of the pitfalls of doing the presentation is not approaching it in the same way as any other assessment... and forgetting the extra element of practising beforehand.**"**

P4 – Present or Perform: Presentation day tips and tricks

Okay – you are going to be nervous. Do not focus on that but think positive thoughts and get on with it. Here are some positive things to do.

Before your presentation

1   Be positive!

 **tip**

Read Chapter 22 'How to Deal with Your Emotions'. Practise your positive thinking. Keep saying: 'I am prepared', 'This is a great presentation'.

2   Be mindful. When travelling to your presentation, run through your main points with and without your cue cards. Reassure yourself that you do know it.

3 Be early. Get to the room early so you will be as cool, calm and collected as you can be. Rushing in late will increase your stress levels.

4 Be organised. Take control of the environment. Organise the seating. Where will you want people to sit so that you feel good and they can all hear you? Do you want them in rows, in a semi-circle, sitting on the floor?

tip

Arrange to stand behind a desk or a lectern. This small barrier between you and your audience will help you feel safe and in control.

5 Be in control. Check that the equipment is working.

tip

Have a back-up system in place – have print-outs of your PowerPoint slides to circulate as handouts if the computer does not work.

6 Be alert. Use your adrenalin – it will help you think on your feet.

7 Be positive again. Say, 'I am prepared' and, 'I can handle this'.

8 Be physiological. Stress has a biofeedback effect where the things our bodies do when we are stressed actually increases our stress. We have to learn to de-stress our bodies. If too stressed before or during your presentation:

- Stop.
- Sigh.
- Drop your shoulders. (We hold our shoulders up when tense and this increases tension.)
- Wriggle your toes. (We clench our feet when stressed and this increases our blood pressure and hence our stress levels.)
- Unclench your fists – this is a typical anger/fear reaction – let it go.
- Take a few deep, slow breaths (deep quick ones and you will pass out).
- Start again more slowly. (Stopping and refocusing never counts against you, it can even impress your tutor.)

9 Be on the ball. Write your agenda on the board, on a handout, on an OHT or on the flip chart.

During your presentation: remember to:

- Introduce yourself and your topic.
- Give a brief introduction and say your agenda even if it is written up.

- Speak slowly and clearly. Let people hear and follow you.
- If you get lost – don't panic! Pause, look at your prompts, and carry on.
- Remember to use linguistic markers: We have looked at… now we are going to cover… moving on to…
- Make good eye contact – look at everyone in the room.

 **tips**

- Do stand so that you can see everyone and everyone can see you. Don't stare fixedly at one person so that they want to get up and leave.
- Use your AVA with confidence. Make sure everyone can see everything. Allow people to notice what is there – then take it away.
- Remember your conclusion – re-visit and re-state your main points… no matter how silly it seems. Your audience does not know the topic as well as you do – they will need to be reminded of what you have talked about and what it means.
- Thank people for listening – ask for questions.
- Chair the Q&A session fairly – keep those answers short and sweet. Bring the Q&A to a firm conclusion. Thank people again.
- After your presentation, review your performance.

SWOTing your presentation

As with the essay and the report, it is useful for you to be able to review and evaluate your own presentations. However, because of the especially emotional dimension of presentations, we recommend that you undertake this in two stages:

1   Immediately after your presentation, tell yourself what a wonderful presentation it was and how brave you were for giving it. Do not dwell on anything that went wrong; this just makes it harder to do a presentation next time. So make this first review a very positive one.

2   After some time has elapsed undertake a more detailed SWOT analysis of your presentation.

- What were your strengths? What did you do very well? What sections of the presentation were you particularly pleased with? Why?
- Sometimes we are so busy correcting our faults that we forget to repeat our strengths. Make notes so that you remember.
- What were your weaknesses? What did not go so well? Why was this? Was it form – perhaps it was not structured or presented properly? Was it content – was it a poor

➡

331

➡

argument unsupported by evidence? Did you forget to discuss your evidence? Did you forget to refer back to the question? Make notes.

- Opportunities: Now, go on, try to think of just how good you can become at presentations and of all the opportunities this gives you, both as a student and in future employment. Make notes.
- Threats: If you are still feeling threatened by presentations, what are you going to do next? Will you practise more? Do you need more support with your positive thinking? Do you need to find a study partner? Do you need to seek out Learning Development or Academic Support and get some more help? Make notes.

 **tips**

- Make notes of your strengths – repeat them.
- Make notes of your weaknesses – repair them.
- Use your tutor feedback.
- Use video play-back to refine your performance.

Make a difference

The presentation can be a more flexible form than the essay. Whilst it is not usually a good idea to write a poem when you have been asked to write an essay, it can be a good idea to be creative with a presentation. Though do be careful and make sure that your tutor is the sort of person who will appreciate a little creativity. We have seen tutors really impressed when students have performed a mini-play instead of giving a straight presentation. So when thinking of your presentation, do think about the topic and how to communicate information logically and effectively – with argument and evidence – but also think whether a different sort of performance would actually get you a higher mark – and go for it.

❝One presentation that really impressed me was one on Fibonacci numbers in maths. The group used real flowers and fruit – a pineapple – to illustrate the numbers in nature. One played the flute to illustrate the link between maths and music ... I thought it was excellent!❞

Presentations – things to do and think about

1   **The three-minute presentation**: Before delivering an assessed presentation for your coursework, practise by preparing and delivering a three-minute presentation to a friend, study partner or study group. Choose a simple topic like a hobby or a holiday – but something that really interests and engages you. Use your energy and enthusiasm for the topic. With this presentation get the form right: introduction, agenda; body (logical structure – AVA); conclusion; Q&A. This will build your confidence for your assignment.

2   **Rehearse, rehearse, rehearse**: Practise with a critical friend before an assignment presentation. Use their feedback.

 tip

Use the presentation checklist to evaluate yourself and ask your friend to complete one for you, too.

3   **Team work**: If asked to prepare and deliver a group presentation: make the AVA together, practise with your group.

 tips

- Do look like a group – this could mean dressing in similar colours.
- Do act as though you were a good group that worked really well together (even if you dislike each other).
- Do listen to each other – do not chat whilst someone is speaking – look fascinated.
- Do learn each others' sections – be ready to carry on if someone disappears.

4   **Role-play**: Build some element of dramatic performance into your presentation, especially with a group. When students act out a scenario or role-play a point to illustrate it, tutors are usually really impressed and give higher marks.

5   **Poster presentations**: Even if not asked to prepare a poster for your presentation, make one anyway. Research indicates that audiences find it easier to follow, and understand and enjoy a presentation that has been backed up by a well-designed and beautifully illustrated poster.

❝ I feel that you need to really emphasise group presentations, as they can differ greatly and rely heavily on the success or failure of the group. My group presentations worked because we got on – we worked together well – and we rehearsed together. **❞**

Group presentations

Working in groups can be a pain and many students will be able to recall a bad experience participating in group assignments.

Example

You are standing in front of the class, ready to present with three other people. As you begin speaking, you realise that another member has put up the wrong slides. After you finish, you listen to the next speaker and realise her points have nothing at all to do with what you were saying before. By the time the third member speaks, the audience is lost and confused, spoiling the presentation and resulting in a low grade.

Group presentations will run smoothly and help to improve your grade if you follow these basic tips.

Working as a group

- Have one person take notes and check in with other members to keep them on track with their tasks
- Consider your members' strengths and weaknesses. If you have someone who is good with computers, you might want to assign them the tasks of creating the visual aids. Also, the strongest writers might be most effective in preparing the outline for the presentation.
- Encourage group participation in preparing the presentation by asking individual members to contribute. This can set a positive atmosphere.
- Decide on a group goal. This includes a strategy, the purpose of the group and the resources needed for the task.
- Develop a group presentation plan that everyone agrees on and that clearly states what will be covered.

Preparing the presentation

- Decide what each member will do during the presentation. One person should run the visual aids until they speak. Choose the most confident speakers for the introduction and conclusion. Decide how you will split up the body of the talk.
- Like all presentations, analyse your audience and consider what they need to hear.
- If the task requires you to introduce each member, decide whether you will do that at the beginning or immediately before they speak.

- Decide how each section fits together. Practise introductions and transitions when moving from member to member so that the presentation flows smoothly.
- Practise, practise and erm... practise!

Group presentations can be challenging because of the effort that it takes to coordinate all of the members and different sections, but if you give yourself time to work together you will be more likely to present a talk that is polished and effective.

Resources

We have work packs online to help you get your presentation ready.

See also this interactive presentation planner: http://www2.elc.polyu.edu.hk/CILL/tools/presplan.htm

Conclusion

We have looked in some detail at the academic presentation: they are talks of set length, on set topics, to set audiences, with a special focus on energetic and interesting performances. As always, we considered the heuristic, active learning, dimension of presentations. We also emphasised that developing good presentation skills will increase your self-confidence while you study – and prepare you for employment when you leave university. We also looked at the four Ps of the presentation: plan, prepare, practise and present, emphasising the specific aspects of oral rather than written communication.

** Now, that was a conclusion – see how it re-visits the main arguments and then highlights the main points? It is as simple as that. **

As always, please make your own key word pattern notes of the points that you wish to remember – and use them. None of this will make a difference unless and until you put it into practice!

Review points

When reviewing your notes on this chapter you might realise that:

- You can now think about presentations with excitement rather than dread
- You have thought about the what, why and how of presentations – and you understand how knowing these will help you to deliver better presentations in future
- You are aware of the importance of oral communications – in HE and for future employment
- You are ready to tackle that presentation!

Presentation checklist

Photocopy this checklist and use it to review your own presentations.

☐ My introduction: tells the audience what I am talking about and why.

☐ It has a 'hook' telling the audience why they should listen – it is….

☐ I have a clear agenda telling people the 'order' of my talk.

☐ I will write my agenda – and speak it.

☐ I have a logical structure – it does answer the question set.

☐ I have thought about my audience – in terms of language, tone, style and interesting AVA.

☐ I prepared a script – made my cue cards – then destroyed my script.

☐ I have illustrated my main points in my AVA.

☐ I have made a poster to support my presentation – and will display that as I speak.

☐ I have made a Prezi presentation and embedded all my resources on that.

☐ I will not pass anything around because that disrupts a presentation.

☐ My slides and handouts are simple and clear – I have used mainly pictures – and few words.

☐ Each part of my presentation follows the paragraph questions.

☐ I have remembered to discuss my evidence.

☐ When I want people to make notes, I will pause and let them do so.

☐ I have concluded each section by making a point that relates back to the overall question.

☐ I have remembered my signposts and my discourse markers.

☐ I have a conclusion that revisits my main arguments and re-states my main points.

☐ I am prepared for the question and answer session.

☐ I have checked my mannerisms or gestures (I won't fiddle with a pen or scratch my nose).

☐ I have practised my positive thinking.

 Photocopiable:

Essential Study Skills, Third Edition © Tom Burns and Sandra Sinfield, 2012 (SAGE)

Section IV

Communicating Effectively in Assignments

21

How to Run Your Own Seminars and Workshops

Aims

To prepare you to run your own successful academic seminars and workshops.

Learning outcomes

After reading through this chapter, and engaging with the activities, you will have:

- considered the nature of the academic seminar and workshop (what, why and how)
- considered the value of collaborative, active and interactive learning
- started the process of organising yourself for successful seminar and workshop participation.

How to run and benefit from excellent seminars

The seminar as assessment is different from the seminars that tutors run – and that you participate in as a student. The academic seminar is run by students for other students and usually occurs as part of a Project or Dissertation. This is often related to final year undergraduate projects or as part of postgraduate work; but you might be asked to run a seminar at any university level as part of active learning.

When you run a Project or Dissertation seminar you share your progress with fellow students – and their feedback helps you to develop your ideas, enhance your research strategies and/or to improve your writing.

If asked to run a seminar or workshop on courses other than Projects or Dissertations, you are usually being expected to teach your fellow students something, but not by just presenting on it and not just by telling them something – but by getting your fellow students *doing* something to help them to learn.

The seminar may be purely developmental – with no marks awarded – or it may be part of formal course assessment. Whether there are marks attached or not it is still an excellent learning opportunity – for we learn best when we teach someone else. In this chapter we are going to look briefly at the what, why and how of the academic seminar – and we will link that to a discussion of the academic workshop.

What is a seminar?

Typically, a seminar is made up of four parts: paper, presentation, discussion, conclusion.

- Paper – prepared by you (seminar leader) and circulated in advance to all participants.

 **tip**

Check with the tutor as to what form the paper should take – essay, report, journal article. Can it be something creative – poem, animation… other?

- Presentation – given by you on the seminar topic. Not just the paper read aloud, but a proper presentation that captures the key aspects of your research to date.
- Discussion – this is not just the question and answer session that normally succeeds a presentation. You must make sure that the audience engages with your ideas in some way.

➡

Give your audience questions to discuss. Divide them into groups and give each group a different question. Allow time for discussion – and hold a plenary where you collect all the feedback.

- Overall conclusion – you, the seminar leader, have to draw together everything that was covered in the paper, in the presentation and in the group discussion(s). If this is part of a research process, you should also say how the seminar will help to shape the next step of your research.

❝ Giving seminars/workshops is also common when participating in extra-curricular academic and Students' Union activities. Our SU used to train people to give seminars/workshops. They help to develop transferable skills and help make you employable... Have a look at the SU packs on 'Key Skills' and their 'Training Games Guide'. ❞

Why engage in seminars?

The seminar is a highly interactive, engaging and productive university activity. It is designed to enhance both individual and group learning processes. If you are giving a seminar you will have to work out how to manage and benefit from each part of the seminar process: paper, presentation, discussion and conclusion. This develops your active learning and communication strategies. For those attending a seminar, it is a chance to participate in their colleagues' research; it can be an interesting and intense active and interactive learning experience. It can model good practice for participants as they get to read other students' papers, hear other students' presentations and engage in lively discussion on a range of topics.

You will have to take control of your own seminar and then think how to manage the learning of your audience. You will have to make sure your discussion topics are useful – to your audience and to your own thinking.

The audience has to commit to engaging generously and enthusiastically with the teaching and learning situation that you create.

You will have to develop inter-personal skills to manage the discussions and make sure that everyone participates positively. They have to learn how to act like an enthusiastic and engaged audience.

By the end of a seminar you should have enhanced your analytical and critical faculties and your communication, team work, inter-personal and leadership skills – and your audience should have had an interesting, engaging and intense learning experience.

How to plan, prepare and benefit from seminars

Five Top Tips

1: When to give your seminar

Seminars often form part of courses that happen over a semester or a whole year. So, you have to decide whether to volunteer to run your seminar early or late in the course.

If you run your seminar early, you may have very little information to pass on to your peers; but you may have useful experiences to share. For example, you may have had difficulty deciding on your research topic or you may not know what methodology to adopt. You may have encountered problems with which you would like some help. Therefore, the focus here might be on outlining your approach to your work, highlighting the opportunities and problems that you have encountered so far – and setting up a seminar where your audience helps you to take your project forward.

If you volunteer to run your seminar late, your research may be almost over, you may not be expecting your peers to suggest further research sources, but you may want them to discuss your findings and conclusions. Input from your peers may help you refine your interpretation of your data and improve the shape of your final paper.

tips

Things to think about:

- Are you researching a topic about which you know very little? If so, go early and hope that your peers will suggest further avenues to explore – further sources to read.
- Are you confident about your ability to find sources, but unclear as to how best to interpret or present data? If so, go late, present your data in rough format and invite critical commentary on your analysis, even on your writing style.

2: Plan the whole seminar

Remember the seminar has four parts to it – paper, presentation, discussion and conclusion. Things to think about here include:

- **Plan the paper**: If you are delivering early, your paper may consist of quite brief notes of what you are going to do in your research and why. You might note the context of your research (what makes it a valuable or interesting topic and what gaps there are already in this field) and the reading and other research activities (interviews, questionnaires) that you have already undertaken. If you are going late, your paper may very well look like a nearly finished draft of what you would expect to hand in. Think about highlighting the areas of the paper upon which you would appreciate critical feedback.

 **tips**

- Think about what the paper could look like: on some courses you may have to present papers that look very similar to journal articles – in others you may be allowed to be more creative. We have seen students who have presented papers in a poetry format; whilst this was a very creative strategy it might not be appropriate in some cases.
- Write your 'discussion' questions on your paper. As the paper is typically circulated in advance, it means that your audience will have already read and thought about your questions before they attend your seminar.

- **Plan the presentation**: Whatever style of paper you have circulated in advance, you should expect your audience to have read it; thus there is no need to cover the whole paper again in your presentation. So, in your presentation you need to focus on the interesting bits. Perhaps you could outline the aims and purpose of your research, say why you were interested in that topic, why you took the approach that you did, highlight any problems that you encountered. You might describe how you overcame your problems – or invite solutions from your audience.

 **tip**

Be interesting! Keep your voice lively, display enthusiasm for your subject and invite real collaboration from your audience. If you have managed to engage and keep the interest of your audience they may well give you really good advice about how to extend, develop or refine your research or how to improve your paper.

- **Plan the discussion topics and discussion strategy**: It is very easy to waste the seminar opportunity by just seeing it as an ordeal to get through rather than the collaborative learning event that it can be. If you want to benefit from your seminar, think really hard about your discussion topics. Set real questions upon which you want your audience to think – and the answers to which could take your own research further forward.

 **tips**

- Do set questions that will help your own research.
- Do divide the audience into small groups and give each group a question (different or the same) to discuss.
- Allow a set time for discussion. Hold a plenary to get feedback from the groups.

    ❝When I gave a workshop I put people into groups and got them discussing different subjects and it meant I was able to work more closely with the people in those smaller groups. **❞**

- **Plan the overall conclusion**: Remember that you will have to sum up your whole seminar at the end. Prepare most of your summary in advance: key points from paper; key points from presentation; discussion questions. Then the only thing you have to capture in the seminar itself will be the discussion points raised by your audience.

 **tip**

Give flip chart paper to your audience (either to individuals or small groups). Invite people to write key points on the flip chart pages and collect these in at the end. Sum up these key points and keep the pages to make sure that you have the ideas to use in your research.

3: Refine your paper, rehearse your presentation and test your discussion topics on a critical friend

Do not forget to practise, practise, practise. Do not expect to be perfect first go – draft and re-draft your work.

4: Run your seminar with confidence and enthusiasm

The most important thing for you to do is to enjoy your seminar. Relish the opportunity of running an interactive learning event that will engage your fellow students – and hopefully take your own research or writing forward in the process.

- If getting students to discuss your questions in groups, move among the groups to check that they really are discussing your topics.
- Give flip chart markers out as well as the paper, so the writing can be seen.
- Allow a plenary session where everyone can briefly discuss each others' points.
- Give that overall conclusion!
- Think about how what you have learned really will help you with your research.

5: Review your own strengths and weaknesses overall

When reflecting on your seminar, think about your:

- Paper
- Presentation
- Choice of topics and management of the discussion
- Summative conclusion
- And then – in the light of the discussion that you managed, and the summative conclusion that you gave – decide what to do and read to improve your research and write a better final paper.

The advantages and disadvantages of seminars

As with any group or collaborative learning experience there are advantages and disadvantages to the seminar.

Advantages:

- Collaborative, collegiate experience
- Active and interactive learning
- Intense learning experience
- Extends knowledge of a topic
- Models good practice – rehearsing your writing, presentation and discussion techniques
- Develops research angles
- Improves grades in associated dissertation and essay work
- Develops personal, interpersonal and communication skills
- Develops organisation and time management skills
- We learn best when we teach other people.

Disadvantages:

- Lack of commitment in the seminar leader produces an uncomfortable event
- Poor techniques – e.g. reading a paper instead of giving a presentation – switches audiences off
- Ill-prepared discussions become embarrassing
- Ill-managed discussions can become exclusive, alienating or confrontational
- Lack of commitment in an audience can mean that little or no learning actually takes place.

Obviously all the disadvantages can be turned into advantages with the proper planning and commitment.

Workshops

These days students are more likely to be asked to run a workshop than deliver a formal academic seminar. The workshop is another mode of active and interactive learning. Typically, you will be asked to 'teach' a topic to your fellow students, but not by lecturing at them – rather you will be expected to develop an event with interactive elements designed to get your audience to think about, explore and understand a particular topic.

Do remember and use all the advice about preparing and delivering an academic seminar – this will help you to prepare, deliver and frame a positive workshop experience. Further, the active learning devices that make work-shops interesting, will also make a more engaging and enriching seminar.

The following are three great things to get to do in workshops – and seminars:

UNIVERSITY OF WINCHESTER
LIBRARY

Play learning games

Set up some form of role-play where participants have to adopt different roles and then act out a learning scenario. For example, if studying refugee education, you might ask some members of the group to be refugees, another to be a passport controller, another to be a member of the public. You could set the scene rolling – and the participants would learn something from the way they developed the scenario.

Draw-to-learn

We have outlined elsewhere how drawing can be a thinking/exploring tool, as well as a reflective or communicative one. You could open a workshop session by asking your group to draw representations of key words, theories or concepts pertinent to your session. Discussion of the drawings would reveal underlying understanding or misconception and can lead to further discussions.

You could conclude a workshop by asking students to draw a representation of everything that they think they have learned. If they are going to write on the topic that you been teaching, you could ask them to make a collage plan of their proposed writing.

Write to learn

As drawing can be creative and exploratory, so, too, can writing. At the beginning of your workshop ask your group to write for two minutes on the topic. Ask them to write for one minute on what they want to get from the session. At the end of a workshop ask them to write a letter to an auntie explaining the workshop to them – or to reframe the whole session for a 10-year-old child.

Workshops and seminars are more effective if you have tried to make them interesting and engaging – and if you have tried to get your group to think for themselves rather than just telling them what they should know. The little activities suggested here give a flavour of what has worked for us. We are sure that you will be able to think of many more of your own once you get started.

 **tip**

In lectures and classes or when other students are giving presentations, delivering seminars or running workshops, make notes of the interesting and engaging things that make learning happen for you. Think how you can adapt those interesting activities in your own sessions.

UNIVERSITY OF WINCHESTER
LIBRARY

Conclusion

The academic seminar – and the workshop – can draw together oral and written communication strategies to form powerful interactive learning experiences for all involved. We really want you to engage positively and enthusiastically in your seminars and workshops; to make the most of them. We have emphasised how these are more productive when you are engaging positively – and when you think creatively about how to get your audiences to interact and think for themselves. In that spirit – when you make notes on this chapter – why don't you try:

- Using only pictures?
- Making an Xtranormal movie?

Review points

When reviewing your notes on this chapter you might realise that you have:

- Understood the nature of the academic seminar (what, why and how)
- Reflected on the joys of running interactive and engaging workshops
- Understood the positive benefits of collaborative learning
- Started the process of thinking about how to be creative, engaging, interesting and interactive in the seminars and workshops that you deliver.

Section V

Emotional Dimension

22

How to Deal with Your Emotions

Aims

To explore the relationship between self-confidence and student success.
To suggest strategies designed to reduce stress and anxiety and to build self-confidence and self-esteem.

Learning outcomes

It is intended that after reading this chapter and engaging in the activities you will have:

- considered the emotional aspect of studying, with a particular focus on building self-confidence
- examined the causes of fear and how to overcome the negative aspects of fear
- covered some very practical things to do to overcome fear and build self-confidence and self-esteem.

How did you feel on your first day?

"Panicky! Suddenly it hits you, because you feel that everyone is looking at you, which is stupid because no one is looking at you. But I remember coming up the steps and all these people sitting down and I felt everybody was staring at me and saying, why is that old woman coming here?**"**

❝ I felt very self-conscious – and terrified that I couldn't find the room. I saw this enormous building and it really scared me … It's frightening. ❞

❝ So I get half way through and I say: Why, why, why can't I just be happy going to work and going home? Why did I start this? I can't bear it! … ❞

❝ I was desperate – I was very nervous. And, the more nervous you are, the less you pick up things. You can't listen and you want everything to go in and nothing's going in. So the first module was awful … ❞

❝ I was quite frightened and I think most of the students were as well! And after I spoke to and got to know a few students we realised that – even though some of the students were sounding confident – they were quite anxious and worried and frightened themselves. ❞

❝ It was really nerve-racking sitting in this room… I did feel nervous, but I thought you're here now, they can't kill you and you can run away if you don't like it. ❞

How does being a student make you feel?

As someone who has chosen to be a student, you have entered an academic environment that may seem quite strange to you. You have committed yourself to your degree programme and much is expected of you: to attend lectures and seminars and benefit from them; to navigate and learn in your university's Virtual Learning Environment; to undertake independent research – to read around your subject; to make usable notes of what you see, hear and do; to demonstrate your learning in assignments – written and oral – and in exams.

Whilst the overall goal of all this activity is that you become a confident graduate, many of the stages and processes involved in becoming this new, confident person can actually feel quite intimidating. Some are so intimidated that they give up on study altogether.

In this chapter we are going to explore the all too human dimension of studying; the emotional elements of being a student. In particular, we will be looking at the roles that fear and positive thinking can play in student success.

❝ Apparently there was a research project at Oxford University that looked at why, given the high A' level grades of all the students, some went on to get first class degrees whilst others did not. They found that it was the students with high self-confidence who achieved the higher grades. ❞

Fear, positive thinking and the student

Actively developing study and academic strategies promotes success and increases student self-confidence – and this is the goal of much of this book. However, focusing directly on how to build self-confidence and self-esteem allows students to immediately and dramatically improve their achievement – and that is the goal of this chapter.

66 After we did that session on positive thinking, I went back to work and was able to speak up in a meeting for the very first time. 99

66 Not only did that session help me with my presentation, I was able to pass my driving test, first go. 99

Students speak up

This is what some of the students quoted above said after learning and rehearsing their study and academic skills:

66 Studying is part of my life now. In fact I think I'm quite a sad person, because when the essay's done and handed in I have to go and put the computer on and stroke it. 99

66 I had some anxieties ... that were partly about my writing skills and structuring essays and a few other things ... I had a lot of anxiety over that ... So I came to study skills. And it all started making sense and when it made sense it all fell into place. And it sort of opened up a new world of knowledge for me as well... 99

66 In the beginning you are all so shy and you're all very self-conscious, but as I said, we all feel the same, but because we don't talk to each other we don't know that the other person feels exactly the same ... Now, it's a great feeling, you belong now; you are part of the university. The whole thing belongs to me. It's my university now. 99

tip

No matter how anxious you may be feeling, you can turn that around and build your self-confidence. Read on.

Does it affect our work?

Do you think that a runner will achieve more by running along thinking 'I am a failure, I cannot possibly win', or 'I am a success, I see myself winning this race'? I think that most of us would agree that the runner who thinks and feels like a success has more chance of winning a race than the one who thinks and feels like a failure. Of course, the physical conditions have to be there, the training, the diet... but basically for the runner to do well s/he must want to do well and must believe that it is possible to do well: s/he must have self-belief and self-confidence.

What is true for the runner is also true for students. You must want to do well and believe that it is possible for you to do well. You, too, must have self-belief and self-confidence. Yes, you need to engage with your subject – and develop your study and academic strategies – but a positive mental attitude will mean that you actually succeed.

What, emotions count, even at university?

Human beings are multidimensional – they are made up of many facets: cognition/intellect/effect and emotion/feelings/affect. Our intellect and our emotions can both play a part in every aspect of our lives, including that of being a student. There is a danger in thinking that because studying is an academic, intellectual activity, there is no room for the emotional dimension. But, you cannot abolish part of yourself as a human being just because it does not seem to fit. In fact, it can be the very ignoring of our emotional side that causes the problem; for what we ignore or deny, we cannot deal with.

There are many things in the educational environment that will affect you emotionally as a student – and as a human being. We hope that some of them will excite, stimulate and even thrill you. Others may frighten, intimidate or horrify you. It is important to notice what is happening to your feelings when you are studying. Ideally, it is advisable to harness your positive feelings and work to overcome your negative ones.

1. Activity: Reactions to studying

Take a few moments to read and respond to the following statement. Write down your reactions to the statement.

➡

➡️

It is in order to return at this point to Jameson's 'loss of the referent' theme, because it is precisely this phenomenology of the everyday that Jameson's work both lacks and consciously relegates to the ethnographic sidelines. (Feather, 2000, *Intersubjectivity and Contemporary Social Theory*, p. 135)

Now compare your reactions with those gathered from some other students:

❝I got really really angry! Why on earth do they have to write like that? It's stupid.❞

❝It made me feel like giving up, it's obvious that I'm not welcome here.❞

❝This is strange and scary; but it's where I've got to get to.❞

❝I read it several times trying to make sense of it.❞

❝I used my dictionary of literary terms and tried to make sense of it piece by piece.❞

❝Well I just laughed and laughed. They've got to be joking, haven't they?❞

> **Query**:
> - Were any of these reactions like your own?
> - What do you notice about these reactions?
> - Perhaps you noticed that there was a whole range of reactions to the statement?
>
> **Discussion**: You can see here a range of different reactions to the same situation. What moves one student to fury, makes another laugh? What makes one student resolved to succeed at all costs, but makes another feel like giving up?

Yet often as human beings, we often think that *our* feelings and *our* reactions are the only possible feelings and the only possible reactions. We do not realise that other people may respond differently to us – and we do not know that perhaps we can learn to *choose* our reactions to situations. We can start to take control of our instinctive negative reactions and build positive reactions to overcome them.

2. Activity: Thinking about positive thinking – SWOT analysis

Take a few moments to think about your reaction to the suggestion that you might be able to affect how you feel about being a student. Now answer the questions in Figure 22A.

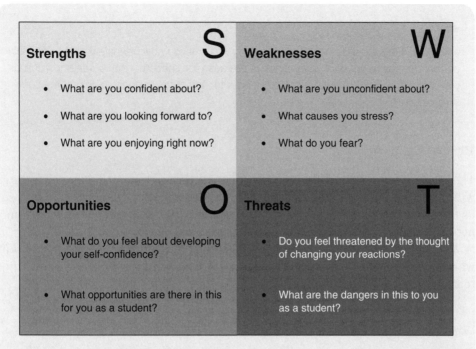

Strengths **S**	Weaknesses **W**
• What are you confident about? • What are you looking forward to? • What are you enjoying right now?	• What are you unconfident about? • What causes you stress? • What do you fear?
Opportunities **O**	Threats **T**
• What do you feel about developing your self-confidence? • What opportunities are there in this for you as a student?	• Do you feel threatened by the thought of changing your reactions? • What are the dangers in this to you as a student?

FIGURE 22A   SWOT analysis – positive thinking

When you have completed this activity, discuss with a friend or your study partner.

Query: Perhaps you noticed that there are opportunities for you in developing your positive thinking? You might have realised that a positive attitude will help you face academic life as an exciting challenge?

On the other hand, you might be a bit frightened of this choice. You know who you are at the moment and you do not want to change. Change is uncomfortable.

Maybe you are doing okay in your work but the thought of success terrifies you, for you do not know what success will feel like or what it might mean.

Discussion: These are all normal feelings. Change will mean entering the unknown – and success may well be a new experience for you – but you can learn to face this positively as well.

➡

Take care: If this exercise has really unsettled you or if you have identified areas that look as though they might give you problems or cause for concern – go to see someone at your university – your personal or academic tutor, the study support people or the counselling service.

The feeling student

The previous activities are designed to illustrate that as human beings our feelings will play a role in our lives as students. Negative feelings can actually prevent us from working to our best ability. At the same time, changing our feelings may not be entirely problem free, we find that we are frightened of change.

We are now moving on to explore the role of fear in our lives; in particular, we will look at what we are frightened of, where fear comes from – and things to do to build self-confidence.

What are you frightened of?

What are you actually frightened of? We're not talking about phobias here (like a crippling fear of spiders or heights), but the sorts of things that make you feel uncomfortable, things that make you sweat or cause you the odd sleepless night. Things that you avoid if you can.

All human beings are frightened of many things. Generally, we are all frightened of the new; we are frightened of change. We may be frightened of ageing, disease and death. More mundanely, we may be frightened of picking up the telephone... of entering a library... of writing our first essay... of giving a presentation... of anything and everything. All these fears are completely normal and yet they can be very inconvenient for us as human beings – and especially awkward for us as students.

Let's face it; to undertake to become a student is to undertake to change. But this change does involve risk – we do not know all the implications of these changes for us as human beings. Risk is frightening. Yet the only way to avoid risk is to do nothing at all – and this really is not an option for you either as a student or as a human being.

It's just me!
There can be another dimension to this fear, and that is whenever we are frightened at school, college or university we feel that we are the only ones that are frightened. We feel alone in our fear – and that just makes it feel

worse. We look at other people and they look fine – they don't appear to feel what we feel. This is especially true for new students. When we ask new students how they are feeling, they all say that they are scared. Moreover, every scared one thinks that they are the only one carrying this burden.

We're all frightened

Here is one student's experience:

"I had been teaching for many years when I took a higher degree programme and became a student again. I thought that everybody else knew what they were doing – but I did not.

When I sat down in my first seminar and the tutor asked us a question, I went red, my heart pounded so much I felt that everyone else must hear it – and I absolutely would not say anything – I was too frightened to look, sound or feel a fool. I found myself experiencing exactly the same fears as everybody else. The fact that I was also a teacher did not help at all.

Later in the course another student asked, 'What on earth does "overarching syntagmatics" mean?' We all looked at each other – we all laughed. We realised that none of us knew – and that we had all been too scared to admit it. We then decided to do something about this. We decided to take control of the course, so we:

- formed a study group and met once a week to discuss our reading. What we couldn't understand on our own, we worked out together
- read one another's draft essays and gave each other critical feedback – our final drafts were so much better – and our marks improved
- read one another's finished essays to get extra ideas for our own work – and for our exams.

Suddenly the whole course was more enjoyable – and all our experiences were more positive."

> **Discussion**: What worked for this student can work for you. Get a study partner – form a study group. Don't suffer your course, don't even just survive it – take control of it!

We are all in the same boat

Everyone tends to feel fear when they start studying. It is normal to be scared of the challenge of becoming a student. It is natural to feel scared if you do not feel like an academic. It is not shameful – it does not mean that you are not cut out for studying – and you really, really are not alone. Everyone else is feeling just the same as you.

3. Activity: The fearful student

1 Work through the questions below. Just respond quickly – do not think too hard about your answers.
2 Then read over what you have written – and think about it. What does it tell you?
3 Discuss with a friend if possible.

The questions:

- Can you think of any situation in life where you have let your fears stop you from doing something? Perhaps you didn't take a subject because you thought you'd be no good at it – or you didn't do a certain sport because you thought it might be dangerous?
- What do you think about that now?
- Are there any aspects of your studying that fill you with fear? What are they? Make a few notes.
- Can you remember times when you have worried and worried over a particular thing, perhaps for months – even for years – then the thing happened?
- What was it like?
- What about all the things that you worried about – and that did not happen?
- What was that like?
- What does this tell you?

> **Query**: How do you feel now? Make some notes to yourself about what you gained from this exercise. If you have a study partner discuss this exercise with them – it can be liberating to realise that you are not alone in your fear.
>
> **Discussion**: It is said that 90% of what we worry about just does not happen at all. It is silly to spend our lives worrying – even more so when what we are worrying about is unlikely to happen.

Being a student can be scary, especially as some of the things that we worry about *will* actually happen. We *will* have to understand the subject and make those notes. We *will* have to write those essays and give those presentations.

Even so, worrying never helps us to cope with life – it is exhausting and makes life harder.

Think positive – believe in yourself – and you will improve your life, not just your life as a student.

" They say that the only things we end up regretting are the things we didn't do. It's true, I've made some terrible mistakes – but I'd rather have had the experience than not. "

Believe in yourself

The overarching theme of most positive thinking books is that fear boils down to a lack of self-confidence and a lack of faith in ourselves. We fear things because we believe that we will not be able to cope with them. We think life will defeat us. And yet, consider the things that we do achieve as human beings.

We managed to learn our language. If we are able-bodied, we learned how to walk, run, dance, play sport... We learned the behaviour that was expected of us in different situations – in the family, with our friends, in school, at work. We managed to go to school and survive that. Many of us then went on to get jobs – maybe even raise families. All of these activities and many more we did eventually take in our stride – no matter how much we feared them beforehand.

Overall, we tend to be much more resilient than we give ourselves credit for. In the end, whatever life chooses to throw at us – we cope with it. Sometimes, we even cope spectacularly well. All we tend to do by doubting ourselves is actually make it more difficult to cope – not easier. Surely, it is not life that we need to fear, but fear itself? All we do when we listen to or, worse, give in to our fears is to damage our own lives.

Students do it in the dark

Perhaps all this worry makes us better students? Well, in our experience the typical answer is no.

We worry about exams so much that we are too scared to prepare for them. Surprise, surprise – we do badly in our exams.

We worry about the final assessment on a course so much, we are too frightened to look at the question. Suddenly, instead of having 15 weeks to slowly work on the assignment and really get to grips with it – we only have two days to prepare the assignment. And, no, we do not achieve the best mark possible for that assignment.

We worry for six months about that presentation that we have to give – it spoils our days and nights – our whole lives. Suddenly it is over. We did not go up in a puff of smoke – we found that we survived after all.

What was the point of all that worry? All it does is blight your life. And it literally blights your life as a student, for it means that you do not give of your best and you do not work to your best advantage.

We have to learn to pass though our fear – not to live with it.

Why do we experience fear?

But, you might argue, surely this fear is there for a purpose? If not, where does it come from? Why do we have it? Evolutionary, cognitive and popular psychology all have something to say in this debate.

Evolutionary psychology

Simon Baron Cohen (1997) argues that fear, anxiety and even depression are a legacy of our animal evolution. He points out that when an animal is on unfamiliar territory it is in danger of its life. As human beings we also have this fear; we, too, are frightened when on unfamiliar territory. But more than that, as humans we have a consciousness. Consciousness means that we are aware of ourselves in ways that no animal is. Birds looking around for a predator are not nervous or scared. They just are. However, as conscious human beings, we are aware of our own nervousness and fear. We can focus on and be really obsessive about our fears – this is what makes fear so dangerous for us.

Remember, to be human is to constantly move into unfamiliar territory. This means that we are constantly moving into fearful situations. The more we focus on our fear instead of the situation, the more we are in danger of avoiding the things that make us frightened. We need to be able to face our fears in order to deal with the unfamiliar – and grow.

Cognitive psychology

Bandura's work on self-efficacy indicates that a complex interplay of personal, environmental and behavioural factors, including one's family background, class, gender and ethnic group, will influence how we will feel in any given situation. Some of us will avoid risk, danger and failure, others will relish those things. Some of us are prepared to persevere and push through problems; others will feel easily defeated and give up.

In terms of being a student, if we are from a group that traditionally does well in education, it will be easier for us to see ourselves also doing well; whilst if we are from a group that traditionally does not succeed in education, it will be easier to see ourselves as failing.

tip

For more information on the role of self-belief in learning, see information on the research of Albert Bandura on self-efficacy: http://www.des.emory.edu/mfp/self-efficacy.html

Popular psychology

Popular psychologists, Susan Jeffers for example, argue that we are accidentally taught fear in the way that we are brought up. You might remember:

- Mind how you cross the road.
- Don't go climbing that tree.
- Don't talk to strangers.
- Don't go too fast.
- Are you sure you can manage that?
- Let me do that for you.

When people say these things to us they are really just expressing their fear (I don't want anything bad to happen to you); but what we hear, and internalise, is that they think that we are inadequate. This can have far-reaching consequences. It can be terribly damaging to our self-confidence to feel that the person who loves us most in the world, does not think much of us. They must think we are pretty useless if they believe that we cannot even cross the road without their advice.

" I was 40 years old and someone gave me a pair of roller skates – I was delighted, I'd always meant to get a pair but kept putting it off. I kept the skates at my mum's so that I could skate around the streets there... One day, my skates were gone. My mum had given them away in case I hurt myself... I was speechless. What sort of an idiot did she think I was? **"**

The fear within

Jeffers (1997) argues that the fears of our carers become our own fears and our own internal negative voice. We no longer need other people to criticise us – we do it to ourselves. After a while every time we do something new, a little voice pipes up inside saying: Watch out! Why are you doing that? You'll only fail! You'll only look a fool...

This is especially hard to deal with if you are a student, for there will be so many new things to face. If we see them only as opportunities to fail, we will never get the most from them.

It gets worse – consider the role of mistakes in our learning. We learn by a process of trial and error, by making mistakes and learning from them. But, if we can't bear the thought of making mistakes, we are going to be afraid of trying anything at all. To learn, we must overcome this.

Studying is an adventure. Embrace it. Realise that you will live through your mistakes and learn from them.

But I'm not really an academic

A fear of making mistakes is particularly harmful if you are a student but you do not *feel* like a student – if you are in an academic environment and you do not *feel* like an academic. If this describes how you are feeling right now, you will have to work to overcome your own negative feelings. You *are* a student. You have been accepted onto a degree programme. If you are interested and motivated and if you work hard you can succeed. You will grow into the role of an academic.

Do these thoughts on fear make any sense to you? Can you now review *your* fears in a different light?

Can we do anything to overcome fear and build self-confidence?

Obviously the whole tone of this section – as with the book as a whole – suggests that you can do something about this state of affairs. Here we are going to take a leaf out of the self-help type book and look at re-framing fear; taking responsibility for our lives; adopting a positive vocabulary; making positive friends; and using positive statements.

Re-framing fear

We have argued that fear, whilst uncomfortable, is a perfectly natural and normal response to life – especially to new or unfamiliar situations. What we can do is *change our response to that fear*. Fear does not have to mean run and hide under the duvet; it can mean something completely different. Here are some new ways to look at fear: see if they help you at all.

- **Fear is good**: Fear is okay, it is part of growth and doing new things. Fear does not mean, 'This is not for me!'; instead fear means that you are doing something new, you are facing a new challenge, you are taking a risk – you are being human. Thus, when we feel fear we should celebrate the fact that we are growing and changing. This is a good thing, not a bad one.
- **Fear affects everyone**: Fear really does affect everyone and realising that we are not alone in our fears can actually help. If Cohen is to be believed, everyone feels fear when on unfamiliar territory. Everyone experiences fear when they do something new. Realising that we are not alone in our fears can take away the stigma of fear, it does not mean that we are cowards, just that we are human. Once we accept this we can move on.

- **The only way to get rid of the fear of something is to do it** ... the quicker the better. You know that this is true. You can spend months worrying about something, and then it takes two minutes to do it. Let's get rid of those months of worry – do it now: you know it makes sense.
- **It is easier to face fear than to live with it**: It is easier to do what we fear than to keep living with the fear. The more we give in to fear the more fearful we become. So, every time you decide to face a fear, remind yourself that this is not a hardship – you are taking the easier option.
- **It takes practice**: Re-framing fear in these ways may not come naturally to you. However, with practice you will find that you can face fear differently, and it will make a big difference – especially to the way that you face the challenge of being a successful student.

We can take responsibility for our own lives

As well as re-framing fear, we can re-frame our approach to life. We can accept responsibility for ourselves. Taking responsibility means dropping for ever a victim mentality: the 'It's not my fault, it's his or hers or theirs!' syndrome. Now we all know that neither society nor nature is fair: class, ethnicity and gender do affect our life chances – a hurricane can destroy a home. But, if we keep blaming everyone else for what happens to us, we end up being trapped by life, instead of being able to live our lives. And if we become trapped, we are the ones that suffer – no one else.

Remember, if it's *their* fault, there is nothing *I* can do to change things. If it's my responsibility, then there is something that I might be able to do to take control of events. I can look to see what I can do – what I can change – what effect I can have.

This is really important as a student. Look at your course, look at the work that you have to do – and do something about it. Discover how to learn and study more effectively; make use of the advice in the rest of this book. All that advice is designed to make you more effective and more successful as a student. And start right now, say, I am responsible:

- for my decisions
- for my actions
- for getting my work in on time
- for getting good grades...

If these things matter to us, we can take steps to make them happen. It may take hard work and sweat, but we *can* do it.

If we don't do it, perhaps it is because these things do not really matter to us, we just say they do because it is expected of us, because it is what our parents, friends or partners want for us or because it makes us look good? In the end, we will only do well in our studies if it is what *we* want. It is our work that has to make it happen, not anyone else's.

So the next time you find yourself blaming someone, anyone, for something that you are not doing, stop and think again. What can you do to make it happen?

Develop a positive vocabulary

A good way to develop a positive and responsible outlook is to develop a positive vocabulary. Just as we can re-frame fear so that it does not mean what it used to mean, so we can also *change the way that we talk about the world*. Here we are going to look at problems, disasters – and choice.

'It's not a problem – it's an opportunity'

If life is a problem, if the world is a series of negative experiences … then life *is* hard for you. Imagine starting a new job – would you see that as a wonderful opportunity to meet new people and face new challenges? Or do you see it as hard work, with horrible new people and a difficult journey…?

And what about being a student? Just think about all that reading – all those lectures – all those essays and presentations. Gulp! It is so easy to think of studying as an imposing mountain of hard work and struggle – a series of exhausting problems.

But, what if you re-framed this into a positive? What if you thought about it as a wonderful opportunity – of time to devote to yourself and your studies. Being a student can be a great time in your life – a time when you can think and learn; when you can make new friends and try out new opportunities; a time to flourish.

Each positive thought will make your life easier – each negative thought that you have makes your problems grow.

tip

If you are that instant negative thinker, how does it make you feel? Try using more positive language. Say, 'This is exciting', 'I'm enjoying this'.

Start now!

Now is the time to try something different. If you normally say, 'That looks really hard!' when faced with a tough assignment, see it as an opportunity not a problem. Say, 'This is an excellent module, it is really challenging – and it takes me much nearer my overall goal'. This very simple and basic re-framing stops it feeling like a burden: once this stops, you can grow with the work rather than being crushed by it.

So, from this moment forward, instead of saying 'That's hard' try saying, 'That looks really interesting' or 'I'm really looking forward to this assignment'.

Keep it up

Do not just try being positive once or twice and then give up. These positive statements start by feeling strange but if you keep them up, you will find that they do make a difference to how you feel about your work. This then improves the work itself – it gets better. Then the only problem you'll have is to accept a more positive you. You will have to accept a change in yourself.

 **tip**

Give this positive re-framing a chance to work. Try not to fear the change in yourself. Try to like the new you – it is still you.

❝ I was moaning about all the hard work I had to do, all the time it was taking... yada yada. When my friend told me to stop it: I had chosen to do the course. If I didn't like it – leave. If I was going to carry on, I had to start seeing it as fun and not work – and I had to leave her ears alone. ❞

It's a learning experience

If problems can become opportunities, similarly disasters become fully blown learning experiences. Nothing is so bad that we cannot benefit from it in some way. Perhaps you lost your job? Surely that left you free to get a better one? Maybe you lost your home? Then there was the whole world of change and excitement open to you.

❝ You know what, this did all happen to me. I gave up my job for an exciting project – and it failed. It cost me so much I lost my flat. This was my nightmare – jobless and homeless! I stayed on my friend's sister's couch... I found some work... I found somewhere else to live... I'm back on my feet – and I know that nothing can defeat me! ❞

> **Query**: What about you – has anything like this happened to you? How did you cope? Hopefully, although it really felt like a disaster when it first happened, you did get something from it. What was it?

Whatever happens to you as a student – see what you can learn from it

- Can't understand the assignment question on your module? Well, ask for help – talk it over with a study partner.
- You get a lower grade than you expected for an assignment? Spend time trying to work out what went wrong.

For every 'disaster' there is a lesson to be learned. And it is irritating but true that we can actually learn more from our mistakes than we ever can from what we do well.

Imagine getting an excellent grade for your very first essay in a subject – but not knowing what you actually did right? This can be a very strange experience. You can end up feeling more lost than successful.

But getting feedback on all the things that you did wrong in that assignment can tell you much that will help you in future assignments. Of course, this will only work if you look for the learning experience and try to get something from it.

Being positive at university

The choice really is yours. You can just choose to sit there and cry and say 'If only...', or you can do something. So, instead of feeling sorry for yourself or blaming other people or just giving up when things go wrong – and things will go wrong – make the effort to find out what went wrong. Work out exactly what you will have to do differently to make sure that next time it is a success.

For example, if you do get a really low grade, use all the relevant sections in this book that might help you do much better next time. In particular, you might look at:

- organisation and time management – so that you manage your time more effectively
- creative and analytical thinking – so that you develop techniques that will open up an assignment question – and a pattern notemaking system so that your research is more active and useful

- reading strategies – so that you develop targeted research and active reading skills and get much more from your reading
- the essay, report or presentation – so that you understand how to present your work most effectively.

I have a choice

Another really important re-framing of the way we speak about the world is to replace *should* with *choice*. Should is a big victim word: I should work on my assignment; I should visit the library... Oh and don't we feel sorry for ourselves and don't we make everyone suffer for it! Remember, that whatever we do or do not do, there is always a consequence, a price to pay. Accept that. Remember, you always have choice; you can do your assignment, visit the library ... or go out and relax.

If you do your assignment or go to the library – go with good grace and work really hard. If you go out, relax, have a good time and try not to worry about your work for one evening.

It's just like when we decide whether or not to become a student:

- If you do choose to become a student, there is a price to pay in terms of time, effort and commitment – and there are the rewards that you have decided for yourself.
- If you choose not to become a student, there is a different sort of price to pay – you may have more time but maybe you will be stuck in a job that you do not like and which does not satisfy you.

Once you do choose to do something, accept that you have chosen to do it, accept the 'price', give 100% and do it with good grace. If you do not do it, accept that, too.

> **Query**: How does this sound to you? What implications does it have for you as a student? Will it change the way you behave?

Change me – change my family?

Once you start changing and becoming more positive, this might have an impact on those around you. What sort of people are in your life at the moment? How do your friends and family view the world? Are the people in your world full of energy and a zest for life? Or do they sit around moaning and grumbling?

If it is the latter, then you will stick out like a sore thumb if you suddenly become all optimistic and positive. They will look at you strangely if you see opportunities instead of the problems that they all see. This can be a challenge for the positive student of whatever age.

Younger students have peer pressure to deal with; for it is not really acceptable to be all positive and enthusiastic as a student. Everyone knows that students have to go around looking bored and suspicious all the time. Enjoying life is ridiculous and enjoying studying is just plain bonkers!

With the *more mature students*, whilst on the surface it may seem okay to be a committed and motivated student, you can find that your family and friends resent you changing. For one thing, the new positive person just feels rather strange to them. They felt more comfortable with the old negative person – they knew who that was, they knew what to expect. They do not want this person to change. It is too uncomfortable.

And whether you are younger or older, this new you has new interests and commitments. Suddenly, you do not have as much time to give to family and friends. Family members have to do things for themselves that you normally did. Friends discover that you do not always answer the phone, you cannot go out with them three nights a week and you do not drop everything whenever they feel like calling. This does not feel like a good change to them.

Gently does it

As we start to become more positive, it becomes easier to make positive friends. Positive friends can reinforce our new positive attitude; positive study partners can make the whole job of studying easier, more rewarding and much, much more enjoyable. At a very simple level, positive people will not be using up your energy just to keep them afloat – you will be able to use your energy to progress.

We are not suggesting that you need to 'divorce' your family and friends – or that you need to challenge and confront them. We just want you to be aware that you may encounter resentment as you do change – and you will need tact and diplomacy to help your family and friends accept you.

If being the new positive student is important to you, it is important to bring your family and friends along with you. You will need to help them to get to like and appreciate the new you. You may well encounter resistance at first – but if it is important to you, you have to work through this somehow.

And finally...

We have already argued that adopting a positive outlook can make a difference to how you view the world. In this last section we are going to take that one step further by exploring more things to do to build self-confidence.

... even more positive things to do

If every time you face something new that little voice in your mind seems to call out, 'watch out! You'll be sorry! That's dangerous! ...', work to drown out that negative voice with a new positive one. You have to learn to respond differently to the things that happen to you. So, instead of immediately saying things like:

- 'I'll never be any good at that' say, *'I can do it'.*
- Wake up in the morning and let your first thought be, *'It's a great day!'*
- Say, *'I am beautiful... I am loved... I am strong... I am a great student'.*
- When you sit down to study do not say, 'I don't want to be here' Or, 'I can't do this'. Say, *'This is great!'*, *'I like this topic'.*

Develop your own statements – the ones that make you feel good, energised and strong.

tip

Put these statements in the positive and in the present tense. So it's not, 'I will not be afraid', but, 'I am brave'. The former only emphasises the thing that you do not want to be, afraid. Putting things in the future tense always seems to put them out of reach somehow. And you want the positive energy now – not in some unrealisable future.

Don't stop

Once you start using these positive statements, it is important to keep them going. You will have had the little negative voice for a long time: when it begins to disappear – to be drowned out by the positive voice – you can get a real sense of euphoria and release. Suddenly it feels as though you don't need your positive statements any more. But if you stop, that old negative voice will come right back. So start the positive statements – and keep them up.

Every time you have a spare moment, maybe as you travel or as you tidy up, repeat your positive statements to yourself. When fear pops out, repeat your positive statements – we promise you will feel the panic subside.

> **"** I always practise positive thinking on my way to do a presentation. I can feel my mouth get dry – and all those butterflies ... But I just keep saying, I can do it, I can do it ... It works for me. **"**

Stick 'em up

Some people write their positive statements on cards and stick them around the house – by the bed, on the bathroom mirror... You can even put a positive statement on the screen saver on your computer. We've got 'joy' on ours. Joy gives a quick boost when it appears – making it easier to get back to work. Immerse yourself in positivity as you immerse yourself in your studies.

Find out – give 100%

When you decide to achieve something, investigate what it will take to succeed – and then do it. Give 100%. You cannot sit in a corner glowing positively and expect that essay to write itself; you *can* investigate what it takes to do a good essay, and then do it. If you want to pass your exams, look at past papers, work out what you need to do and learn to pass – then do it. If you want a new job, find out what they are looking for, put that information in your CV, then go for it. Positive thinking is not about replacing hard work with happy fluffy thoughts; but it is knowing that with research, effort and belief in yourself, you can do it.

A positive conclusion

In this chapter we have explored the human, affective, dimension of the academic environment and of being a student. We have paid particular attention to the role of fear and the benefits of positive thinking, self-belief and self-confidence.

Entering education – the unknown – can be fearful for everybody, and perhaps even more so for those who do not see themselves as typical students or as academics. If this is you, we recommend that you take the time to actively work on developing your positive thinking.

Positive thinking does not just help in your studies, it can give new confidence elsewhere. Suddenly you can speak up in meetings, you can volunteer for things that you would never have dared do before, you can set yourself whole new challenges... you can look for a more exciting and rewarding job... all because you now realise you have more ability than you thought.

Post script

Has this actually made you a little more fearful? Well, you know the answer to that – feel the fear and do it anyway! It is exciting and liberating to be in charge of your own life – enjoy your fear, it means you are still alive.

4. Activity: Active review – think positive

As always, reflect back over this chapter and make your learning conscious.

- What have you read?
- Why did you read it?
- How did it make you feel?
- What have you learned?
- Can you use it in your studies? How? Where?
- What else will you need to find out?
- What else will you need to do?
- When will this happen?

Further reading – self-help

You may like to follow up these ideas by reading some of the positive thinking books dedicated to helping people learn how to face life's challenges more positively. The one that our students particularly like is Susan Jeffers (1997) *Feel the Fear and Do It Anyway*.

 **tip**

Experiment until you find something that appeals to you. Note that there is also criticism of this type of literature – that it can make us feel even more guilty and responsible for our own failures – avoid the negative...

Reading

Bandura, A.: http://www.des.emory.edu/mfp/self-efficacy.html (accessed 18 August 2011)

Cohen, S.B. (1997) *The Maladapted Mind*. London: Psychology Press

Feather, H. (2000) *Intersubjectivity and Contemporary Social Theory*. Farnham, UK: Ashgate

Jeffers, S. (1997) *Feel the Fear and Do It Anyway*. London: Century

Psychology blog – understand your mind: http://www.spring.org.uk/

Ted Talks – Five mindshifting talks on happiness: http://blog.ted.com/2011/08/19/playlist-5-mindshifting-talks-on-happiness/

Review points

When thinking about what you have read and the activities that you have engaged in, you might feel that you have:

- Thought about the impact of fear and a lack of self-belief and self-confidence on you as a student
- Considered the origins of fear in humans in terms of evolution, environment and upbringing
- Explored some steps to take to improve your own self-confidence and assertiveness in the academic environment.

Section VI

Reflective Learning

23

Reflective Learning and the Learning Log

Aims

It is the intention of this chapter to consider the importance of reflection in effective learning – with a special focus on the reflective learning log.

Learning outcomes

By the end of reading this chapter, and through engaging in the activities, you will:

- understand the importance of the reflective review as an essential part of the learning process
- have engaged in specific review activities designed to get you reflecting on your development of the study and academic skills and practices necessary for becoming a successful student
- have utilised the opportunity to practise several review activities.

Introduction

Welcome to this reflective learning section – with chapters on the learning log, memory, exams, PDP, moving on – and the Bibliography, which we suppose is an academic reflection on the contents of this book. Whilst these chapters are separate, their message is uniform: in terms of successful academic practice, reflection (review) is something that you should be engaged in all the time, for without review, there is no learning. In this chapter we are going to suggest you keep a reflective learning diary to make your learning more effective and successful. We will cover the diary in some detail – making links with successful active learning. We will also offer some review activities to get you thinking about different sections of this text.

What is reflective learning?

Reflective learning involves a process of thinking over what you have done – of making your learning conscious – of actively revisiting what you have learned. It is part of the active learning that we have been practising throughout this book: with each chapter we ask you to think about what you know and need from the chapter itself – to set yourself goals. Within the chapter we present information – supported by activities, questions and discussion that are all designed to get you to engage actively with the information. We conclude each chapter with a review of the learning that could have taken place for you. We have suggested that you blog about your learning – or complete a learning log. In this chapter we are going to explore how to formalise this active reflective learning in a learning log, diary or journal.

 **tip**

For Kolb's reflective cycle, linking reflective learning to PDP, see Chapter 26.

Beyond the revision cycle

Active revision = successful study.

- Without a revision cycle we forget 98% in three weeks.
- Revision starts at the beginning of a course – and should be ongoing.
- This is different from what people call revision – which tends to mean giving yourself three weeks or three days before your exams to learn everything on your course.
- A reflective learning diary is a form of reflective writing that will help you to understand, learn and write about your course material.

Why be reflective?

Ongoing review of what you are learning – and of how successfully you are learning – promotes active self-assessment and puts you in control of your own development. This is always useful, but even more obviously so for reflective assignments, especially PDP (Chapter 26). Reflective moments can focus on any aspect of your development that you wish – but remember; whilst your university will expect you to reflect, complete learning journals and engage in PDP, don't just go through the motions. Reflective learning is for you – not the university. Set your own goals. Take control of your own learning.

How to keep a reflective learning diary

Your reflective learning diary (or log or journal) is your own analytical, detailed and concise record of your studies. The process of completing this diary makes your learning active and conscious – which improves the quantity and quality of your learning.

Writing your diary should follow swiftly upon a study session – and the writing itself should be purposeful and concentrated. The structure outlined below works with our students; but once you have tried it, re-shape it so that it takes the form or shape that works best for you.

tips

- Keep a diary for each module that you do.
- Spend a few minutes after each study period – a class, lecture or independent study – completing your journal.
- Keep an online learning diary, blog one of your modules.
- When completing your learning diaries, you could use the question matrix questions – who, what, where, when, how, why, so what, what if, what next, and the diagrams offered in Chapter 13 – or the headings below.

The reflective learning diary

This diary has six parts: what, why, reaction, solutions and problems, learned and goal setting. It does not have to be a rigid thing – experiment until you find a structure that best meets your needs and suits your learning style.

tip

Write your diaries on one side of a piece of paper, use the template offered at the chapter end – or use a pattern note format. Use key words to make them manageable and colour and cartoons to make them memorable.

- **What**: Make brief notes of what you did: the lecture or seminar that you attended, the reading that you have done.
- **Why**: Make brief analytical notes: why did you do it? How was it useful? What learning outcomes did it cover? What part of the assignment question is it helping you with? Knowing why you are doing something helps you move from being a passive to an active learner.
- **Reaction**: Make brief notes on your emotional response to the activity: notice the affective dimension to your learning. This allows you to build a picture of yourself as a learner and as a student. (See Chapter 22 'How to Deal with Your Emotions'.)

This reflection allows you to notice what and how you like to learn: the subjects and topics that you enjoy – and the ones that you do not like so much; whether you like lectures or reading, whether you enjoy group work or independent study. This means that you can choose modules and teaching and learning strategies that suit you.

tips

- Be honest. You will not get a true picture of your own likes, dislikes and preferences if you paint a rosy picture of yourself.
- Use the discoveries that you make here to inform your subject choices.
- Use the information to help you refine your own learning style.

- **Successes and Problems**: Note how you solve the problems that you encounter as you study. It is all too easy just to focus on our failings – note your successes.

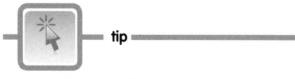

tip

If you are submitting a reflective account as part of an assessment, reflecting on how you overcame problems demonstrates that you are a successful, reflective student.

➡

- **Learned**: Make brief notes on all that you think that you learned from the lecture, class or reading. These notes are where you make your learning conscious, which improves both the quantity and quality of your learning. When we do not do this we are in danger of leaving the learning behind as we walk away from that lecture or close that book. You can make this section of your review as detailed and/or concise as you wish.

tips

- When making the learning conscious, make links with the assignment question.
- Use this section of your review to practise your academic writing.
- Diaries, as with all academic writing, get easier with practice.

- **Goal setting**: Make brief notes about what you will do next... nothing will ever give you 'all you need to know' on a subject. Therefore, you should always be thinking: What next?

Resources and Tips

Set dates in your diary – if you do not make a date it will not get done.

Make it creative and fun: a sketchbook of ideas, thoughts and learning. See 'Creative Learning in Practice Sketchbook' site for advice on reflective learning, podcasts from staff and students – and beautiful images of what a journal could look like: http://www.arts. ac.uk/cetl/visual-directions/

Reflective writing leads to successful writing in assignments. This is the reflective writing section of the Queen Mary's University of London 'Thinking/Writing' site: http://www.think-ingwriting.qmul.ac.uk/reflect.htm

This takes you to examples of real students' reflective writing: http://www.thinkingwrit-ing.qmul.ac.uk/reflect3.htm

Remember the 'Evolving Essay' wiki and blog that demonstrates reflective writing as part of the assignment process: http://evolvingessay.pbwiki.com/

Reflecting on ESS3

We have included some reflection activities here that are designed to help you think about how ESS3 is helping your development as a student. Use the Diary template in Figure 23B and use these activities positively – enjoy them.

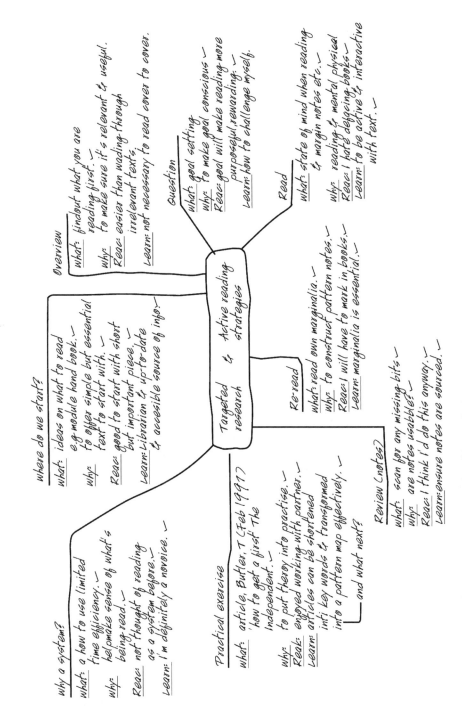

FIGURE 23A Example of a pattern review completed by student

Reflective learning diary – template	
What	Make brief notes of what you did: the lecture or seminar that you attended, the reading that you have done.
Why	Make brief analytical notes: why did you do it? How was it useful? What learning outcomes did it cover? What part of the assignment question is it helping you with? *Knowing why you are doing something helps you move from being a passive to an active learner.*
Reaction	Make brief notes on your emotional response to the activity: notice the affective dimension to your learning. It allows you to build a picture of yourself as a learner and as a student. NB: This reflection allows you to notice what and how you like to learn: the subjects and topics that you enjoy – and the ones that you do not like so much; whether you like lectures or reading, whether you enjoy group work or independent study. This means that you can choose modules and teaching and learning strategies that suit you.
Learned	Make brief notes on all that you think that you learned from the lecture, class or reading. These notes are where you make your learning conscious, which improves both the quantity and quality of your learning. When we do not do this we are in danger of leaving the learning behind as we walk away from that lecture or close that book. You can make this section of your review as detailed and/or concise as you wish.
Goal setting	Make brief notes about what you will do next… nothing will ever give you 'all you need to know' on a subject. Therefore, you should always be thinking: What next?

FIGURE 23B   Reflective learning diary template

 Photocopiable:

Essential Study Skills, Third Edition © Tom Burns and Sandra Sinfield, 2012 (SAGE)

1. Activity: Self-assessment – What have you done with ESS3 – the chapters?

When reading and working through ESS3, write a reflective account of each chapter that you have read.

Discussion: If you do this, you should be more aware of what you are learning – and be feeling much more in control. If you do still have any remaining issues, why not:

- Go to see the Learning Development or Support Unit at your institution?
- Visit the Student Support Services people?
- Sort things out with your study partner?

2. Activity: Self-assessment – What have you done with ESS3 – the book?

When you have finished reading and working through the whole book – re-read your chapter dairies and reflect on what you have learned from the book as a whole. Write a report on your own progress (like the student report in Chapter 18).

Discussion: This would also help you to write your PDP. If unclear of how to make the most of this read Chapter 26.

"Without doing my review, I wouldn't even have understood the class, let alone remembered it!**"**

Conclusion

We have prompted you to reinforce your active learning by using the reflective learning diary – an ongoing and detailed review system that will allow you to make your learning conscious. This will improve both the quantity and quality of your learning and help you with your academic writing and other assignments.

We argued that this particular review structure will also enable you to notice the subjects and learning strategies that suit you best. This is information that can inform your module choices, your learning strategies and your development as a successful student.

We moved on to include a couple of activities designed to get you actively reviewing your engagement with this text – we do hope that you enjoy those activities. Good luck with the rest of the book.

Further reading

For creative ideas see 'Creative Learning in Practice Sketchbook' site: http://www.arts. ac.uk/cetl/visual-directions/

For links between reflective writing and assignment success see: http://www.thinking writing.qmul.ac.uk/reflect.htm

For examples of real students' reflective writing: http://www.thinkingwriting.qmul.ac.uk/ reflect3.htm

For an online essay and accompanying reflective blog: http://evolvingessay.pbwiki.com/

Review points

When reviewing this chapter you might notice that:

- You are much more aware of how active you have to be to make learning happen
- You have practised the learning log – and are ready to use a reflective learning journal as part of your active learning on your course
- You will explore how to make your journal creative and stimulating so that it inspires you
- You have made a connection between reflection, active learning – success in assignments – and PDP.

Section VI

Reflective Learning

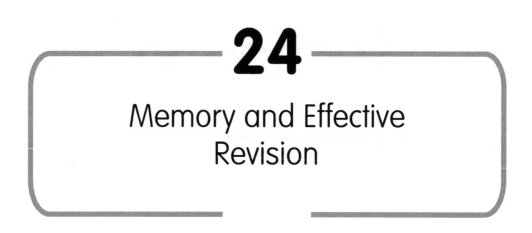

24

Memory and Effective Revision

Aims

In this chapter, we aim to enhance your learning and memory strategies so that you revise effectively and pass your exams. (See also Chapters 5, 22 and 25.)

Learning outcomes

After reading this chapter and engaging with the activities, you will have:

- considered your own memory and memorisation strategies
- reflected on how to harness your memory to pass exams
- re-visited learning styles and linked this to revision and exam success
- been introduced to successful memory, learning and revision strategies.

Memory and learning style

This whole book is about improving your learning and maximising what you can get from your studies – here we are going to link that to successful revision techniques.

Do you think that you have a good memory?

Whenever we ask that question of a group of students, the majority say they have a bad memory, usually because they have not consciously developed effective learning and memory strategies. We can all develop a good memory – with practice.

Memory

Tony Buzan has explored the psychology and dynamics of memory with respect to study and learning. He argues that we need *active revision* if we want to remember, if we want to learn. Learning does not happen by accident or chance. Buzan states that, without active revision, we forget 98% of what we encounter after just three weeks. This means that if we do not *act* to remember we forget, almost immediately. This is obviously a real problem for those students who revise only three weeks before an exam: this is not revision; it is learning it all from scratch. And no, you cannot do that in three weeks.

The revision cycle

Buzan recommends an active revision cycle when encountering new and important material:

1 The same day that you encounter the new material, spend 10 minutes making a short, dynamic version of your notes. Build in mnemonics – triggers to jog your memory. These might be cartoons, illustrations or diagrams that are funny, bizarre or bawdy – these are what make the memory work.
2 A day later spend two minutes recalling your memory trigger – and the notes attached. Mentally recall the information or actually re-draw the notes. The more active you are the better. Find and highlight what you forgot.
3 A week later spend another two minutes reactivating the memory – plugging those gaps.
4 A month later spend another two minutes reactivating the memory.
5 Reactivate every six months for as long as you want to keep the memory alive.

The revision cycle is a 'use it or lose it' cycle. It is a system based on transferring information from our relatively ineffectual short-term memories into our infinitely more useful long-term memories. In the process of doing this, we are actually building memories chemically into our brains.

   And, we get quicker with these revision strategies with practice.

➡

Each week reduce your lecture and reading notes onto index cards. This will develop your memory – and the cards will be the building blocks of your revision.

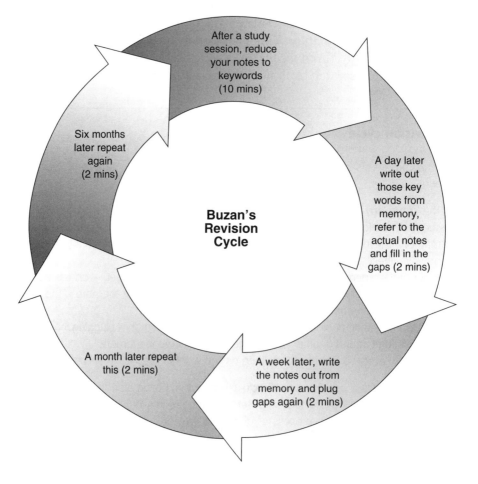

FIGURE 24A   Buzan's revision cycle

Short- and long-term memory

Buzan's research refines our notions of the short and long-term memory. The short-term memory is a very small and immediate working memory. This allows us to function day to day. Our long-term memories are memories that we create and build and reinforce over time. It could be argued that these allow us to function in our lives – they become who we are. In terms of studying, the short-term memory is good for picking up pieces of information, but we need to get that information into our long-term memories if it is to be of any use to us. Getting information into our long-term memories does not happen by accident or chance. It does not happen quickly. It does not happen unless we do something to make it happen. Basically, if we do want to learn something, then we have to:

- Choose what to remember
- Decide how we are going to remember it (our memory triggers)
- Be prepared to reactivate the memory immediately, then a day, a week and a month later (use the revision cycle).

1. Activity: Think back to how you learned things in primary school or kindergarten

Spend five minutes jotting down how you learned things in your earliest days at school. Now compare your list with points taken from other students:

"I learned the alphabet by singing a little alphabet song. It is still the way I remember the alphabet."

"We were taught our sums by reciting the times tables. But I don't actually remember them now. I don't think I wanted to learn my tables – so that didn't work so well."

"I remember the colours of the rainbow, you know: Richard of York Gained Battle In Vain. If you take the first letters you can get back to Red, Orange, Yellow, Green, Blue, Indigo, Violet."

"One that my little girl came home with the other day was the spelling of 'because' – big elephants can always understand small elephants."

"And then there is that other one – Never Eat Shredded Wheat – which gives you the points of the compass... North, East, South, West."

"I went to a Montessori school, we would see it, hear it, say it and do it."

➡

> **Query**: How do these compare with what you have written?
>
> **Discussion**: What is happening here is that the teacher is designing the mnemonics, the memory systems or triggers, for the students. Where the trigger involves rhythm and rhyme (the alphabet song), it seems to be more successful; where the trigger involves something unusual or bizarre (Richard of York – or the big elephants) it is more memorable; where the student does not want to remember, all the repetition in the world is not making it happen.

We put aside childish things

Unfortunately, most of us did not realise that this *was* learning how to learn. What seems to happen as we get older is that we stop using these successful memory strategies, strategies that work with the way that our brains actually work. We grow to be adults and instead of becoming more proficient learners, we put aside these successful learning strategies. It is as if we deliberately forget how to learn. What we need to do once we are students, is to relearn how to learn. When we apply learning strategies to our studies, we must *want* to learn and we must be *active*: working out *what* it is that we want to remember – and deciding *how* we are going to remember that – using the systems that work with our brains.

 **tips**

- Design your own mnemonic systems for all the things that you need to remember.
- Use rhythm and rhyme.
- Use the bizarre.
- Reduce key information onto index cards, carry them about and revise in odd moments.

Learning is key

We are emphasising just how active you have to be in your own learning and remembering: choosing what and how to learn. However, we are not saying that you have to learn textbooks, your lecturer's PowerPoint slides or essays by heart. Indeed a key to successful learning is not to try to remember whole

Short-term memory	Attribute	Long-term memory
Relatively small – holds 5–9 pieces of information	Capacity – size	Infinite – can build an infinite number of memories in the brain
Brief – piece of information number 8 comes along – and a piece of information falls out	Persistence – how long information stays	Infinite – with reactivation and barring brain trauma – information can stay there for ever
Is immediate – either it goes in or it does not	Input – how to get information in	Relatively slow – see revision cycle. It takes time and effort to build memories
Is immediate – if it is there you can access it	Access – how to get information out	Depends on input. How you put it in is how to get it out (alphabet song)

FIGURE 24B   The main attributes of short- and long-term memory

chunks of information. It is not an advantage to try for word-for-word recall of whole lectures or seminars, of whole essays that you or other students have written or whole passages from books. This is ineffective: you are remembering padding rather than key information; you are being passive rather than active; and it can trap you in the way that other people have used information and stop you from being able to use it yourself.

To be both active and effective in our learning we have to develop our ability to strip back what we need to learn to the bare essentials: to the skeleton. Once we have learned the bare bones, we need to be able to use information ourselves: in discussion, in presentations and in our writing – including our exam writing. If we simply remember how other people have used the information – in lectures or in textbooks, for example – it will never be our own.

❝ I saw this student in the library preparing for the exam by trying to learn the PowerPoint slides from my lectures – all of them and in the same order that I had delivered them! I tried to explain that it's not about learning my lectures – it's about understanding and extending them – and then using the data to answer the questions set in the exam. **❞**

Add flesh to the bones – later

So, the trick is to reduce information to its bare essentials, the skeleton – which we do learn by heart. We then practise using the information for ourselves over the whole programme of study. We do this by talking, reading, listening and writing – not just by rote learning handouts or lecture notes.

What we can do as we move through a course towards the exams, is, week by week, to reduce handouts, lecture notes and notes from our reading to ever fewer words. We understand these key words because we have been *using* them constantly over the course: we reduce the quantity of what we have to learn (the amount) but improve the quality (we can use it ourselves, with confidence).

tip

As you reduce information to the bare essentials, utilise 'see, hear, say and do' strategies. Use all the learning styles to develop your revision strategies.

Use your learning style to learn your key words

See
If you are visual, you may enjoy learning by reading and using visual aids (television, film or video). It will help if you made revision notes as colourful as possible – visual triggers will definitely help you to remember.

Hear/say
If you prefer an auditory learning style, then lectures, discussion and audio-tapes will all help you to learn. For revision purposes, put your key word data into jingles or songs – use funny voices when revising.

Feel/do
If you favour a kinaesthetic learning approach, you will benefit from building a physical dimension into your learning – this could be really simple, like moving about as you study (very different, though from the notion of the good student sitting quietly in one place for hours on end). *Make* your pattern notes – make collage notes.

But to learn it all, you need to see it, hear it, say it and do it.

tip

Explore BBC Scotland's Brain Smart website which has animations and information on the brain, memory, dealing with stress, successful learning strategies – and brain games: http://www.bbc.co.uk/scotland/brainsmart/

390

2. Activity: Have some fun!

Make a game of your learning – inject some fun into the proceedings. Designing revision games really helps learning.

If you had to design a revision game for one of your programmes of study, what would you do? Think for five minutes – then compare your ideas with those below.

Typically, students have designed:

- **Quizzes** – here the students researched a specific programme (sociology, psychology, history), examining the aims and learning outcomes. Once they identified the key data (names, dates, information) that ought to be learned by the end of the course, they designed questions and answers for them. A competitive edge was set up for the quiz by having several teams competing against each other. Answering the questions or not revealed to the players both the information they had learned – and that which they had forgotten.
- **Board games** – here again, the students researched a programme examining the aims and learning outcomes. They constructed questions and answers that covered all the learning outcomes (the key data – names, dates, and information). But here they designed a colourful board game that could be played as the questions were answered.

> **Discussion**: Both these strategies are very effective with respect to learning the key information on a course.

The quiz utilises 'see, hear and say' strategies, and the playing of the quiz can become an emotional and even a physical experience.

The board game scenario is especially good, as to play the game you will be working with other people and using see, hear, say and do!

3. Activity: Learning style revision games

Choose one section of this book. Reduce the information to key word points. Design a revision game that would help you learn the material. Play the game with your study partner.

4. Activity: Get Ready for Exams Checklist

If you have not already done so, complete the 'Get ready for your exams checklist' in Chapter 25, for each course that you are studying.

Conclusion

We have explored how to develop your memory and utilise your learning style as part of successful revision and learning strategies. The trick now is for you to actually do something with this information. It will not work for you if you do nothing about it. A next step is to read Chapter 25 to see how to draw all these things together into a whole course strategy for passing exams. You can build your memory, whatever you think of it now – and enjoy learning your course material and passing those exams.

Further reading and resources

If you are interested in taking the ideas in this chapter further, the following might help:

BBC Scotland Brain Smart: http://www.bbc.co.uk/scotland/brainsmart/
Buzan, T. (1989) *Use Your Head*. London: BBC Publications
Buzan, B. and Buzan, T. (1999) *The Mind Map Book*. London: BBC Publications
Rogers, C. (1992) *Freedom to Learn*. Upper Saddle River, NJ: Merrill
Rose, C. and Goll, L. (1992) *Accelerate your Learning*. Aylesbury, UK: Accelerated Learning Systems

Maths resources

Video tutorials: http://www.sigma-cetl.ac.uk/index.php?section=92
Pdfs: http://www.sigma-cetl.ac.uk/index.php?section=102
Revision tips for Maths students: http://www-users.york.ac.uk/%7Edajp1/Exam_Hints/Exams.html

Review points

When reviewing this chapter you might realise that you now have:

- A better understanding of the role of memory in learning
- A sense of how to use learning styles to develop your memory and learn course material
- An understanding of successful learning and revision strategies
- A sense of how to inject some fun into your learning.

Section VI

Reflective Learning

25

How to Understand and Pass Exams

Aims

Exams are not a universally popular form of assessment – this chapter explores how to adopt a positive approach to exams – with advice and guidelines on how to prepare for and succeed in exams.

Learning outcomes

After reading this chapter and engaging with the activities, you will have:

- considered exams – and how you feel about them
- been introduced to a whole course approach to exam success
- been introduced to successful learning, revision and exam strategies.

Introduction

In this chapter we are going to explore the what, why and how of exams – but the big focus will be on:

- A practical whole-course approach to passing exams
- Essential examination day information
- 'Get ready for exams' checklist.

Reflective learning is covered in Chapter 23 and memory, learning style and revision in Chapter 24; see also Chapter 5 on effective learning and Chapter 22 on dealing with the emotional aspects.

---

1. Activity: Goal setting

As always, before you read this chapter, pause and reflect:

- What do I already know about exams?
- What would I like to know?
- What do I like about my exam techniques?
- What would I like to improve?

Once you have brainstormed and set your own goals, you are ready to get the most from this chapter.

Exams are good for many things...

Or to put it another way, we know you will probably have to sit exams – so this is what they are good for and how to survive them.

❝ I hated the very idea of exams. They left my stomach in knots at the sheer thought of them. The fear of them paralysed me, which probably resulted in my getting a 2:1 instead of a first. **❞**

Many students have a fear of exams – but often the problem is not with exams at all, but lies in how we were taught at school and college. That is, whilst we are taught subject *content* we are not taught *how to learn* that content. Content is good – and it is important to know *what* we ought to learn – but it helps if we also know *how* to learn the material for ourselves. Without this, many people admit defeat and give up on exams, thinking that they are not cut out for them, they are not clever enough, that they have poor memory... whatever. The reality is that they have either not been taught how to learn or they do not realise that they were taught this in primary school, but forgot. And they have not learned how to take control of their emotional responses to exams – and still fear them.

Fear can have a negative effect on the brain releasing stress hormones cortisol and adrenalin which reduce short-term memory and create a tunnel vision effect – great for fight or flight – but unhelpful in exams. If this describes how you feel about exams, you really will have to change your basic negative approach before you will be able to move forward.

tips

- Look at material on positive thinking – see Chapter 22 to start you off.
- Understand that exams are a test, not a trick.
- Work towards your exams with a study partner.
- Use the learning development (learning support, study skills or study development) at your university to help you prepare for exams.
- Use the counselling service to help you get over your fear of exams.

It's learning, Jim – but not as we know it

Exams are designed not to test your surface learning, your memory of key facts and data. Exams test your deep learning, your *understanding* of key facts and data; they are designed to see how you *use* the information that you have learned over a whole course in a new situation. As this whole book has been about learning how to learn, this aspect – the learning bit – should not be a problem for you now.

tip

Try to enjoy the exam as a way to prove yourself and show what you know.

❝I know I'm unusual but I really love exams and hate coursework. With exams I get to pace myself throughout the whole year – as opposed to everything I write counting! Then I can psych myself up to perform really well for three hours or so. It's brilliant!❞

Many people feel that they have a bad memory, often because they have not actually learned how to use their memories; they have not learned how to learn. Moreover, contrary to popular opinion, revision is not something that you should be doing just before your exams. Revision is part of active learning. You should be learning material as you go through your course – not just before the exams. Doing this should sort out your worries about your memory. What you do just before the exams is practise that timed writing.

" I've got a really bad memory: How can you learn a whole year's work in three weeks? **"**

— **tips** —————————————————————————————

- Check out Chapter 24 on memory and learning styles.
- Check out Chapter 5 on effective learning.
- Summarise and learn key points as you go.
- Read the whole course approach to passing exams, below.

" How long should the answer be? I'm dyslexic and write slowly. **"**

There is usually no set length to an exam answer; in the end there is only what you can write in the time you have. Everyone has to discover how much they can write in the time allowed – and then get better at writing an answer in that many words.

For the dyslexic student who writes more slowly perhaps this can feel like a problem. However, there are many positive things to do.

First, if you think that you are dyslexic, you must get a proper test done. Go to the Student Support Services at your college or university to find out how this happens.

If you are dyslexic you will get extra time in exams. Typically another 10 minutes per hour in an exam – but check.

More importantly, lobby to take exams on a PC, as this can have a marked effect on your grades. We know students who moved from FAIL to FIRST doing this – perhaps because:

- Word-processed work looks so much neater, it overcomes any unconscious prejudice in the mind of the examiner towards untidy handwriting
- The student feels much more confident on the computer and therefore produces better work
- The student practises more.

 **tips for slow writers** ——————————————————

- Practise timed writing.
- Practise answering assignment questions, but where you would normally be allowed upwards of 1,500 words, give yourself half an hour.

- Practise preparing perfect answers with your study partner.
- If using a computer – learn to touch type.
- Practise timed writing on the computer.

Putting it all together – a practical guide to exam success

In this section we will bring together the learning to learn information from the whole book into a very practical revision and exam technique: survey, question, predict, plan, prepare and practise (SQP4). This will be followed by essential examination day information and a 'get ready for exams' checklist.

2. Activity: Thinking about exams

In this brief activity, we want you to compare academic exams to other things that you might choose to do:

- Running a marathon
- Passing a driving test
- X-Factor or a dance competition.

1 Choose one of the activities above and think how you would prepare for it (5 minutes).
2 Now compare your answer with that given by the student below:

66 When planning for my driving test I sorted out the written test first. I got the book with the questions in and tested myself 'til I thought I'd got them right. Then I got my friends to test me 'til I was sure I'd got it right. I only lost two points in the test itself.

With the driving part, I had lessons 'til my instructor thought I was ready. When I was confident that I knew how to do it, I booked the test.

Then my instructor and I practised all the things that would definitely come up in the test – you know emergency stop, three-point turn, and parking properly.

When I could drive a car in my sleep – I took the test and passed first time. **99**

Query: Did you cover much the same ground as this student?

Discussion: When it comes to the sorts of 'test' that we choose to do in our everyday life, we do know what to do. We:

- find out exactly what will be required of us in the test
- learn the things that we need to learn

- practise often
- want to do well.

That is the essence of our system.

Survey

As soon as you start on a course, make sense of it straight away – get the overview – the big picture (see also Chapter 4):

- If you have a course booklet or handbook, check the aims and learning outcomes. Make key word notes summarising all the things that you will have to do and learn to pass the course.
- If supplied with a syllabus, read it and cross reference with the aims and outcomes – what is being covered when?
- Read the assignment question to give yourself specific learning targets, and again cross reference with the course. Each week you study you should know what you are learning and why – and which bit of the assignment or exam you are tackling.
- Find and read past exam papers: How many questions will you have to answer – in how much time? How difficult or complex are the questions? What topics always appear? Be prepared!

 **tips**

Write an 'exam' list for each course that you are taking, note:

- How long will the exam be?
- How many questions will you have to answer?
- Whether it is a seen or unseen exam (where you get the paper in advance).
- Whether or not it is an open book exam (where you may be allowed to take textbooks into the exam).

Where are my papers?

Sometimes past papers are given to students, sometimes they are not. Sometimes they are kept in the library – sometimes they are kept in your VLE.
   The trick is to find them and read them. ➡

❝I have a website for all my students to use – and I put resources up there. I also have a counter to see which pages students look at the most.

I suppose you've guessed it, they look at past exam papers and model answers the least!**❞**

Question

Once you have spent real time surveying the course to gain your overview, you need to sit down and ask yourself: what exactly do I need to do and learn to pass this course? Make a list – pin it up in your study space. Do this for every course, module or unit that you are taking.

tips

- Draw up your lists with your study partner.
- For each exam, make a list of the topics that will come up.
- Link to learning outcomes.
- Link to course weeks.
- Link to assignment question.
- Put the lists on your wall and in your coursework folders.

Predict

Once you have examined all the course information that you have been given and all the past papers that you can find, predict the questions that will come up on the exam paper. Then decide which questions you will answer. Follow your interests and you will learn more: it is very difficult to learn if we are totally uninterested.

tips

- An exam question usually combines two or more of the topics set in the coursework assignments.
- If possible, do assignment questions that lead to an exam topic.
- If you are prohibited from answering an assignment question and an exam question on the same topic work out a strategy with your study partner. (Write your coursework on A and your exam on B – your partner does the opposite and you share your research.)
- Open a revision folder on each exam topic that you intend to answer.

Plan

Once you have chosen your exam topics, you must plan your learning and revision strategy for each topic, drawing on what you now know about effective learning, memory and learning style.

Useful things to do to pass exams

1. Have a revision folder for each topic – in each exam.
2. Put relevant class, lecture and reading notes into each folder.
3. Answer assignment questions linked to exam topics.
4. Put assignment notes into the relevant folders.
5. Put the assignments into the folders.
6. Put any extra work that you do following your tutor's feedback on your assignment in the folders.
7. Put in press cuttings.
8. Start a revision cycle for each of the topics that you want to learn – from week one of each course!
9. Build a big picture, pattern note for each topic (see Chapter 11).
10. Add information to your own 'big picture' every week.
11. Spend a few minutes reviewing your big picture every week.
12. Reduce key information – summarise as key words on index cards. Carry them with you – learn them in a supermarket checkout queue, learn them on the bus, learn them in the lift.
13. Fill in the 'Get ready for your exams' checklist.

Prepare for your exams

It is not enough to *plan* to pass your exams – you must actually do everything that you have planned to do: you must *prepare* for your exams. So, to prepare properly you have to:

- Keep a revision cycle going for each exam topic.
- Keep your revision folders and your big picture revision pattern up to date.
- Go through each revision folder from time to time, throwing out excess material.
- Each week add key points and illustrations to your big picture.
- Keep your index cards up to date. As you learn the material, reduce your notes, make your index card notes shorter.
- Each time you make your notes shorter, you are revising the material.
- Illustrate your notes with memorable cartoons.
- Make key word tapes using rhyme and music. Play these as you go over your big picture notes.
- Design quizzes – test your friends.

Successful exam preparation tips and tricks

- **Want to do well**: Be interested, know what you want from the course, know why you want to get a good grade.
- **Learn the bones**: Only learn key word points, don't fill your memory with padding. You want the skeleton, not the whole body.
- **Memorise**: Take time each week to memorise key facts.
- **Practise turning key words into essays**.
- **Study partner**: Make sure you do have a study partner. Plan and prepare perfect answers together.
- **Board games!** Get Trivial Pursuit or some other board game. Put the questions to one side. Devise question and answer cards for all your exam topics – play the game with your study partner.
- **See it, hear it, say it, do it!**

Practise

At last, we have come to something that you can do three weeks before your exams! All the above strategies emphasise learning key data – names, dates, key points of information – from the beginning of each course. What you need to do just before the exam is to practise using the information that you are learning *under exam conditions*. Typically, this involves practising timed writing.

What, squeeze 3,000 words into half an hour!

As you study, you use information in class discussion, in group-based learning activities, in presentations and other assignments. You have time to plan and research your answers. You have anything from 1,500 to 3,000 or more words in which to answer a question. Suddenly in an exam, you have just half an hour or an hour to plan and write a perfect answer.

You now have to work completely differently from the way you have worked before. As with a driving test, you will not be able to do this unless you have practised doing it. You will not be able to plan and write a good essay in a time limit unless you have practised both planning and writing under timed conditions. It is as simple as that.

Practising for exams

- Practise brainstorming and planning: Develop the 10-minute brainstorm technique.
- Go through all the questions in your course handbook – allow 10 minutes per brainstorm, plan an answer for each one.
- Find past exam papers: Allow 10 minutes per brainstorm; brainstorm every question on the paper.
- See how much you can write in half an hour.
- Practise writing something good in half an hour.
- Practise turning a long assignment essay into a half-hour version of the same essay.
- Practise timed writing with notes.
- Practise timed writing without notes.
- Practise preparing and writing 'perfect' answers with your study partner.

Essential examination day information!

No writing on revision and exam techniques is complete without a look at the actual exams themselves. Here we are going to give some practical advice for examination day. So whatever you normally do around exam time, next time you have an exam try to do some of the following.

Using time in exams

Each exam is different. For each you will have to know how long the whole exam is and how many questions you will have to answer: this tells you how long you will have for each question. Time per question needs to be divided between preparation time, writing time and reviewing time:

- **Read the paper**: Always read the questions carefully. This is another reason why it is important to see past papers; so that the actual wording of the question does not intimidate or confuse you.
- **Plan each answer** (allow five to 10 minutes per plan): As with your assignment questions, analyse all the key words in the question: brainstorm each word in the question. Use the brainstorm to plan the answer: number the different points in your brainstorm to plan your essay. Always plan before you write. Time spent planning is never wasted. Time spent writing without planning can be very wasted indeed.
- **Start each answer**: You must begin to answer every question that you are supposed to. It is more important to begin than to finish (law of diminishing returns).
- **Write something for each question**: Do not run out of time – give the same amount of time to each question. Time yourself.
- **Review what you have written**: A few minutes checking your answer can make a phenomenal difference to your marks!
- **This all takes practice!**

Handling the exam

Read the paper, identify which questions you will answer, then try the following:

1   Brainstorm and plan each answer before you write anything. The advantage of this is that as you brainstorm one question, you may recall additional information for another question.
2   Brainstorm/plan and write your favourite question. Then brainstorm/plan all the others and then write in order of preference. The advantage of this is that you feel good once you have a whole question out of the way.
3   Brainstorm/plan and then write one question at a time.

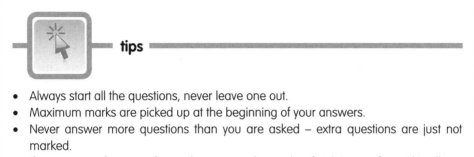

tips

- Always start all the questions, never leave one out.
- Maximum marks are picked up at the beginning of your answers.
- Never answer more questions than you are asked – extra questions are just not marked.
- If you run out of time – refer marker to your plan and/or finish in note form. This allows you to pick up points for key facts.
- Always cross out material that you do not want the examiner to mark.

Think smart – think positive

You need to mentally prepare for exams. You must want to do well – and you have to work at believing in yourself. See Chapter 22 on dealing with your emotions and building self-confidence – but here are a few tips for examination time:

- Remember that fear is normal – it does not mean that you cannot do well.
- Enjoy your fear – it means you are facing a new challenge.
- Think positive thoughts – I can handle this! I'm looking forward to this exam! I'm so well prepared!
- Act positive – find out what it would take to do well in your exam and then do it. Give 100%.
- Have a positive study partner – encourage and support each other – no moaning!

Relaxation

We recommend that as a student you build in stress relief activities from the beginning of your course, if not throughout your life. If you are in the habit of running or exercising, of meditating or doing yoga, then it will be easy for you to just do more of this around exam time.

If you are not in that habit, it is unlikely that you will suddenly develop good habits in the nick of time. So here we would just like to reiterate our advice – build exercise and stress relief into your life from the start. If you feel that you will become sleepless around exam time, practise using a sleep audiotape before the exams come up, then your body will know how to use the tape when you really need it.

The night before

If you have been putting successful techniques into practice over your course, you should feel confident that you do know your material and that you can plan and write an answer in the time allowed. So the night before the exam, you should not be trying to cram in new information, neither should you be panicking.

You should be quietly confident. You may wish to go over your key word notes – whether you have them on a big pattern on the wall, index cards or summarised onto sheets of paper. You may wish to practise a few 10-minute brainstorms – but the essence is on quiet confidence and rest. Have an early night.

On examination day

Get up early and have a light breakfast even if you do not feel like eating. Exams are hard work and you will need energy. But do not eat so much that all your blood goes to your stomach – you need a good supply getting to your brain.

Arrive at the examination room in good time. Do not cram in new information. Avoid people who are acting nervous or scared – they will only unsettle you and it is too late to help them now. Worse, we have heard of students who deliberately behave negatively in order to unsettle others to make them do badly in the exam. They feel that this increases their chances of doing well.

Make sure you have working pens and a watch. Take some chocolate with you or a glucose drink – for that extra energy boost mid-exam.

Think positive thoughts. Read through the paper carefully and choose your questions with confidence. Brainstorm and plan before you write. Recall your revision notes by sight, sound or feel. Time yourself through each question – and *start* every question. Leave time to quickly review what you have written.

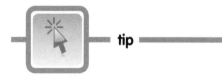 **tip**

The law of diminishing returns means that it is better to start every answer than to finish. If you are a slow writer, don't finish a single one – but do start them all. More marks are picked up at the beginning of an answer.

What examiners like to see

- Correct use of key words, phrases, terms and concepts from your subject.
- Questions answered in the correct format – essays where they want essays and reports where they want reports.
- Not writing 'all you know' on the topic but identifying the key words in the question and addressing those in your answer.
- Focus on the question set – appropriately drawing on course material.
- Discussing course material critically.
- Using the time well.
- Neat presentation.

After the exam

Avoid discussing the exam with other people, especially if you have another exam later that same day or the next day. Comparing answers with others can lead to panic – and you do not need that if you have other exams for which to prepare. If you do have another exam the following day, treat yourself to another relaxed evening and an early night.

---

3. Activity: The three minute test

Settle down and give yourself just three minutes to work through this short test:

Name:

Class:

Date/Time:

Read the paper carefully before answering any questions. This is a timed test – you have three minutes to complete the paper.

1 Before answering any questions, read through the whole paper.
2 Print your name, class, time and date in the appropriate sections of this paper.
3 Draw five small squares in the bottom right hand corner of this sheet.
4 Circle the word 'name' in question 2.
5 Put an 'x' in each of the five squares.
6 Sign your name at the top of this paper.

➡️

---

7   In front of your name write 'YES, YES, YES'.
8   Loudly, so that everyone can hear you, call out your name.
9   Put a circle around question number 3.
10 Put an 'x' in the lower left-hand corner of this paper.
11 Draw a triangle around the 'x' that you have just put down.
12 In your normal speaking voice count down from 10 to one.
13 Loudly call out, 'I am nearly finished, I have followed directions!'
14 Now that you have finished reading everything, do only questions one and two.

End of exam

Query: Well, how did you do? Were you that student bobbing up and down and calling things out? What does that tell you?

Discussion: Another name for this test is 'Can you follow directions?' It is a simple way of illustrating that you really do need to read an exam paper carefully before you start to answer the questions. The problem with not following directions in an exam could be that you do the wrong things. Typically, this would be in the sort of exam that states answer one question in section A and then one in B and then choose one question from either section – or something like that. If you do not read these instructions very carefully you can answer the wrong questions and throw marks away!

If you would like more practice at reading exam papers and brainstorming and writing answers, we have put a short Study Skills exam at the end of this chapter for you to use.

Conclusion

How to pass exams links several of the active and effective learning strategies covered elsewhere in this text with exam success. Specifically we discussed a whole course strategy for success. We finished with a detailed look at the examination day – things to do before, during and after the exam. You should now be ready to put these ideas into practice in your own learning. Do use the checklists and sample exam papers that have been included (also at the end of this chapter) to help you. Good luck with your exams!

Further reading

If you are interested in taking the ideas in this chapter further, the following might help:

BBC Scotland Brain Smart: http://www.bbc.co.uk/scotland/brainsmart/
Buzan, T. (1989) *Use Your Head*. London: BBC Publications
Buzan, B. and Buzan, T. (1999) *The Mind Map Book*. London: BBC Publications
Rose, C. and Goll, L. (1992) *Accelerate Your Learning*. Aylesbury: Accelerated Learning
    Systems

Review points

When reviewing this chapter you might realise that you now have:

- An understanding of exams and a chance to shine
- An introduction to a whole-course strategy for successful examination day strategies
- A time set aside for a practice exam and completing your exam preparation checklist (below).

4: Activity: Optional – the Study Skills exam

Just for fun, we have included a possible exam paper for students of this book. If you want to see how well you would do under timed conditions, why not have a go at this exam. Afterwards you can reflect on how well you did – and what that tells you about yourself as a student.

Study Skills Exam

Name:

Date:

Candidates must answer two questions: ONE question from Section A and ONE question from Section B. You have 90 minutes for the whole paper.

Section A

1 Evaluate the usefulness of this Study Skills book to you as a student.
2 In what ways have you been able to use your whole study programme as a Study Skills laboratory? With this in mind, what advice would you give next year's students?
3 What aspects of Study Skills will you take with you either into further study or into your work? Give reasons for your answer.

➡

Section B

1 Which is better – coursework or end of year exams? Justify your answer.
2 What are learning styles and how can you harness them to promote academic success?
3 Evaluate the usefulness to you as a student of one or more of the following: active learning; trial and error; reflective learning; creativity in learning. Give examples to justify your answer.

Exam ends

Query: How well did you do? If you are not sure, ask your study partner to mark your answers and to give you feedback. Here are some things for you to think about:

- Did you follow instructions? Did you answer one question from each section? If not, you know that you will need to keep practising this.
- Did you brainstorm/plan before you wrote your answer? Did this help? Do you need more practice at brainstorming? When will you do this? If you did not brainstorm – why not? If in doubt go to Chapter 12 on creative learning. Remember that brainstorming, like everything else we do, does indeed get better with practice.

 **tip**

Why not brainstorm every question on this paper just to practise brainstorming? Do this with your study partner – allow yourselves 10 minutes per question, then compare brainstorms at the end.

- Did you manage your time well? What have you learned about your ability to manage time? What do you need to practise to get better at managing your time?
- Overall: what have you learned about yourself as an exam taker? Make sure you do something with this information.

	Exams checklist		
	Subject		
Survey	*I have:*		
☐	received the course outline		
☐	read the course aims and learning outcomes		
☐	read the schedule and thought about the course structure and design		
☐	found and analysed past exam papers		
☐	paper is.......hours		
☐	I have to answer.........questions		
☐	I know the typical language used in exam questions		
☐	I know the topics that come up every year		
Question	*I have thought about this programme*	*Predict*	*I have:*
I need to know...		☐	predicted the likely questions for this subject
I need to learn...		☐	chosen … topics to revise in depth
Plan	*I have:*		
☐	opened a revision folder on:		
☐	Topic 1:		
☐	Topic 2:		
☐	Topic 3:		
☐	Topic 4:		
☐	Topic 5:		
☐	Topic 6:		
☐	made links between learning outcomes, coursework, assignments and my revision topic		
☐	placed coursework notes, press cuttings, assignment notes and assignments into the topic folders; on a big pattern on the wall; and on my index cards		
☐	*Discovered that I prefer learning:*	☐	*Thus, my preferred revision system will utilise mainly:*
☐	by sight	☐	pattern notes of the key points
☐	by sound	☐	tapes of me reciting the key points
☐	by feel/movement	☐	making condensed charts of the key points
☐		☐	I will see it, hear it, say it, do it.

Prepare	I have:		
	gone through my exam folders and have prepared condensed notes of everything that I need to remember for the exam for:		
☐	Topic 1:		
☐	Topic 2:		
☐	Topic 3:		
☐	Topic 4:		
☐	Topic 5:		
☐	Topic 6:		
☐	I am learning this by:		
☐	memorising my key point patterns/charts		
☐	reciting my key points along with my tape		
☐	testing myself and friends		
☐	carrying index cards with the key points on them		
Practise	I have drawn up a revision timetable for this exam subject. It includes the following:		
☐	positive thinking	☐	writing with notes
☐	brainstorming and planning answers	☐	writing without notes
☐	planning and writing 'perfect' answers with friends	☐	timed writing without notes
I am ready and confident!			

FIGURE 25A   Exams checklist

 Photocopiable:

Essential Study Skills, Third Edition © Tom Burns and Sandra Sinfield, 2012 (SAGE)

Section VI

Reflective Learning

26

Personal Development Planning (PDP): Becoming Who You Want to Be

Chris Keenan

Aims

To demonstrate how engaging with PDP can help you to help yourself be successful in your academic, personal and professional life.

Learning outcomes

After reading this chapter and engaging with the activities, you will have:

- started to develop your own ideas of what PDP is all about
- understood how engaging with PDP can give you a clear idea about the kind of life and work that you want for yourself
- linked the idea of PDP to developing confidence in your skills, qualities and attributes
- developed a positive attitude and approach associated with success
- understood many of the terms associated with PDP
- thought about how to effectively promote your skills, personal qualities and competencies: from PDP to CV.

Introduction

In many ways, this whole book is about Personal Development Planning. Each chapter has a number of learning activities such as:

- how to learn and study – where you complete a personal study skills review
- organising yourself – where you think about the skills you have and what you would like to improve on
- how to research and read academically – where you think about how to access the information you need and develop your information literacy
- how to use computers to help you study anywhere, any time or develop your ICT skills
- how to understand your course – where you examined how the overview, or big picture, helps you to become a more effective student by really understanding what your course is all about, including how it will be assessed
- how to pass exams – including goal setting and thinking about learning styles
- how to work with others in groups
- how to build your confidence – and develop positive thinking
- how to transfer the skills you have developed to both work and life.

If you stop to think about it, you will see that these activities are about:

- understanding yourself and personal organisation
- the management and handling of information
- managing tasks including academic work
- managing and working with others
- self-awareness in applying for and succeeding in work.

In other words, the PDP attributes. And, these involve skills such as:

- reflection
- goal-setting, objective-setting and forward-planning
- collaboration and negotiation
- being able to respond to different situations, contexts and people
- persuasion
- managing time
- critical thinking.

Are these terms and phrases familiar? It is important that you feel comfortable with these as they will continue to be used throughout this chapter. If you come across terms that you do not fully understand, jot them down and gather definitions for them – but here's an activity to get you thinking about them right now.

1. Activity: Learning about terms and phrases often associated with PDP

Reflection

What is reflection? Generally, we learn through experience, thinking about that experience and then making adjustments for the future. Some professional bodies require reflective practice to be included in the curriculum.

But what is it? Think about a new recent experience. It might have been travelling abroad on your own for the first time, or learning to drive a car.

Reflect back on how you felt about it. Were you nervous? What planning and preparation did you do? How did you feel about it later? What will make for a better experience next time?

There have been a number of attempts to help describe this process. One of the most famous is what is known as the 'Kolb Cycle'.

The Kolb Cycle suggests that learning is a process, and that there are no fixed timescales for each phase, but that they all flow into each other in a cyclical way. There are criticisms of this model, some suggest that it is too simplistic in trying to describe a very complex process in a mechanistic way; nevertheless, the model is quite useful in attempting an explanation of the role of reflection in learning.

There are four phases to the Kolb Cycle:

- **Concrete experience**: What happened? What took place? What was the experience?
- **Reflection**: Your own personal analysis. What skills, attributes, competencies, did you draw on? Reviewing what happened, thinking about how you, and others, felt about it.
- **Abstract conceptualisation**: Coming to an understanding of what happened. Being able to make generalisations from the experience, and thinking about whether more information is needed before coming to conclusions.
- **Active experimentation**: Planning for the future, based on experience and reflection. What would you do differently next time and why? What would you do in exactly the same way, and why? Who could you get help from next time to improve something? What resources do you need?

Leading on to the next concrete experience...

> **Query**: Can you see how to use these descriptions in your own learning – and in your PDP process?

tip

If you come across other terms that are new to you, jot them down and find out about them in a similar way. You can then come to your own conclusions about how useful they will be, for you.

See also:

Kolb, D.A. (1984) *Experiential Learning: Experience as the Source of Learning and Development.* Upper Saddle River, NJ; Prentice-Hall

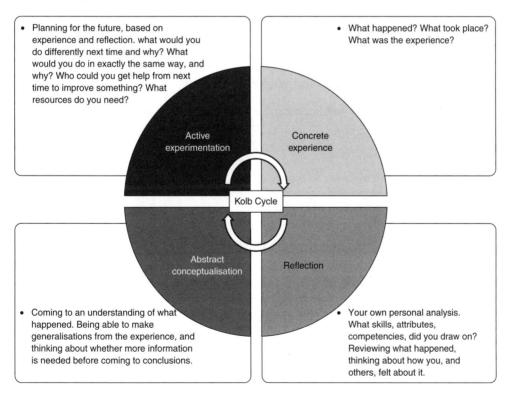

- Planning for the future, based on experience and reflection. what would you do differently next time and why? What would you do in exactly the same way, and why? Who could you get help from next time to improve something? What resources do you need?

- What happened? What took place? What was the experience?

Active experimentation

Concrete experience

Kolb Cycle

Abstract conceptualisation

Reflection

- Coming to an understanding of what happened. Being able to make generalisations from the experience, and thinking about whether more information is needed before coming to conclusions.

- Your own personal analysis. What skills, attributes, competencies, did you draw on? Reviewing what happened, thinking about how you, and others, felt about it.

FIGURE 26A   Kolb cycle

Me and my CV

Don't wait until three weeks before the end of your degree, have a look at some job advertisements right now. What do you see? What sort of person is being looked for? What sort of skills or qualities are required of them?

Whatever the post being advertised, there will be some consistent themes. The employer may ask for specific skills, for example 'Must be a fluent French speaker', but will also be seeking someone with transferable skills, for example 'Candidates should have experience of working in a management role with a track record of solving administrative problems'.

This is your opportunity to let your CV do the talking for you. For example, see how your skills in goal setting, planning, collaboration and negotiation, being responsive to different situations, working with people, persuasion, managing time, and critical thinking can be applied to an example from your experience:

> In my first year at University I joined the snowboarding society which I enjoyed very much. In the second year I became a Students' Union rep for the snowboarding society which meant I accompanied first years on trips during the vacations. This involved sorting out any problems that the students may have had whilst on holiday and taking responsibility for making the travel arrangements, including sorting out itineraries, insurance and accommodation.

You can see that this is more compelling than a simple skills list like,

- I am a good team player
- I have strong leadership skills
- I have good organisational skills.

What is Personal Development Planning?

It's interesting to think about the term 'Personal Development Planning'. This can indeed be very 'personal', something that you 'do' for yourself, in order to think more deeply about your life, how you do things, your goals, ambitions and how you perceive yourself. 'Development' implies that PDP is a process that happens over time. If you really work with it, it will become a way of life and not just an add-on that you are required to do. 'Planning' suggests that you will be careful to make sure you gather the right information to work with, that you know who or what can help you achieve your goals and the resources you may need. From this 'reflection' you can plan for developing the knowledge and skills that you will need in order to help you to achieve your ambitions and hopes.

Sometimes, PDP may be a process required by a tutor, or an employer, in which case your development plans will be developed in consultation with others and it can be very helpful to share your reflections with fellow students. For example, if your university covers aspects of PDP in tutorial sessions, make sure you know what to ask the tutor, what you want to get from the session – and how you can use the tutorial to develop your PDP. If you have a study partner, compare your PDP with each other – make plans for how to improve your portfolio. Whatever your motivation, active engagement with the process of PDP will ensure that you have a clear idea of:

- who you are
- how you like to learn
- your strengths and weaknesses
- and how to achieve your desired goals, whether they be personal, academic or professional.

 **tip**

Many employers and professional bodies have clearly defined activities that you may be required to work through in order to progress. Make sure you know what these are.

2. Activity: WiiFM: What's in PDP for me?

Do you have mixed feelings or purely positive ones about PDP? Take a little time to reflect on what PDP could do for you.

1 How do you want to get started?
2 What are your priorities at the moment?
3 How can you maximise your own potential and how will PDP help you to do this?
4 What are your time scales?

This can be the start of a general action plan.

❝I didn't want to do PDP, I don't have any time – and this just felt like more hard work.**❞**

❝I doubted the point of it at first – but actually it did help me to produce a better CV.**❞**

Time

Engaging with PDP can be a very time-consuming exercise.

❝ I can imagine that reflecting on my strengths and weaknesses would be useful but it's the rest of the work around it which I find a bit scary ... Such as action plans, listings, e.g. hobbies, etc. **❞** (First year, service industries' student)

So, you might well be asking:

What's in it for me?

PDP can be seen as a set of building blocks on which to develop your academic understanding, deepen your knowledge of yourself and build your self-awareness and self-confidence. Taking control of and responsibility for all your learning and development in this way helps you get the most from your studies and enhances your independent learning capacity – and your self-confidence. Whether you view PDP as an investment, or a waste of time, is entirely up to you. Engaging with PDP can be time consuming and can also be challenging, but, the payoff is that you will find out more about yourself, you will get more out of your studies, and you will be better prepared as a graduate seeking employment.

❝ I wish I had known about this at the start of the year. It is something that I will definitely get involved with now that I am more aware about it. **❞** (First year computing student)

If you think about it, it is actually a framework for life. Throughout life, we face new challenges and when doing so, we reflect on previous experiences. We think about what went well and what didn't go so well, and about what we might want to do differently in future. This can apply across any situation and at any time in our life, and underpinning this are what are often termed *transferable skills*, when we apply the skills or competencies that we learn from one situation to another. These are lifelong strengths that will help with your studies, your personal relationships and in your professional life. The rest of this chapter will give some ideas on how to do this.

Why do we think PDP is important?

If you are reading this, you probably want to be a successful student – and a successful professional. Elsewhere, this book talks about motivation and commitment and visualising yourself as a successful person. That you have already made a commitment to studying at university and reading this book indicates that you have motivation to succeed. But, have you stopped to think about, or reflect on, what 'success' means to you?

3. Activity: Planning to succeed

- Before you read further jot down your own definition of 'success' – you might find that you have more than one!
- If you are just starting out at university, jot down how you think it will be different from school or college, what you want to get out of the next three or four years there, what you think your strengths are and where you think you can improve, and what you enjoy doing now (e.g. hobbies, sports, pastimes) that you want to keep on doing.
- Then, jot down a quick plan of what you need to do make all your goals happen.
- Finally, keep this in a safe place and refer back to it from time to time.

> **Query**: What is the point of this?
>
> **Discussion**: Well, what is happening here is that you are taking time to pause, and reflect on what you want for yourself, what is happening to you right now, what your aims and goals for yourself are and reflecting on your strengths and acknowledging any weaknesses that you might want to work on as well.

This is the basis of PDP. You will see that it reflects on you as a person in your own right, you develop an honest self-evaluation and in doing so, will have the basis for an action plan or personal progress file, or portfolio.

Your definition of success might have concentrated on your own academic development, or you might have mentioned making friends and making the most of university life, or you might have mentioned getting a good job after graduation. These are all legitimate and form the basis of this chapter. In other words, PDP is not just about ticking the boxes in your academic life, but is all about becoming the whole person that you want to be.

Be positive

Some students do think that PDP is boring – perhaps they are disenchanted because of their previous experiences. But, the aim of this chapter is to try to turn that perception around and help you to see that it can be a very positive, exciting, illuminating and yes, also, challenging process with many positive outcomes.

❝ PDP will be appropriate when designing my CV as personal development will help me look back at what I have achieved. ❞ (Psychology student)

Me and my CV

Keep a notebook or a spreadsheet handy where you can jot down reminders, or evidence, of things that might be useful to recall for your CV.

For example, if you have just completed a group work task, you could note things like: your role in the team; what went well, what didn't go so well and why; how disagreements were handled; whether team members all contributed equally and if not how was this resolved; whether the work was completed in time.

This review is more than just a diary. It reflects on how you interacted with the team and how you all worked together to meet a target. This can later be drawn on for your CV, for example, you are applying for a job with a prospective employer looking for someone who must be a good team worker.

❝ In my final year we had to do a group work assignment. We had a very tight deadline and negotiated between ourselves which tasks we would take on based on our strengths. I was the programmer in the team and had to negotiate the end user requirements with the client, ensure that the team were kept up to date with any changes to the spec, and work together to minimise the impact of any changes. So, I set up brief daily meetings either in person or on email at least once a day in order to ensure we were on brief and on schedule. We completed the task successfully and on time. ❞

This is much more effective than:

- I am a confident team player
- I can prioritise
- I have strong communication skills.

PDP and universities: A little bit of politics

Every UK university is required to provide PDP opportunities to its students and all universities are free to interpret this in their own way.

In 1997 a far reaching document, the Dearing Report, was published. This made a number of significant recommendations about universities, including several in connection with providing structured support to students in developing lifelong learning skills.

In 2003 the government published a White Paper entitled *The Future of Higher Education*, which set out its plans for HE. These plans included enabling 'learners to understand and reflect on their achievements and to present those achievements to employers, institutions and other stakeholders'.

The 2011 Higher Education White Paper entitled *Students at the Heart of the System* again states that students are entitled to 'leave their course equipped to embark on a rewarding career'.

A definition provided by the Quality Assurance Agency for Higher Education is probably the most widely used:

A structured and supported process undertaken by an individual to reflect upon their own learning, performance and/or achievement and to plan for their personal, educational and career development.

The primary objective for PDP is to improve the capacity of individuals to understand what and how they are learning, and to review, plan and take responsibility for their own learning, helping students to:

- Become more effective, independent and confident self-directed learners
- Understand how they are learning and relate their learning to a wider context
- Improve their general skills for study and career management
- Articulate personal goals and evaluate progress towards their achievement
- Develop a positive attitude to learning throughout life.

(Source: QAA (2000) *Recommendations for Policy on Personal Development Planning*)

4. Activity: How does your university tackle PDP?

- How is PDP referred to in your university prospectus, on your university website and in your course documentation?
- Look at the detailed information provided about each of the units or modules that you will be taking on your course, and list all the terms that might come under the PDP umbrella, e.g. group project (working in groups), research skills (information handling), etc.

➡

➡

- Jot these down and think about your previous experiences, think about what went well last time you worked in a team, what didn't go so well, what you could do to make yourself a more effective group member, what resources or support do you need to do this?
- You may also find that your university provides you with a progress file, or portfolio, where you can record your goal setting, skills audits, action plans, transcripts, etc. This is a very useful way of recording your reflections, action plans and achievements and can be drawn upon when preparing your CV or planning for an interview. For example, this could be where you record and reflect on your experience of group working, or developing your critical thinking skills, or information literacy skills, recording examples as evidence. Find out if your university has an e-portfolio, if not, find out whether they can support you in setting one up for yourself, or, alternatively, create your own paper or online record.
- In some universities, the Students' Union is actively engaged with facilitating PDP activities, e.g. leadership courses, volunteering, representation, etc. These extra-curricular activities are an excellent way of 'adding value' to your time at university. Find out what happens where you are and perhaps get involved.

Transferable skills

Universities often develop their PDP resources around what are known as transferable skills. You may find that your university has a list of the transferable skills on its website. The term 'skills' can sometimes be contentious in higher education – some prefer the term 'attributes' and some use the term 'competencies'. Nevertheless, the development of these 'skills' continues throughout our lives and will also contribute hugely to your employability.

Employers often look for a range of skills which will transfer from your experience of higher education into the world of work. Remember also that there are transferable skills within the curriculum (often termed academic skills) and outside of the curriculum (often termed life skills) – you have probably started to think about this already.

It is useful now to have a think about a range of transferable skills typically referred to in higher education, and then carry out a personal audit – and remember it is important that you provide the evidence (the record associated with the activity) that you can refer to. This is where your progress file, or portfolio, comes in useful.

All the boxes below are designed to get you to actively think about your transferable skills – and in the process set yourself manageable targets for developing them. This highlights the need to record this development as you work through your degree – from your first year to your last.

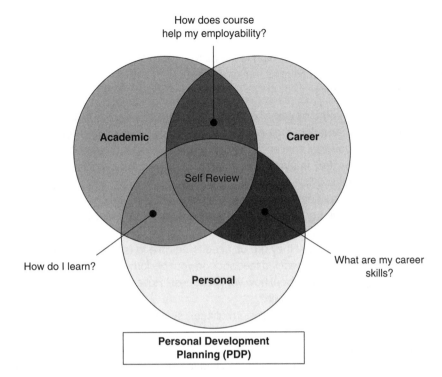

How does course
help my employability?

Academic

Career

Self Review

How do I learn?

Personal

What are my career
skills?

Personal Development
Planning (PDP)

FIGURE 26B   Personal Development Planning

Of course, the transferable skills do not separate neatly into skills for work, skills for study and skills for life – they overlap and interconnect: plan to make the most of your experiences in as many of the 'boxes' as possible.

Transferable skill: Learning

At university, learning is about building up valid knowledge for a particular situation but remaining open to other views, and being able to:

- extract general concepts, principles and procedures
- critically evaluate, select and present ideas/arguments/evidence
- connect ideas and knowledge
- form your own opinions
- apply theory to practice
- seek and use feedback

➡

➡

- evaluate your own work according to the relevant criteria
- find and adopt study techniques that work for you
- identify learning needs.

Let's think about this in the context of academic learning. At university in the UK, students are encouraged to formulate their own ideas by critically evaluating a range of ideas, scholarship and theoretical concepts and approaches. There is more about this in other chapters in this book. But, in terms of learning as a lifelong transferable skill, you might want to think about this a little more:

How do you have confidence in what you are learning? Where do ideas come from? How do abstract ideas transfer into experience and how can reflecting on experience lead to abstract ideas and concepts?

All learners, whatever level they are at, need to be able to reflect on feedback to their work – how do you feel and react to feedback on your performance?

Have you stopped to think about how you learn best? Have you identified areas of your learning that you need support with?

Learning is often described as 'transformational', so why not record and reflect on the journey that you are undertaking.

You might not previously have thought about this as a transferable skill, but it is an area of our own development that is really interesting to reflect on once you get started on it.

Transferable skill: Information Technology

This refers to using electronic means to find, record, manipulate and present information (see also Chapter 7), and refers to your ability to:

- use a word processor to create documents and use functions to add value to work, e.g. Word
- create and use a spreadsheet and manipulate data within it, e.g. Excel
- create a database from a set of data, work with it to produce reports, e.g. Access
- create effective presentations using a graphics package, e.g. PowerPoint
- produce transparencies or visual aids for a presentation
- research topics of interest on the internet
- use email to maintain effective links with colleagues and clients

It is very difficult these days to think about any aspect of our lives that does not interact with information technology. This is a very broad life skill that is seen as being very necessary in our everyday interactions. Even those who do not consider themselves to be IT literate will usually be comfortable with email and simple web searching. Most universities will have workshops and tutorials available to help less confident students develop these essential skills.

Transferable skill: Self management

This is about understanding, using and developing our own abilities to effect good outcomes in life and work. You could look to:

- set appropriate targets and goals
- organise tasks to meet deadlines – prioritise and plan
- know your own strengths and weaknesses
- apply strengths to weaker areas
- reflect on progress and outcomes
- find support or develop new strategies where necessary
- accept and act on feedback
- evaluate your own performance.

Some hints on how to apply this: Your transferable skills audit may have highlighted a weakness in the area of self management. Your action plan will help you to address these weaknesses and identify resources and help that may be needed. But, why is this an important skill to develop?

Being able to set manageable and achievable targets and stick to them, and having a clear understanding of your strengths and weaknesses can help you maintain control over your life.

The evidence you collect in your portfolio or progress file can be drawn on as a reminder to yourself of the journey you have undertaken to improve, enhance, or develop that skill. It will also provide a reminder of an achievement that you can include in a job application or in preparation for a job interview.

Transferable skill: Critical thinking

This is often a difficult concept to grapple with. Critical thinking is about the development of logical thoughts and ideas about a subject; or coming to a reasoned solution of a problem or dilemma. When you think about it, we do this all the time in our daily lives. We make decisions about important things – for example, what were the things that you took into account when choosing your course and university?

Critical thinking involves being able to:

- critically analyse a line of reasoning
- identify bias, distortion, illogical reasoning in arguments and texts
- challenge taken-for-granted assumptions and existing practice
- evaluate evidence presented in support of a conclusion

➡

427

➡️

- identify and address gaps in knowledge or understanding
- identify and analyse key points/issues within a problem
- generate creative/innovative ideas using techniques such as brainstorming, mind-mapping, critical path analysis
- consider alternatives/implications/wider or local contexts
- plan/implement a course of action
- take calculated risks as necessary to achieve goals
- organise sub-tasks appropriately
- monitor/control activities
- assess outcomes and incorporate the lessons into future planning.

Many of our day-to-day decisions are based on thinking about the pros and cons of something – for example, what influences us to open an account with one bank rather than another? What influences us to buy our groceries from a particular supermarket? Do we know enough about ethical shopping to help us make purchasing decisions that our conscience is comfortable with, or, don't we care?

Most people over the age of 18 have the right to vote. How do we choose the causes we want to support and follow? How do we differentiate between political ideals? Critical thinking allows us to recognise bias and take this into account when coming to our own decisions, whether decisions about life style, politics or education.

In academic life, we are encouraged to review or evaluate competing ideas or approaches and come to a conclusion based on our analysis and evaluation of them.

Critical thinking helps us to come to an understanding of where we stand in relation to something – whether it be challenging the status quo, or, evaluating a number of sources of evidence in order to make our own mind up about something.

This is why critical thinking is often considered to be a key transferable skill and one that is very important in enabling us to identify key issues, analyse them, and come to a conclusion based on them.

Transferable skill: Information handling

This includes being able to:

- locate and use a variety of sources – print, electronic, people
- exploit bibliographic databases – conduct searches using keywords
- sift through information to identify key points
- appraise information using relevant criteria

- reference material correctly and understand plagiarism
- organise and store information so it can be retrieved when needed
- organise information into a logical and cohesive format that can be communicated easily to others.

This transferable skill is often quite tricky. In a world where there is so much information at our finger tips, how can we possibly manage, handle and store information in a way that makes sense to us? This is a huge area, and you may decide that you need to break it down into manageable chunks.

A way to start may be to speak to your subject librarian and ask them to give you an introduction to searching for information relevant to your subject. In this way, you can learn to get the most out of the electronic resources available to you through your library.

Don't forget to record what you are doing and how the new skills that you are acquiring are facilitating your personal development.

Transferable skill: Numeracy

This is about understanding and applying mathematical techniques when handling problems and projects. It involves your ability to:

- make fundamental calculations – estimating, adding, subtracting, multiplying and dividing
- use a calculator confidently
- have a grasp of statistics and percentages, fractions, decimals and ratios
- derive conclusions and reason with the use of numerical data
- create and interpret spreadsheets, graphs, charts, tables and diagrams
- develop mathematical models using complex equations in order to find solutions to problems.

Many university courses and professional bodies have a basic requirement of maths or numeracy, but, how important is numeracy to you? You may find that people are often quite comfortable admitting that they have a weakness with numbers and maths, but would be reluctant to admit a weakness with literacy. Why is this and does it matter?

Well, you need to think about this for yourself. Even those people whose daily lives do not involve the requirement of working with mathematical formulae or concepts still need to have a basic understanding of how to calculate their change and how to understand their utility bills and their bank statements.

➡

429

➡️

Numeracy and literacy are often quite emotive topics and many adult education centres offer short courses in them – this tends to suggest that this is a skill worth thinking about and addressing, particularly if working with numbers is problematic for you.

Many universities recognise this and offer support sessions in numeracy and maths. If your skills audit demonstrates a weakness in this area, why not challenge yourself to tackle this area and beat this problem?

See also the following maths resources:

- Video tutorials: http://www.sigma-cetl.ac.uk/index.php?section=92
- Pdfs: http://www.sigma-cetl.ac.uk/index.php?section=102
- Revision tips for maths students: http://www-users.york.ac.uk/%7Edajp1/Exam_Hints/Exams.html

Transferable skill: Career management

Here, you will need to have:

- good organisational awareness
- an awareness of trends that are emerging in the business or professional world
- effective communication of your skills and experience to others, in order to gain employment or develop your career
- future targets in mind regarding your career and education.

It's never too early to start being aware of career opportunities and to start thinking about directions in which you might want your future career to develop.

Often we think about a general area of a career, for example, teaching, working with computers, health and social care, but, we may not exactly know quite how that will materialise yet. This is fine, and university careers offices are on hand to alert you to the range of opportunities within a particular field, for example, emerging technologies may present opportunities that you had not thought of when you set out on your computing degree.

Whether your goals are already firmly established, or whether you are still unsure about your career aspirations, you can start thinking now about who you are and the sort of career that will suit you. Are you a vocational person with a passion for social justice or working with people in difficulties? Do you consider yourself to be highly ambitious and aspirational? Do you want to do something creative or earn a lot of money? Are you interested in something else all together? Some jobs offer relatively low salaries, but bring a sense of value and self-worth; others may be challenging and highly paid; still others (university teaching!) may be challenging and not very well paid…

An understanding of the broad aspects of PDP can help you to understand who you are and will help you to make decisions about what life you want – and to be comfortable with and validate the decisions you make.

You can start now by keeping a note of what your goals and ambitions are for yourself, and how these might change and adapt over a period of time. You will then find that the evidence you collect in your portfolio or progress file will begin to help you picture the sort of career that you want for yourself.

Transferable skill: Team working

This is about being able to:

- understand the basis of group behaviour and team roles
- motivate yourself and others to the achievement of common goals
- respect feelings, views and values of others – take on board other opinions
- assist and support others
- collaborate and negotiate
- take the initiative when necessary
- delegate where necessary
- review progress and alter plan if necessary
- accept and carry out agreed or delegated tasks.

Team working is not easy for everyone and very often it might feel much quicker and simpler to just get the job done on your own. But, if you scan the situations vacant columns, you will soon see how important team working is. Many large organisations hold assessment days as part of their recruitment process when applicants are required to demonstrate their team working capabilities.

Often at university you will get the opportunity to develop these skills by working on group projects, and many students will engage with extra-curricular activities where working together in teams is a key principle in getting the job done.

Your transferable skills audit results will give you an indication of your strengths and weaknesses in this area. It is important sometimes to be able to achieve common goals in co-operation with others, and this requires a number of the skills described in the list above.

Transferable skill: Communicating

Communication is about being able to:

- use a variety of modern communication tools
- listen positively and respond to both verbal and non-verbal messages
- present a well-structured and evidenced argument
- express self and ideas clearly, concisely and logically in speech and writing
- influence others and gain agreement or acceptance of plan/idea/activity
- understand other viewpoints and appreciate cultural differences
- evaluate how well your message is received.

There have already been a number of examples indicating how important this transferable skill is and it is unlikely that you will see a job advert that does not highlight the importance of good communication skills – of being able to persuade, influence, encourage, motivate, engage others. It is difficult to imagine the opposite, where an advert will ask for an insular person unable to communicate effectively with others and with no confidence in their communication skills.

Some things to consider:

- Who do you need to communicate with? Depending on the context you are in, you may be required to deal with members of the public (and will probably have been developing these skills if you have had part-time jobs to help fund your studies), you may be required to deal with other professionals, you may be required to communicate with a range of people in a range of positions in your own organisation.
- What do you need to communicate? Are you able to present what you need to communicate in a clear and well-structured way?
- How do you need to communicate? You will need to be able to adapt your communication styles to meet the needs of your 'audience'.

(Source: www.pdp.bournemouth.ac.uk)

5. Activity: Conduct your own PDP Skills audit

Now, that we have worked through the PDP goals, try an activity in order to 'audit' yourself in these transferable skills. Go to: http://pdp.bournemouth.ac.uk/documents/u-transferable_skills-self_assessment.doc

Because we all develop and grow all the time, it is useful to carry out a regular reflective review of your transferable skills.

Then, you can create an action plan to help you plan for improving areas of weakness, and to maintain and develop your strengths. You should also consider how you will do this, what resources you need to help you achieve your goals, and, importantly, give yourself time scales that are manageable.

Here's an example of an action plan, however you may prefer to design your own:

http://pdp.bournemouth.ac.uk/documents/u-my_goals-goal_setting_and_action_planning.doc

---

Me and my CV

A recent job advert for a worker with young people, called for candidates with an 'excellent skills base, including communication, organisational and group work skills'.

Yes, they were also looking for someone with an understanding of the particular requirements of that area of work, policy and experience – but why did this job advert, and many others, emphasise these particular skills as well? What does it reveal about the sort of person they are looking for and what is the something extra that would make you stand out as a candidate for this post?

If you are going to be looking at job adverts that emphasise these skills why not start right now – make a record of your starting points. Did your audit reveal that communication is a weakness for you? What did it tell you about your organisational and group work skills? What have you done to improve these, have you attended any workshops or tutorials to help you? Can you provide examples of how you have improved your organisational skills through a better understanding of self management?

" I organised the student conference at my university. I had to book the rooms, get students to run sessions – and other students to attend. I organised the budget and sorted out the catering. I got marketing students to design the posters and flyers for me... I had to manage the day itself and make sure that it ran smoothly.

This is obviously something that I can use to demonstrate my organisational skills – and I had to use so many different communication skills as well – from setting up a Facebook site to advertise the conference and allow people to book a place, to getting those posters and flyers produced – and in the right places at the right time. I had to email, phone and meet people from every level of the university hierarchy – and I had to make sure that all the student participants felt supported and had the rooms and resources they needed to run their workshops. I had a great time – and I think this is going to be an excellent activity to use in my PDP and in my CV. **"**

PDP and CV tips

You may decide that some of the transferable skills described above are more important in your life than others; you may think that it would be very time consuming to develop all of them all at once.

Depending on your own plans you might want to scan job opportunities in the press (including jobs and careers that you are not necessarily interested in) and get an impression of which skills are the most regularly sought after.

Also, have a look at the websites of the professional bodies, particularly where they express their mission and values to see how they articulate the skills and values you are interested in. For example The British Computer Society values include:

- respecting the individual
- advocating fair treatment
- rewarding exceptional performance
- showing commitment to personal and professional growth
- encouraging teamwork (www.bcs.org)

If you are an aspiring computing professional, you will find that these values can be developed, recorded and evidenced through your own attention to your personal development planning.

Me and my CV

Self-awareness and self-understanding are valuable assets in life. Universities use terms like Lifelong Learning, Learning for Life and PDP in the hope that these equip you with the tools to transfer your knowledge and skills to novel situations. Understanding yourself as a learner transforms you from *being taught* to taking ownership of your learning: a powerful platform for your personal development and employability.

Be your own person

Think about other things that are important to you:

- Check out your course documentation for PDP opportunities.
- Do you have paid work? If so, what skills are you developing when balancing work and study? Reflect on how these can be transferred to other aspects of your life.

434

- Do you play sport? Reflect on the many ways that playing sports can enhance your life, think about the skills and qualities that you are acquiring.
- Are you a member of any clubs and societies?
- What extra contributions are you making in your local community?
- Are you prepared to get involved? For example, are you an elected course representative, or elected Students' Union official?
- What hobbies do you have and how do these contribute to the whole you?

ff PDP encouraged me to take greater advantage of resources to improve my skills and capabilities. **"**
(First year media production student)

Conclusion

PDP really is an opportunity, not a problem. Think about how you want to record your reflections, achievements and goals and ambitions. This may be in your own personal journal or your university may offer a template for a progress file or portfolio. It is really important to remember to keep examples as evidence of what you have done and what you have achieved.

Engaging with personal development planning at university will help you to reflect on the skills you are developing within your programme of study. It will also enable you to reflect on your strengths and weaknesses in relation to academic work and plan for improvement. PDP can be time consuming, and hard work. However, PDP is much more than just reflection on your academic work.

Everything you do and all your achievements, disappointments, ambitions and aspirations are key to you being who you are. Reflecting on all of these experiences can help towards your future growth. It's important also to remember that the whole university experience and making the most of all aspects of your life will contribute to your overall development.

If you have worked through all the activities you will start to see how much time this can take up, but it does become second nature with practice. Find ways of engaging with PDP that suit you and your work, study and personal commitments. The rewards will become clear and obvious over time.

Further reading and resources

Bournemouth University: http://pdp.bournemouth.ac.uk/u-transferable_skills-i.htm
Centre for Recording Achievement: http://www.recordingachievement.org/
Higher Education Academy: http://www.heacademy.ac.uk/ourwork/learning/pdp

Review points

When reviewing this chapter you might notice that you have:

- Started to think constructively about yourself as an independent, self-confident and moti-vated learner and how to achieve this through PDP
- A much better understanding of yourself as a person in your own right
- Started to think constructively about how to reflect on your experiences and plan for the future
- A much clearer idea about your skills, personal qualities and competencies and how to articulate them to potential employers
- A clear set of personal, academic and professional goals, a positive attitude and a clear sense of who you want to be
- A better understanding of some of the terms associated with PDP and know where to find out more if you wish to.

With thanks to Bournemouth University for allowing the use of their PDP website to provide a basis for much of the content of this chapter.

Section VI

Reflective Learning

27

Moving On: What to Do When You Finish University

Aims

This chapter explores how to plan your next steps with special reference to building your CV – and using online sources.

Learning outcomes

By the end of this chapter you will feel that you:

- understand the purpose of careers and job search websites – and you know how to use them
- will use your whole course and PDP to gather evidence for your CV
- are prepared to explore extra-curricular activities to enhance your job prospects.

“'Moving on' ... but in fact your future career should be planned from very early on. Whatever you do, don't do what I did and hope something turns up.”

Moving on: Careers, CVs and PDP

Taking control of your learning, managing yourself, finding and evaluating information, communicating effectively – in written and in oral forms – performing

under pressure and managing stress IS this book – and this is how you prepare for, find and get that great job. This chapter briefly reviews some top
tips for preparing CVs and gives some case study examples of what a mature
student, a careers adviser and a subject tutor have to say about getting the
job that you want. We also discuss what employers are looking for, and refer
to some key resources that can help you find the job you want – and then get
it, with a special focus on the Careers Service Prospects site.

" There are ways an undergrad can stick out from a crowd, including extra-curricular academic and
community activities, general volunteering, work-experience, involvement in sport teams and
development projects, Students' Union and cultural pursuits (choir/drama and other cultural-type
stuff). You could do a meaningful internship over the summer after your second year or get involved
in Erasmus programmes. **"**

Employability: University as a way of getting that job

We want to get you thinking about your whole degree as an adventure
designed to develop you as a person – and as an employable person. In that
light, we suggested that you embrace the employability opportunities both
within and outside the curriculum that your university provides as a process
designed to get you the job that you want.

Typically, most universities do not leave employability completely up to
student motivation and initiative. Instead, you will be expected to engage in
employability activities across your time at university – and usually these
will articulate with your PDP (Personal or Professional Development)
Portfolio or Process.

This is such a key issue that we have a whole chapter on this, so please also
look at Chapter 26. However, this is too important a subject to leave for your
university to organise or to wait until the last few weeks of your degree before
you actually make your thoughts about your future a reality. Talk to Careers
early and this may give you clues as to which modules to choose, which societies to join or what volunteering activity to get into in order to make the
most of your time at university and beyond.

" Towards the end of your degree students should also start looking for blue-chip graduate
opportunities. Many institutions will host presentations from corporations and work fairs for the
smaller companies and organisations. There are also massive three-day exhibitions at places like
Earl's Court. **"**

What to do right now

- Go to Careers; see what jobs are available to someone on your degree programme.
- Look up a job advert in your possible career – see what sorts of skills and experience you will need to get such a job. Discuss with Careers how you can get that experience whilst at university.
- Write your CV and take it to Careers for feedback. Give the same time to writing your CV that you give to your assignments – it's that important.
- Practise job interviews with other students: predict questions from the job description – then rehearse how you would handle yourself in a real job interview
- Visit the Prospects careers website early in your course and set yourself the goal of working through the different sections and benefiting from them.

But it's never too late:

❝I didn't realise I could use the careers service after I graduated. I could have really used their help and support, because at times I felt quite lost.**❞**

Improve your prospects

The Prospects Website: http://www.prospects.ac.uk/careers.htm

This is an excellent site that has been developed with exactly you in mind. We give a quick overview here – but the real trick is for you to use it as you work through your degree programme. Put reflections on different parts of this site into your PDP file to show how you are indeed managing your life and career in positive ways.

Other sites to explore include:

- http://www.totaljobs.com/
- http://www.monster.co.uk/

Prospects covers:

- Starting out
- CVs and covering letters
- Job application guidance
- Interview tips

- Interview tests and exercises
- Job hunting
- Options
- What do graduates do?
- Using your language skills
- Country profiles
- Careers fairs
- Careers services
- Forum
- Leaving your course.

I don't know what I want to do next

You may already know what you intend to do after you leave university – but not everybody does. Some come to university and expect that a career will just sort of manifest itself at the end of their degree; others have a particular career in mind, but over time this changes and by the end of their degrees they want something very different; some have clear goals at the start – work towards them and get exactly what they planned.

Do you know what you want to do when you leave university? If not – the Prospects' section on *Starting out* has advice for those unsure about what work they might be interested in – and on how to plan and develop their careers. Check out their career planning tool: 'what jobs would suit me?' Try also the psychometric testing site and personality questionnaire to get you thinking about who you are and the sort of work that you would enjoy doing and would be a good fit for. If you are not sure how to answer the following questions – use this section of the site:

- What jobs would suit me?
- What am I interested in?
- What does my personality, interests and motivation suit me for?

CVs and covering letters

The information in your CV and your covering letter is a key aspect of getting an interview – and without an interview you stand no chance at all of getting that job. Be aware though that most job applications will not want you to

441

send your CV – they will want you to complete their own application form – typically online.

As with your assignment questions, an application form is not asking you to tell them everything you know about yourself. They are not after your autobiography. What they do want to see is that you have understood the job requirements, you have read the person specification and that you have written something about each of their requirements. Employers want you to write about what you can do that is what they want.

tips

It is always useful to see what a successful CV or covering letter looks like so that you can model – but not copy – them, so do use the websites to find some.

Keep a meta-CV: an overarching CV file online – which you update regularly. In it you should have sections on:

- Education and training
- Employment
- Extra-curricular activities

You need to maintain this file regularly, updating it as you do new things – including at university. When you apply for a job copy and paste relevant sections of that into your online application forms – changing the wording to make it better fit the actual job you are applying for.

Problems with CVs and covering letters

The employability people at our university tell us that the big issues with CVs and covering letters include:

- not doing the research: not knowing the company and not addressing exactly who they are in your application
- poor spelling, punctuation and grammar
- poor layout and a sloppy and careless appearance
- writing a general covering letter that is not interesting and not tied to the specific job you are applying for.

You MUST know the company that you are applying to work for. Search their website – see what they do and what they are known and respected for.

Check out their values and any Social Responsibility statements they have made, or their commitments to equality or sustainability. You must tailor your application to who they are, otherwise you are naively thinking that they are going to adapt to fit you.

If you are not good at spelling, punctuation and grammar – or at laying out information – then get someone to do this part of the process for you. If your application form looks messy and uncared for, it goes straight in the bin!

We told you it was about PDP!

The Prospects site says the following about what employers want – and what they are looking for in their employees and new recruits:

Graduate employers recruit motivated applicants who have relevant skills and the capacity to 'fit in'. Many also require a good degree.

Some jobs require specific technical expertise but others are open to graduates of any discipline, as employers often focus on potential.

Transferable skills: These are competencies that can be carried over from one activity to another. They are key attributes within graduate recruitment.

You should get involved in a wide range of activities and work experience while you are at university to develop these skills so you can promote yourself to employers.

Every vacancy requires a unique set of competencies but some transferrable skills are commonly requested, these are listed below:

self-awareness: knowing your strengths and skills and having the confidence to put these across;

initiative: anticipating challenges and opportunities, setting and achieving goals and acting independently;

willingness to learn: being inquisitive, enthusiastic and open to new ideas;

action planning: prioritising, making decisions, assessing progress and making changes if necessary;

interpersonal skills: relating well to others and establishing good working relationships;

communication: listening to other people and clearly getting your point across orally, in writing and via electronic means, in a manner appropriate to the audience;

teamwork: being constructive, performing your role, listening to colleagues and encouraging them;

leadership: motivating others and inspiring them to take your lead;

customer service: being friendly, caring and diplomatic with clients and customers;

networking: building effective relationships with business partners;

foreign language: specific language skills;

problem solving: thinking things through in a logical way in order to determine key issues, often also including creative thinking;

flexibility: ability to handle change and adapt to new situations;

commitment/motivation: energy and enthusiasm to achieve goals;

numeracy: competence and understanding of numerical data, statistics and graphs;

commercial awareness: understanding business and how it affects the organisation and sector;

IT/computer literacy: office skills, ability to touch type and use common software packages.

You can develop these skills during your work experience, your studies and your extracurricular activities. For example, you could improve your customer-service skills by working on the customer service desk in a supermarket or demonstrate your teamwork skills in a group project at university. (http://www.prospects.ac.uk/careers.htm accessed August 2011)

... And of course, the whole of your PDP process is designed to make you aware of which of these skills or attributes you are developing – and to give you information to use in your job applications.

Employers' perceptions of the employability skills of new graduates

A report that has recently emerged from the University of Glasgow (Kevin Lowden, Stuart Hall, Ely Elliot, Jon Lewin, 2011, SCRE: http://www.edge.co.uk/media/63412/employability_skills_as_pdf_-_final_online_version.pdf) summarised employers' attitudes to graduate skills – and highlighted what they wanted from universities and from the students themselves.

From the universities they wanted employability skills that were embedded throughout the whole curriculum – and they wanted a focus on work placements, work-based learning, experiential learning and graduate award programmes that recognised achievement beyond the curriculum.

From students they wanted the normal transferable skills: team working, communication, leadership, critical thinking and problem solving – but they elaborate upon these. They want proactive employability skills, the ability to engage in multi-layered communication – and innovative team work capable of transforming organisations. Moreover, they wanted graduates to be work ready.

" So there I am waiting for the new boy to turn up – and his mum phones: 'Sorry he can't come in today, he's taking me to the doctors!' The boss told me to let him go... **"**

Case studies – student; careers adviser; computer lecturer

What a recent graduate said

As a so-called mature student, I was already thinking about my future career before I started my course. I wanted to get the most out of university as I thought that it would benefit me when I later had to find a job, so I was determined to experience and participate in things I had never done before and looked out for extra-curricular activities. I joined clubs at the SU, learnt to play volleyball, went to lectures from visiting academics, politicians and celebrities and generally immersed myself in uni-life. I did a bit of volunteering, helped out at the drama club behind the scenes and in my final year got the opportunity to participate in academic research (they even paid me for it!).

In my final semester I actively looked for companies recruiting graduates – and I visited the careers service. They translated some of the experiences I had had into actual skills I could put on my CV, plus they gave me tips for where to look for work. I participated in a mock interview, which helped build my confidence. Probably the best thing they gave me though, was an email address which I could use to contact them when I was struggling.

After leaving uni I sent out my CV and a letter to companies I was interested in working for, applied for graduate positions and joined agencies. I used Facebook, LinkedIn and Twitter to promote what I was doing, which resulted in friends looking out for jobs for me and sending advice/links, etc.

After four months of looking, I finally got an offer and I have been working there for seven months now.

My main advice to other people looking for work is to plan ahead, make use of what facilities the uni offers and don't be afraid to ask questions when you need help. If you are determined, you will find that job sooner or later.

General advice from a university careers person

The best web resource is probably still Graduate Prospects. It is a huge website with masses of good stuff on it all aimed at new and recent graduates (www.prospects.ac.uk). My favourite little book of totally sound advice for students is *Questions of Degree* by Colin MacGregor – he is a designer who is approached by students/grads all the time and it is an 'employer's eye' view of how NOT to behave. It is very sane and sensible and beautifully and simply designed (www.questionsofdegree.co.uk).

Someone has recently written up to the Employability Developers' jisc-mail with this Canadian resource – Blueprint4life which includes competencies, including relationship building: http://206.191.51.163/blueprint/competencies.cfm.

What a computing lecturer said

The following URLs are helpful and have helpful advice and tools:

General job sites:
http://www.totaljobs.com/
http://www.monster.co.uk/

Specific to IT Industry:
http://www.theitjobboard.co.uk/

Specific to type of IT – see Jobs Boards on Networking sites like:
http://www.escapestudios.co.uk/ (for 3D Animation)

The three most important points when searching on these websites (or in newspapers etc) are:

(a) Industry sectors
Don't just look for Computing or IT. They may have the job you want down under Information Systems, Media and IT, New Media, Databases, Creative Industries, Telecommunications, and even... Infrastructure, Marketing, Advertising, Management, Publishing, Manufacturing, etc.

(b) Job titles

Get to know the various titles the job you want can have, e.g. Web Developer, Web Designer, Graphic Designer, Content Developer, Graphic Creator/ Artist... and even Communications Developer. These titles can mean essentially doing a similar job, when you look at the tasks of the job spec. You can research sectors, job profiles and job vacancies using: http://www.prospects. ac.uk/jobs_and_courses.htm

(c) Research your specific professional sites

Network. Become a member of the site. Search the Job Boards, contribute to blogs, etc. You don't always have to become a member to search the Jobs Board.

Be targeted and flexible

Obviously in our Computing Faculty we have Computing, Communications Technology, Maths and Multimedia – so each area would have their own specific ways of finding employment, e.g. the BCS (British Computer Society) which now calls itself the Chartered Institute for IT (http:// www.bcs.org) and which is really important for Computing and IT students but less so for Creative Computing and Animation and Maths. So the big tip for ICT students – and for all students – is to find the sites for *your* professional society or organisation and see what advice they have to offer new graduates, what skills they want and where they advertise the jobs.

Big tip: Prepare for a job the way you prepare for university assessments

Work out what you are interested in and how the university as a whole can take you there: degree programme – specific modules – embedded employability opportunities and PDP – Students' Union – careers, placements, volunteering and peer mentoring... If your university offers students the opportunity to go for a graduate award, to engage in research projects with staff, to engage in enquiry-based or problem-based learning – grab these opportunities. These are very useful when getting employment.

   Plan a strategy that makes the most of all of these opportunities – open a CV file – open a PDP file – open a job search file.

➡

➡

Find websites for the professional bodies you will become a member of, research companies that you would like to work for and jobs that you would like to do. Connect what is happening on your course and at your university as a whole to what you will need to demonstrate in a job application.

Engage in your degree programme and your extra-curricular activities with energy and enthusiasm – collecting data for all your files as you go!

When you do complete a job application give the same effort – or more – that you gave to your best ever assignment. It's that important. If you cannot convince at the application stage you'll never get that interview.

Once you have the interview you must prepare all over again – as though for the hardest and most important assignment that you did.

And all the while... Enjoy yourself!

Postscript: Further study?

Of course, you may decide that you do not want to move straight into work – you may have a taste for studying and find that you want to do a postgraduate course. Discuss this with a sympathetic tutor on your degree programme – ask if your university does what you want. Speak to your postgraduate unit. Speak to students in the Students' Union. Explore the options for that on the Prospects site, and again, prepare for that the way you would prepare for an especially tricky assignment.

Conclusion

The whole of ESS3 is designed to enhance active and proactive learning – and to develop you as someone who can succeed on a course and at any task that you set yourself, including finding and getting that great job. We have tied some of the strategies highlighted in the book as a whole to locating and applying for the job you will want to get to be the person that you want to be. We have focused on some of the big things that stand out for us – finding out exactly what it is you want to do; reflecting on how to harness your whole university experience – on-course and extra-curricular – to help you develop the qualities required by employers. We have captured top tips from a past student, a careers adviser and a subject lecturer – the rest is up to you. Use and enjoy your time at university – find and get that great job. Good luck and good wishes...

Review points

We hope that you now:

- Understand the purpose of employability activities within your course, the potential of extra-curricular activities, of Careers services and websites… to help you become who you want to be and to get the job that you want
- Will use all your time at university – your whole course, PDP and beyond – to gather evidence for your CV and get that great job.

Bibliography

Ahearn, A. (2006) 'Engineering writing: Replacing "writing classes" with a "writing imperative"', in L. Ganobcsik-Williams (ed.) *Teaching Academic Writing in UK Higher Education*. Basingstoke: Palgrave Macmillan

Akerlind, G.S. and Trevitt, C. (1999) 'Enhancing self-directed learning through educational technology: When students resist the change', *Innovations in Education and Teaching International*, 36(2): 96–105

Anie, A. (2001) *Widening Participation – Graduate Employability Project*. University of North London (now London Metropolitan University)

Archer, L. (2002) 'Access elite', *Times Higher Education Supplement*, 18 January 2002

Archer, L. (2003) 'Social class and higher education', in L. Archer, H. Hutchings and A. Ross, *Higher Education and Social Class: Issues of Inclusion and Exclusion*. London and New York: RoutledgeFalmer

Archer, L. and Leathwood, C. (2003) 'Identities, inequalities and higher education', in L. Archer, H. Hutchings and A. Ross, *Higher Education and Social Class: Issues of Inclusion and Exclusion*. London and New York: RoutledgeFalmer

Barrow, M. (2006) 'Assessment and student transformation: Linking character and intellect', *Studies in Higher Education*, 31(3): 357–72

Barthes, R. (1957/1972) *Mythologies*, trans. A. Lavers. London: Paladin

Barton, D. and Hamilton, M. (1998) *Local Literacies: A Study of Reading and Writing in One Community*. London; Routledge

Beck, U., Giddens, A. and Lash, S. (1996) *Reflexive Modernization*. Cambridge: Polity Press

Beetham, H. and Sharpe, R. (2007) *Rethinking Pedagogy for a Digital Age: Designing and Delivering E-Learning*. London: Routledge

Belbin, R.M. (1981) *Management Teams: Why They Succeed or Fail*. London: Heinemann

Bennett, N., Dunne, E and Carré, B. (2000) *Skills Development in Higher Education and Employment*. Buckingham: Open University Press/Society for Research into Higher Education

Bennett, R. (2002) 'Lecturers' attitudes to new teaching methods', *International Journal of Management Education*, 2(1): 42–58

Blalock, A. (1999) 'Evaluation research and the performance management movement: From estrangement to useful integration?', *Evaluation*, 5(2): 117–49

Bourdieu, P. (1977) *Reproduction in Education, Society and Culture*. London: Sage

Bourdieu, P. and Passeron, J.-C. (1979) *Reproduction in Education, Society and Culture*. London: Sage

Bradley, C. and Holley, D. (2011) 'Empirical research into student mobile phones and their use for learning', *International Journal of Mobile and Blended Learning*, 3(4): 38–53

Brockes, E. (2003) 'Taking the Mick', *Guardian*, 15 January. Available at: http://www.guardian.co.uk/politics/2003/jan/15/education.highereducation (accessed 20 September 2009)

Burke, P.J. (2005) 'Access and widening participation', *British Journal of Sociology of Education*, 26(4): 555–62

Burns, T. and Sinfield, S. (2004) *Teaching, Learning and Study Skills: A Guide for Tutors*. London: Sage

Burns, T., Sinfield, S. and Holley, D. (2006) 'The silent stakeholder: An exploration of the student as stakeholder in the UK government e-learning strategy 2005', paper presented to the International Corporate Social Responsibility Conference, Idrine, Turkey, May

Buzan, T. (1989) *Use Your Head*. London: BBC Publications

Buzan, B. and Buzan, T. (1999) *The Mind Map Book*. London: BBC Publications

Cohen, S.B. (1997) *The Maladapted Mind*. London: Psychology Press

Conole, G., Smith, J. and White, S. (2006) 'A critique of the impact of policy and funding', in G. Conole and M. Oliver (eds) *Contemporary Perspectives on E-learning Research*. London: RoutledgeFalmer

Cottrell, S. (2001) *Teaching Study Skills and Supporting Learning*. Basingstoke: Palgrave Macmillan

Crème, P. (2003) 'Why can't we allow students to be more creative?', *Teaching in Higher Education*, 8(2): 273–77

Curry, M.J. (2006) 'Skills, access and "basic writing": A community college case study from the United States', in L. Ganobcsik-Williams (ed.) *Teaching Academic Writing in UK Higher Education*. Basingstoke: Palgrave Macmillan

Department for Education and Skills (now Business, Innovation and Skills) (2005, revised 2008) *Harnessing Technology: Transforming Learning and Children's services*. London: HMSO

Devine, T.G. (1987) *Teaching Study Skills*. Newton, MA: Allyn and Bacon

Feather, H. (2000) *Intersubjectivity and Contemporary Social Theory*. Farnham, UK: Ashgate

Fergusson, R. (1994) 'Managerialism in education', in C. Clarke, A. Cochrane and E. McLaughlin (eds), *Managing Social Policy*. London: Sage

Finnigan, T., Burns, T. and Sinfield, S. (2009) 'Tell us about it', workshop presented at ALDinHE Symposium Bournemouth

Foucault, M. (1980) *Power/Knowledge*. Brighton: Harvester

Foucault, M. (1988) *History of Sexuality. Vol.3: The Care of the Self*. Harmondsworth: Penguin

Freire, P. (1977) *The Pedagogy of the Oppressed*. Harmondsworth: Penguin

Freire, P. (1996) *Pedagogy of Hope*, 3rd edn. London: Penguin

Gamache, P. (2002) 'University students as creators of personal knowledge: An alternative epistemological view', *Teaching in Higher Education*, 7(3): 277–294

Gibbs, G. and Makeshaw, T. (1992) *53 Interesting Things To Do in Your Lectures*. Bristol: Technical and Educational Services

Giddens, A. (1996) *Consequences of Modernity*. Cambridge: Polity Press

Gravett, S. and Henning, E. (1998) 'Teaching as dialogic mediation: A learning centred view of higher education', *South African Journal of Higher Education*, 12(2): 60–8

Haggis, T. and Pouget, M. (2002) 'Trying to be motivated: Perspectives on learning from younger students accessing higher education', *Teaching in Higher Education*, 7(3): 323–36

Hodge, M. in C. Saunders (2003) 'Fact: term jobs damage grades', *Times Higher Education Supplement*, 7 February 2003

Holmes, L. (2009) www.graduate-employability.org.uk (accessed August 2010)

Holmes, L. (n.d.) http://www.re-skill.org.uk/grads/grademp.htm for research into the emergent graduate identity (accessed 3 August 2011)

Hutton, W. (1995) *The State We're In*. London: Cape

Jeffers, S. (1997) *Feel the Fear and Do It Anyway*. London: Century

Kapp, R. and Bangeni, B. (2005) 'I was just never exposed to this argument thing: Using a genre approach to teach academic writing to ESL students in the Humanities', in C. Moran and A. Herrington (eds) *Genre Across the Curriculum*. Logan, UT: Utah University Press

Kirkpatrick, I. and Lucio, M. (1995) *The Politics of Quality in the Public Sector*. London: Routledge

Kolb, D.A. (1984) *Experiential Learning: Experience as the Source of Learning and Development*. Upper Saddle River, NJ: Prentice-Hall

Krueger, R.A. (1994) *Focus Groups*. London: Sage

Land, R. (2010) 'Threshold concepts and troublesome knowledge: A transformative approach to learning' (variations presented at Leeds 2008, NTU 2010, Dundee University 2010)

Lea, M. and Stierer, B. (eds) (1999) *Student Writing in Higher Education: New Contexts* Buckingham: Open University Press/Society for Research into Higher Education

Lea, M. and Street, B. (1998) 'Student writing in higher education: An academic literacies approach view', *Studies in Higher Education*, 23(2): 157–72

Leathwood, C. and O'Connell, P. (2003) 'It's a struggle: the constructions of the "new student" in higher education', *Journal of Education Policy*, 18(6): 597–615

Leathwood, C. and Read, B. (2009) *Gender and the Changing Face of Higher Education: A Feminised Future?* Maidenhead: Open University Press

Lillis, T. (2001) *Student Writing, Access, Regulation, Desire*. London: Routledge

Lillis, T. (2003) 'Student writing as "academic literacies": Drawing on Bakhtin to move from *critique* to *design*', *Language and Education* 17(3): 192–207

Lyotard, J. (1984) *The Postmodern Condition: A Report on Knowledge*, trans. G. Bennington and B. Masumi. Minneapolis, MN; University of Minnesota Press, in M. Barrow (2006) 'Assessment and student transformation: Linking character and intellect', *Studies in Higher Education*, 31(3): 357–72

Macherey, P. (1990) 'The text says what it does not say', in D Walder, *Literature in the Modern World: Critical Essays and Documents*. Oxford: Oxford University Press. pp. 215–23

May, T. (2003) *Social Research: Issues, Methods and Processes*. Buckingham: Open University Press

Medhurst, A. (2000) 'If anywhere: Class identifications and cultural studies academics', in S. Munt (ed.) *Cultural Studies and the Working Class*. London: Cassell. pp. 19–35

Medhurst, N. (2010) 'Collaborative online design: A pedagogical approach to understanding student multiliterate creative practice'. Available at: http://www.londonmet.ac.

uk/fms/MRSite/acad/foc/research/seminars/09-10/nigel-abstract.html (accessed August 2010)

Mitchell, S. and Evison, A. (2006) 'Exploiting the potential of writing for educational change at Queen Mary, University of London', in L. Ganobcsik-Williams (ed.) *Teaching Academic Writing in UK Higher Education*. Basingstoke: Palgrave Macmillan

Moon, J. (2005) 'Coming from behind: An investigation of learning issues in the process of widening participation in higher education', abstract of the final report published November 2008 at http://escalate.ac.uk/1109 (accessed August 2010)

Morrice, L. (2009) 'The global in the local: Issues of difference (mis)recognition and inequity in higher education', paper presented at the ESRC seminar series: Imagining the University of the Future

Mullin, J.A. (2006) 'Learning from – not duplicating – US composition theory and practice', in L. Ganobcsik-Williams (ed.) *Teaching Academic Writing in UK Higher Education*. Basingstoke: Palgrave Macmillan

Munt, S. (ed.) (2000) *Cultural Studies and the Working Class*. London: Cassell

Murray, R. (2006) 'If not rhetoric and composition, then what? Teaching teachers to teach writing', in L. Ganobcsik-Williams (ed.) *Teaching Academic Writing in UK Higher Education*. Basingstoke: Palgrave Macmillan

Newman, J. and Clarke, J. (1994) 'Going about our business? The managerialism of public services', in C. Clarke, A. Cochrane and E. McLaughlin (eds) *Managing Social Policy*. London: Sage

Noble, D. (2002) *Digital Diploma Mills: The Automation of Higher Education*. New York: Monthly Review Press

Northedge, A. (2003a) 'Rethinking teaching in the context of diversity', *Teaching in Higher Education*, 8(1): 17–32

Northedge, A. (2003b) 'Enabling participation in academic discourse', *Teaching in Higher Education*, 8(2): 169–180

Norton, L.S. (2009) *Action Research in Teaching and Learning: A Practical Guide to Conducting Pedagogical Research in Universities*. Abingdon: Routledge

Paczuska, A. (2002) 'The applications process', in A. Hayton and A. Paczuska (eds) *Access, Participation and Higher Education*. London: Kogan Page

Palmer, R. and Pope, C. (1984) *Brain Train: Studying for Success*. Bristol: Arrowsmith

Pollitt, C., Birchall, J. and Putman, K. (1998) *Decentralising Public Service Management*. London: Macmillan Press.

QAA (2002) *Subject Review for Business*, London Metropolitan University

Quinn, J. (2003) *Powerful Subjects: Are Women Really Taking Over the University?* Stoke-on-Trent: Trentham Books

Quinn, J. (2004) 'Understanding working-class "drop-out" from higher education through a socio-cultural lens: Cultural narratives and local contexts', *International Studies in Sociology of Education*, 14(1): 57–74

Ridley, P. (2010) 'Drawing to learn: making ideas visible', workshop for staff and students – see GetAhead 2010 http://www.catsconsulting.com/getahead2010/# (accessed August 2010)

Rogers, C. (1994) *Freedom to Learn*. Upper Saddle River, NJ: Merrill

Rose, C. and Goll, L. (1992) *Accelerate Your Learning*. Aylesbury, UK: Accelerated Learning System Ltd

Satterthwaite, J., Atkinson, A. and Martin, W. (eds) (2004) *The Disciplining of Education: New Languages of Power and Resistance*. Stoke-on-Trent: Trentham Books

Schwandt, T. (1997) *Dictionary of Qualitative Enquiry*. London: Sage

Seale, C. (1999) *The Quality of Qualitative Research*. London: Sage

Silverman, D. (ed.) (1997) *Qualitative Research: Theory, Method and Practice*. London: Sage

Silverman, D. (ed.) (2004) *Qualitative Research: Theory, Method and Practice*, 2nd edn. London: Sage

Sinfield, S., Burns, T. and Holley, D. (2004) 'Outsiders looking in or insiders looking out? Widening participation in a post 1992 university', in J. Satterthwaite, A. Atkinson and W. Martin (eds), *The Disciplining of Education: New Languages of Power and Resistance*. Stoke-on-Trent: Trentham Books

Skillen, J. (2006) 'Teaching academic writing from the "centre" in Australian universities', in L. Ganobcsik-Williams (ed.) *Teaching Academic Writing in UK Higher Education*. Basingstoke: Palgrave Macmillan

Stierer, B. and Antoniou, M. (2004) 'Are there distinctive methodologies for pedagogic research in higher education?', *Teaching in Higher Education*, 9(3): 275–85

Tett, L. (2000) '"I'm working class and proud of it": Gendered experiences of non-traditional participants in higher education', *Gender and Education*, 1(2): 183–94

Thomas, E. (2001) *Widening Participation in Post-compulsory Education*. London: Continuum

Thomas, L. (2002) 'Student retention in higher education: The role of institutional habitus', *Journal of Educational Policy*, 17(4): 423–32

Willetts, D. (2010) Speech to the CBI. Available at: http://news.bbc.co.uk/1/hi/uk_politics/6662219.stm (accessed September 2010)

Wingate, U. (2006) 'Doing away with study skills', *Teaching in Higher Education*, 11(4): 457–69

Winnicott, D.W. (1971) *Playing and Reality*. London: Tavistock, cited in P. Crème (2003) 'Why can't we allow students to be more creative?' *Teaching in Higher Education*, 8(2): 273–77

Wyatt, A. and Cash, C. (2010) 'i-write: animating essay writing', presented at ALDinHE

Index

UNIVERSITY OF WINCHESTER
LIBRARY